India in the World Economy

Cross-cultural exchange has characterized the economic life of India since antiquity. Its long coastline has afforded India convenient access to Asia and Africa as well as trading partnerships formed in the exchange of commodities ranging from textiles to military technology and from opium to indigo. In a journey across two thousand years, this enthralling book, written by a leading South Asian historian, describes the ties of trade, migration, and investment between India and the rest of the world and shows how changing patterns of globalization have reverberated in economic policy, politics, and political ideology within India. Along the way, the book asks three major questions: Is this a particularly Indian story? When did the big turning points happen? And is it possible to distinguish the modern from the premodern pattern of exchange? These questions invite a new approach to the study of Indian history by placing the region at the center of the narrative. This is global history written on India's terms, and, as such, the book invites Indian, South Asian, and global historians to rethink both their history and their methodologies.

Tirthankar Roy is Reader in the Economic History Department at the London School of Economics and Political Science. His publications include *The Economic History of India, 1857–1947*, Third Edition (2011); *Towards a History of Consumption in South Asia*, coedited with Douglas Haynes, Abigail McGowan, and Haruka Yanagisawa (2010); *Company of Kinsmen: Enterprise and Community in South Asian History, 1700–1940* (2010); and *Traditional Industry in the Economy of Colonial India* (1999).

This dynamic new series will publish books on the milestones in Asian history, those that have come to define particular periods or to mark turning points in the political, cultural, and social evolution of the region. The books in this series are intended as introductions for students and can be used in the classroom. They are written by scholars whose credentials are well established in their particular fields and who have, in many cases, taught the subject over a number of years.

Books in the Series

1 Judith M. Brown, *Global South Asians: Introducing the Modern Diaspora*
2 Diana Lary, *China's Republic*
3 Peter A. Lorge, *The Asian Military Revolution: From Gunpowder to the Bomb*
4 Ian Talbot *and* Gurharpal Singh, *The Partition of India*
5 Stephen F. Dale, *The Muslim Empires of the Ottomans, Safavids and Mughals*
6 Diana Lary, *The Chinese People at War: Human Suffering and Social Transformation, 1937–1945*
7 Sunil S. Amrith, *Migration and Diaspora in Modern Asia*
8 Thomas DuBois, *Religion and the Making of Modern East Asia*
9 Susan Mann, *Gender and Sexuality in Modern Chinese History*

India in the World Economy

From Antiquity to the Present

TIRTHANKAR ROY

London School of Economics and Political Science

CAMBRIDGE
UNIVERSITY PRESS

CAMBRIDGE UNIVERSITY PRESS

Cambridge, New York, Melbourne, Madrid, Cape Town, Singapore,
São Paulo, Delhi, Mexico City

Cambridge University Press
c/o Cambridge University Press India Pvt. Ltd.
Cambridge House
4381/4, Ansari Road, Daryaganj
New Delhi 110002
India

www.cambridge.org
Information on this title: www.cambridge.org/9781107401471

First published 2012
First South Asian edition 2013

This South Asian edition is based on Tirthankar Roy / India in the World Economy /
9781107401471 / 2012

Printed in India at Sanat Printers, Kundli, Haryana

A catalogue record for this publication is available from the British Library

Library of Congress Cataloguing in Publication data
Roy, Tirthankar.
India in the world economy : from antiquity to the present / Tirthankar Roy.
p. cm. – (New approaches to Asian history ; 10)
Includes bibliographical references and index.
ISBN 978-1-107-00910-3 (hardback) – ISBN 978-1-107-40147-1 (paperback)
1. India – Commerce – History. 2. India – Economic conditions. 3. India – Foreign
economic relations. I. Title. II. Series.
HF3785.R69 2012
337.54–dc23 2011035574

ISBN-13   978-1-107-03639-0 (Hardback)

For
Mrinmoyee Roy

Contents

Figures and Tables

Figures

Tables

Preface

This is a book about transactions between South Asia and the rest of the world in the very long run. I show the antiquity of long-distance intercultural economic exchanges conducted from South Asia, and also show how external factors such as new technology or new partnerships and internal factors such as geography shaped these exchanges, allowing us to mark out distinct epochs in the history of these transactions.

The idea of writing this book occurred to me some years ago while I was taking part in the proceedings of the Global Economic History Network, an international collective of economists and historians, now concluded. The conversations started during those proceedings exposed me to interesting current research on other regions, especially other Asian regions. Useful though the experience was, however, this book does not implement the intellectual program of the network with Indian material. In fact, I formed the idea of this book partly in reaction to the main item on the network's agenda, namely, to search for the causes of international economic inequality in the modern world. It seemed to me that by placing the inequality problem at the center, we risked making the history of India's globalization too dependent on the history of Europe's globalization, which would be a wrong thing to do because every region did business with other regions in a somewhat autonomous and distinctive way, depending on local factors such as politics and geography. And because some of these local factors were extraordinarily durable, a *longue durée* India-focused narrative of transactions was possible. I did not wish to get into the sterile rhetoric about which region – Asia or Europe – was the center of the world in the seventeenth century. My point was, rather, that it should be possible to write a history of transactions that is mindful of the distinctive qualities of India. This book implements that idea.

The scholars with whom I have discussed my interest in global history since the network began, and who have indirectly contributed to the making of this project, are too numerous to be named. I should thank especially my current and former global history colleagues in the Department of Economic History, London School of Economics and

Political Science. I wish also to thank Douglas Haynes, Giorgio Riello, and the readers for Cambridge University Press, who saw earlier versions of the manuscript and the book proposal and made many useful suggestions on structure, presentation, arguments, and citations. I am grateful as well to Mina Moshkeri for drawing the maps at short notice. Debanjan Dasgupta supplied helpful tips on procuring images for the book, and Rangan Datta, a photographer of historical monuments in West Bengal, kindly provided me with a set of rare pictures representing European trade in Bengal from his impressive collection.

1   Introduction: India and Global History

Global historians remind us that the cross-cultural exchange of goods and ideas by means of trade, conquest, migration, and investment forms an important part of human history. Almost all significant examples of change in the conduct of material life contain elements of borrowing. Equally, the desire for goods and services acts as a strong motivation behind attempts to establish new channels of transaction, sometimes by force.

The Indian subcontinent has long enjoyed a pivotal place within overlapping webs of cross-cultural exchange. A coastline thousands of miles long; convenient access from West Asia, Central Asia, Africa, and East and Southeast Asia; the presence of skilled artisans; a robust mercantile tradition; states created by warlords and nobles of foreign origin; and kings who sponsored and protected merchants all secured the strategic position of the world economy in Indian life and of India in the world economy. Classics of Indian literature are replete with the heroic undertakings of the itinerant trader. Sanskrit and Persian works on statecraft set out kingly duties toward the merchant. Medieval ballads recorded how fortunes were made, and lost, in a business environment that posed great risks and yet promised huge returns for those intrepid enough to take the risks.

From the sixteenth century, Portuguese mariners, followed by English, Dutch, French, Danish, and American merchants, joined the commercial world of India. At first lured by the extraordinary profits that Asian spices and silk fetched in European markets, they found in Indian cotton cloth both a means of payment for the spices and a promising consumer good in Europe. As states in Europe, as well as those in India, plunged into warfare in the eighteenth century, rivalries in trade spilled over into contests for territory and led to the colonization of large parts of India by the English East India Company. Directly or indirectly, the company's empire enormously expanded channels of transaction. Even after Indian cotton cloth ceased to be in demand, new channels of transaction emerged as Indian labor and markets for new commodities came in contact with British

1

capital and technology. India became a force in global capitalism once again, if this time on a different foundation.

India, this sweeping view would suggest, was a point of intersection for many transactions across many cultures and, therefore, is a useful example for global historians. And a useful way to examine Indian history is to study the region in its interactions with the world. Indeed, there is hardly any other way of reading Indian economic history. The present book explores this two-sided relationship. A number of questions arise, each one quite wide in scope. The history of India's transactions with the outside world is thousands of years old. Can we fit all these years into one narrative? What are the common threads that run through such a narrative? Are there elements that make it a distinctively Indian story? Would that story tell us when the big transitions occurred? How do we distinguish the modern from the premodern pattern of exchange?

These questions have yet to be addressed as a group. Most writing on Indian economic history emanates from region-bound scholarship and has been preoccupied with issues of land control and land revenue. Within that intellectual tradition, however, there have been notable attempts to discern long-term patterns of change. Thus the pioneering works of William Moreland and D. D. Kosambi come to mind.[1] But these attempts focused on the relationship between the land and the state, confining foreign trade to a place on the margins of a fiscal system dominated by the taxation of agriculture. The capacity of the plow to sustain urban societies drove these visions of the rise and fall of states, dynasties, empires, and civilizations. The two pioneers just named, and other scholars influenced by a reading of long-range history, did not exactly neglect trade; but they did not offer a definite perspective on long-distance trade before European entry either. This oversight persisted into the historiography of the Aligarh School, which dealt with medieval Indian economic history. A good argument can thus be made that shifting the focus of economic history from land to trade should enable us to bring into the story of economic change over the long run a relatively neglected, and yet a very important and dynamic equation, that is, the one between the land and the sea, or between the settled and the mobile components of society. We should, then, see how the world of coastal commerce both responded to and contributed to state formation in ancient, medieval, and modern

---

[1] William H. Moreland, *India at the Death of Akbar: An Economic Study*, London: Macmillan, 1920; Moreland, *The Agrarian System of Moslem India: A Historical Essay with Appendices*, Cambridge: W. Heffer & Sons, 1929; D. D. Kosambi, *An Introduction to the Study of Indian History*, Bombay: Popular Book Depot, 1956.

India, eventually reaching the point at which seafaring merchants could take control of land-based states.

If such is the situation with Indian economic history, few global historians would dispute the proposition that the Indian subcontinent holds interesting lessons for their discipline. But few global historians venture beyond the last two or three hundred years to draw out the lessons. Few have asked the kinds of long-range questions that the Indianists have. The frameworks of interaction used by most global historians concentrate on the problem of "the modern" and tie the notion of the modern to European ascendance in the Indian Ocean, as if only one epochal transition should really matter in the study of Indian history. In other words, these historians have not yet tried to tell the story of globalization from a regional perspective.[2] To see why a regional perspective should matter, a fuller discussion of the existing frameworks is necessary.

Envisioning contacts

Serious interest in cross-border economic exchange goes back to the classical economists of the nineteenth century. The *Wealth of Nations* by Adam Smith often refers to the English East India Company and the trade between Europe and Bengal in the eighteenth century. Such interest stemmed from the belief that market integration, unencumbered by monopoly and regulation, was a foundation not only for modern economic growth but also for the transmission of the growth impulse worldwide.[3] The theory predicted a convergence among countries' average level of living the more the countries traded with each other.

---

[2] I use the term "globalization" in the generic sense of an increase in the long-distance exchange of goods, services, labor, capital, and knowledge. Recent attempts to define the term employ it to explore the implications of increased transactions for the nation-state, a problem not relevant to this book. See J. Osterhammel and N. Peterson, *Globalization: A Short History*, Princeton, NJ: Princeton University Press, 2005, for more discussion.

[3] "Modern" economic growth is defined as growth based on the productivity of resources rather than on the accumulation of resources. Much of comparative economic history today explains the genesis of modern economic growth and the uneven spread of growth in the world with reference to the uneven distribution of factors necessary for modern economic growth to start. Such factors include energy resources, fertile land, private property rights, and the cultural makeup of entrepreneurs. For further readings on entrepreneurial culture and institutions, see Douglass North, *Institutions, Institutional Change and Economic Performance*, Cambridge: Cambridge University Press, 1991; and Avner Greif, *Institutions and the Path to the Modern Economy: Lessons from Medieval Trade*, Cambridge: Cambridge University Press, 2006. On a modern argument about resources,

Although this idea found some relevant fields of application internationally, it encountered a problem in that the world did not become more equal as it traded more. Most critiques of liberalism inserted a political element into the story of market integration to explain this anomaly. Usually, this political element came from a concept of European state systems and politics.

According to one of the more widely held conceptions, the rest of the world was "incorporated" into a process of politico-economic development that began in early modern Europe and culminated in the European empires.[4] Whereas the economic relationship between the ruling core and the colonized periphery in the premodern empires was often based on fiscal and military ties, in the modern European empires the relationship was capitalistic, that is, based on commodity trade, capital export, and labor migration. Cross-border economic exchange was an explicit aim of these empires, which are seen as expressions of a type of state that lived to advance capitalistic market integration.

Using the nineteenth-century empire as a tool of economic history can be questioned on the grounds that the empire itself is left unexplained and somehow unconnected to trade and empire in other times. The concept of the "world system," introduced in the 1970s, bypasses this difficulty by tracing the origins of modern forms of international economic exchange to European commercial expansion, which took off in the 1500s. The emergence of a worldwide pattern of exchange dominated by European agents and supported by European states defined the modern capitalist world economy.[5] This is largely where the "grand narrative" of globalization in the long-term stands today.

I take from these formulations the insight that states make a crucial difference to market integration. Beyond that point, these ideas – empire and world system – do not suit the purpose of this book. First of all, the pursuit of a grand narrative in global economic history is more or less driven by a need to explain the genesis of world economic inequality. The present book is not about world inequality. If our main interest is not inequality, then looking at the world through the prism of hierarchical arrangements between places, as the economic history of empires and world system theory tend to do, is not very useful. Rather than a model of a

see Kenneth Pomeranz, *The Great Divergence: China, Europe, and the Making of the Modern World Economy*, Princeton, NJ: Princeton University Press, 2000.

[4] See, for example, Immanuel Wallerstein, "Incorporation of the Indian Subcontinent into Capitalist World-Economy," *Economic and Political Weekly* 21(4), 1986, pp. PE28–PE39.

[5] Immanuel Wallerstein, *World-Systems Analysis: An Introduction*, Durham, NC: Duke University Press, 2004.

European core and an Indian periphery, a more flexible conception that allows for economic emergence all the time would suit this project better.

Furthermore, the histories of empires and world capitalism tend to explain inequality using the concept of the "incorporation" of a region into a Europe-centered world economy. This approach, which places a single huge epochal change at the center of the history of transactions, has been questioned by sympathetic critics.[6] For a region like India that has been doing business with the outside world for two thousand years, we cannot assume that the history of its interactions had only one turning point. Such a belief would entail reducing all of the "premodern" into one featureless period and would be, as well, a misreading of what the "modern" has meant in Indian history.

Through the mediation of concepts such as "empire" or "world system," the world enters Indian history via a stylized "Eurocentric" idea of the world rather than through a historically and geographically particular idea of India. The aim of global history, then, is to show how the world economy was constituted and how it changed. We run the risk of losing a specific sense of the region when we try to fit the many diverse units that make up India into the larger picture of exchange between Europe and India. This is a serious issue if a region is in fact as large and as heterogeneous as India is. We need, instead, an account of transactions that can avoid creating cleavages between a region's history and global history.[7]

This book, it should be clear, hopes to offer a somewhat different narrative of globalization in the long run. It is global history with the axis located in one region, rather than in a conception of the world. Its goal is to show how a people that tended to share some cultural practices, institutional traditions, and resource endowments, as well as a political

---

[6] Major recent works have moved away from the idea that significant forms of interaction in Asian regions began in 1500 and with the coming of the Europeans. See Janet Abu-Lughod, *Before European Hegemony: The World System, A.D. 1250–1350*, New York: Oxford University Press, 1991; and André Gunder Frank, *ReOrient: Global Economy in the Asian Age*, Berkeley and Los Angeles: University of California Press, 1999. Such rethinking also finds that South Asia is a poor fit in any model of the world economy. Christopher K. Chase-Dunn, Thomas D. Hall, and E. Susan Manning, "Rise and Fall: East-West Synchronicity and Indic Exceptionalism Reexamined," *Social Science History* 24 (4), 2000, pp. 727–54. The lack of fit is owed to the geographical positioning of India, which meant that the region could access a variety of trading networks not necessarily connected with the Eurasian ones.

[7] An interesting example of such cleavage is the divergent ways that leading texts in global history account for the decline of the Indus Valley civilization, though all relied on region-centric archaeology. See Padma Manian, "Harappans and Aryans: Old and New Perspectives of Ancient Indian History," *History Teacher* 32(1), 1998, pp. 17–32.

heritage, engaged in transactions with those who hailed from different backgrounds. It shares with global history the premise that a great deal of what any "settled" population consumed or made productive use of arose from its contacts with more "mobile" and "foreign" elements. And yet, what was borrowed from those elements, and with what effect, depended on institutions, geographies, cultures, and traditions that were often deeply rooted in space. I cannot claim that all these regional markers are adequately discussed here, but they do play a relatively larger role in the present narrative than do exchange relations as such. Using Patrick O'Brien's distinction between analytical narratives of global history, I would place the present work nearer a history of "connections" than of "comparisons."[8] It is, however, a story of connections mediated by a host of local constraints upon which the emphasis of the present work falls.

In spirit, this project is closer to the scholarship on the Indian Ocean in its preoccupation with a large region's endogenous structures and dynamics.[9] But this is not a maritime history. It is as much concerned with the land as it is with the sea and, even more, with the relationship between the land and the sea. Nor is this a history of trade; its interests encompass all axes of globalization, including trade. In its orientation, the present work is distinct from Indian Ocean scholarship also in its interest in the premodern and the postcolonial, whereas Indianist maritime history remains anchored in the European era in the Indian Ocean.

The scope of this book is comparable to that of the region-centric studies of globalization offered by Anthony Reid on Southeast Asia or Joseph Inikori on Africa.[10] Like them, I aim to write a "longue durée" narrative wherein the world is one of the main ingredients in a large region's economic transformation. I find Inikori's distinction between a trading system and an economic system, and the suggestion that the one did not necessarily induce changes in the other, useful. The distinction between land and oceans, which is a frequently used organizing concept in this book, likewise shows us that the two worlds followed sometimes

---

[8] Patrick K. O'Brien, "Historiographical Traditions and Modern Imperatives for the Restoration of Global History," *Journal of Global History* 1(1), 2006, pp. 3–39.

[9] K. N. Chaudhuri, *Trade and Civilisation in the Indian Ocean: An Economic History from the Rise of Islam to 1750*, Cambridge: Cambridge University Press, 1985; Abu-Lughod, *Before European Hegemony*; Kenneth Macpherson, *The Indian Ocean: A History of People and the Sea*, New Delhi: Oxford University Press, 2004; Ashin Dasgupta, *The World of the Indian Ocean Merchant, 1500–1800*, New Delhi: Oxford University Press, 2001.

[10] Reid, *Southeast Asia in the Age of Commerce*, vol. 1, *The Lands Below the Winds*, New Haven, CT: Yale University Press, 1988; and Inikori, "Africa and the Globalization Process: Western Africa, 1450–1850," *Journal of Global History* 2(1), 2007, pp. 63–86.

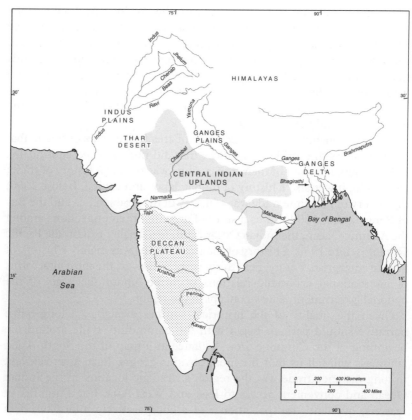

1.1. Geographical zones.

independent and sometimes intersecting pathways. That being said, this book does not share Inikori's particular interest in the modern era defined by European intrusion or Reid's in "the age of commerce."

The easiest way to launch a project like this one is to start with geography.

Early trade

It is a cliché, but it bears repeating, that the Indian subcontinent is not one homogenous region. It is geographically diverse, and partly because of this geographical diversity, culturally diverse as well. All parts of this complex whole did not engage in transactions with the outside world quite to the same extent or in a similar fashion. Even as late as 1700, it was mainly the littoral regions that engaged in foreign trade; the Gangetic plains traded with the littoral regions, and the central and southern Indian uplands traded with few, if any, outsiders. The nature of merchant firms and their interests diverged between the coastal regions, where merchants engaged in maritime trade, and the capital cities, where they served the fiscal system and the grain trade.

The relationship between the parts of the Indian subcontinent that did transact with outsiders and those that did not, changed continually. Before 1800, a history of their transactions was mainly a history of trade; after 1800, it was also a history of mobile labor and capital. Before 1600, the history of maritime trade was a history of the Arabian Sea and the Bay of Bengal; after 1600, it was a story of growing interconnections among the Atlantic Ocean, the Indian Ocean, and, to a smaller extent, the Pacific Ocean. Before 1950, a history of the transactions was mainly a history of private enterprise. For the next thirty years, however, the most vital forms of international economic relations occurred under the aegis of the national government, a new concept in the region.

Given the quality of the historical sources available, a long-range narrative should perhaps begin with the commodity trade around the beginning of the Common Era. A glance at a map of the South Asian landmass will tell us that the most obvious geographical asset relevant to long-distance trade was the region's strategic location in the Indian Ocean and convenient access to East and West Asia. For a number of reasons, overland transportation was a comparatively minor business and a weak integrative force almost anywhere in the region before the railways in the nineteenth century. Overland transportation at this time can be divided into three classes: wheeled carriages, caravans of pack animals, and boats plying rivers. The wheeled carriage was of marginal use in the uplands of Central and South India, and the numerous large rivers made the deltas unsuitable for road traffic. Caravans of bullocks and camels traversed the east-west and north-south roads. But even in the best of conditions, caravans did not carry more than a tiny proportion of what the land produced (see also Chapter 6). If much later data are any indication, the costs of carrying goods per ton per mile were several times more for caravan traffic than for carts, and the costs for carts several times more than those for boats. Industrial raw materials such as iron ore and major agricultural produce such as grain, therefore, moved across space only to a limited extent.

From the beginning of the Common Era, if not earlier, trans-Himalayan caravans carried valuable goods such as horses and silk along the six major trade routes that connected the plains of India with Tibet, China, and Central Asia. But under the best of conditions, the cargo capacity of cross-border caravan traffic was extremely limited. Ordinarily, a horse or a camel could carry one hundred kilograms of goods, but much less than that quantity on a Himalayan journey. On that assumption, one average-sized oceangoing ship of the early era would be equivalent in cargo capacity to several thousand animals. The peak scale attained by the Himalayan caravans in the more recent times would not exceed one hundred thousand animals. In volume, then, trans-Himalayan trade was small compared with maritime trade. Such a comparison, however, should not mean that it was unimportant. Overland trade was essential to the consumption and livelihood of mountain societies. For them, it carried such basic necessities as salt and wool. For the plainspeople, it carried such valuable and coveted merchandise as warhorses.

The corollary to the marginality of roads was that navigation was, relatively speaking, a more effective and more widely used means of bulk transportation, whether we look at the interior of the subcontinent or consider foreign trade. The ancient trading zones in India formed around two critical resources: a navigable river, and a port located on the estuary of the river or near it. Coastal trade, caravan trade, and port-to-port "looping" trade increased the options for moving cargo, but in the main, the ports used the rivers adjacent to them to bring in supplies of food and traded goods from the interior. The physical link between the sea and the land was achieved by means of the rivers more than by the roads. Cambay/Khambat on the river Mahi, Surat on the Tapi, Broach/Bharuch/Bharukacchha/Barigaza on the Narmada, Arikamedu on the Ponnaiyar, Tamralipti/Tamluk on the Rupnarayan, Saptagram on the Saraswati, Masulipatnam in the Krishna delta, Hooghly on the Bhagirathi, Balasore/Baleshwar with easy access to Budibalang and Subarnarekha, Sonargaon on the Shitalakhya, Old Goa on the Mandovi, the Malabar ports of Muziris (exact site still debated) and Kollam/Quilon on the inland waterways – all of these sites were simultaneously within easy reach from the sea and from inland via the rivers on which they were situated.

The positioning of ports on inland waterways carried advantages other than easy access by river to the interior. The delta soil was usually better than soil further inland for cultivation, so that much food and even some raw materials could be grown locally. A slightly inland location, as opposed to one that opened out to the sea, provided a shelter from storms and pirate attacks. In the Ganges and the Indus plains, maritime trade was well connected with river-borne trade deep into the plains because these rivers were navigable with boats for hundreds of miles. Even when the river itself was not navigable for more than a few miles, the river valley supplied easy access to the interior by land. Many caravan roads followed the course of a river. Such a pattern for the location of commercial hubs also carried risks, however. One common reason for the decline of the ports was the silting of the rivers, which happened often in the Gangetic delta. Changes in the navigability of the rivers affected the integration of regional and maritime trade networks, even when such circumstances did not necessarily stop contacts with overseas trade.

This pattern of land-and-sea integration imposed a seasonal rhythm on trade. River-borne trade was seasonal, and so was trade at the seaports. Historians of trade have noted the significance of the monsoon wind for sea navigation, a field of knowledge that seventeenth-century European visitors to India needed to master. Another source of seasonality, which the Europeans did not need to know and the modern historians tend to overlook as well, was that inland navigation depended on the rains. The summer months did not bring many valuable goods from the interior because most peninsular rivers dried up. Owing to the pronounced seasons, large and permanent urban settlements did not always form at the sites of even the most considerable ports. Many ports had the character of a seasonal fairground. Further, the spatial reach of rivers was limited in peninsular India. Even the largest of the rivers were not navigable beyond a hundred odd miles, and some of the smaller ones were not navigable beyond a few miles.

Although the port-hinterland nexus enabled valuable trade, it was biased in favor of articles with high value-to-bulk ratios. Spices, silks, pearls, diamonds, fine ceramics, and gold entered trade easily; cotton cloth became a favorite where there was local cultivation of cotton. But grain was virtually absent except for meeting the needs of the mariners and merchants in the port cities. Trade remained largely unspecialized. It was necessary to distribute risks over many commodities. A huge variety of goods, individually or in small quantities, was sold at the seasonal fairs and carried by ships into maritime traffic. The opportunistic nature of trade made for commercial relationships of a contingent and impermanent kind. Auctions and spot sales were far more common than were long-period bulk contracts in the fairground trade.

The limits on volume imposed by dependence on rivers meant that only simple ships and rudimentary harbors were needed. A study of the design and size of the ships that plied the Indian coasts suggests that shipwrights concentrated on building vessels that relied on monsoon winds rather than on ocean currents. This preoccupation with adapting to local geographical constraints made Indian shipping less attentive to long-distance voyages and the challenges that such voyages entailed. Although adding a lot of value through what it did, the Indian trading system was technologically incapable of either venturing beyond the Indian Ocean or embarking on voyages that might take months rather than weeks.

Ships built in India were, with some exceptions, much smaller than those being built in Europe after 1400 CE. Indian ship design was very diverse and resistant to change until the seventeenth century. Some design variations commonly found among the different maritime communities on the coast could be explained by local geography, by, for example, such factors as the height of the tides or the force of the monsoon. In addition, there were institutional obstacles to the exchange of knowledge among artisan communities involved with shipping. Barriers took the form of limited social intercourse when artisan guilds coalesced with caste and community and thus restricted the exchange of apprentices among communities engaged in similar or related activities.[11] The technological standard for the harbors was also rudimentary. In most of the ancient ports of India, the harbor was a makeshift affair, destroyed in storms and rebuilt quickly. The prospect of weather-induced damage, the small size of the ships, and the makeshift nature of the harbors reinforced each other.

A similar diversity characterized internal navigation. In this sphere too the shipbuilding tradition was a fragmented one. The average scale of construction was small, and numerous local techniques existed side by side seemingly without borrowing ideas from one another. Once again, the diversity of models was at least partly an effect of adaptation to extremely variable local conditions. Within a relatively small region like Bengal, the larger-sized boats that plied the Ganges were ill suited for the rapid and shallow waters of the rivers of Chotanagpur, where small, flat, clinker-built boats served better; and the boats that managed the Ganges or the Damodar could not be used in the narrow creeks of the Sundarbans, where low but deep boats worked better. Furthermore, neither of these boat types was suited for the treacherous waters of the deltaic eastern Bengal rivers.

---

[11] Tirthankar Roy, "Knowledge and Divergence from the Perspective of Early Modern India," *Journal of Global History* 3(3), 2008, pp. 361–87.

With shipping and harbor technology so tied to meeting local needs, direct Indian participation in maritime trade remained confined to the Indian Ocean. But having to be restricted to Asia was hardly bad news. The intra-Asian trade was sufficiently lucrative given the extraordinarily wide range of valuable cargo that could be carried among West, South, and East Asia. Wealthy urban centers in West Asia offered attractive markets for merchants operating from the western coast of India, and culturally proximate civilizations in Southeast Asia were equally attractive destinations for merchants operating from the southern Coromandel.

Whereas the littoral was the center of commercial activity, most states, especially the larger ones, were formed inland, with at best a presence in the delta. Because of this disjuncture, the commercial towns in India acquired a particular character. Few of the port towns were also politically central. Land tax pulled the capital to the interior, but commerce pulled the trading center to the coasts and the estuaries. Political integration between them remained limited. This distance gave merchants more room to maneuver. Certainly, merchants often maintained multiple bases. Far-flung merchant networks, buttressed by powerful codes of conduct, had a long presence in the region. These codes could be so powerful that community elders were known to punish violators with death. Much of the evidence for a symbiotic coexistence of merchants and rulers, as well as of the guilds that operated over long distances, comes from medieval South India.

But states tended to grow bigger and try to encompass the coast or build more secure contacts with the coastal world of commerce. In this way, politics either eased or reinforced geographical constraints. States that depended primarily on land taxes had an interest in building roads and opening military supply routes along the rivers or over the land. The formation and disintegration of states, therefore, strengthened or weakened traffic between the interior and the ports. From time to time, empires also secured large chunks of overland routes that connected them to the sea. Before the Christian era, the Satavahana Empire achieved this integration, which fed the Indo-Roman trade. The Kusanas at the turn of the Common Era secured overland traffic between the upper Indus plains and Central Asia. The Gupta Empire in west-central India controlled traffic between the political center and the Gujarat littoral. And, in the twelfth century, Cholas achieved an unusually extensive spatial integration too.

The immediate impact of an empire on long-distance contact can be seen in its roads. The roads shown in the map (Fig. 2.2) in the next chapter stood as symbols of major empires, and carried soldiers, pilgrims, monks, and merchants. Early in the Common Era, the two main roadways in India were established – the Mauryan capital Pataliputra in the east to the Punjab plains in the north, where the commercial-cum-pilgrim town Taxila was located, and the other from the Gupta capital Ujjain in Malwa going up north to the Punjab plains. The roads met at Mathura. These two roads, or rather road systems, for surely they received numerous feeders as well, made use of natural tracks along the river valleys and therefore served as conduits for trade and conquest for centuries to come. In the nineteenth century, the railway lines linking Calcutta with Peshawar and Delhi with Bombay more or less followed these tracks established two thousand years previously. Not all roads were built and protected by the empires, of course. Several others, again geographically determined, especially in mountainous areas, were theoretically sponsored by the local states, but they carried more caravans than soldiers. Such arteries could be found in all parts of the Himalayas.

A more broad-based and permanent integration of India's roads and the sea began to take shape from the thirteenth century onward, with the consolidation of Turko-Afghan empires in northern India. Over the next four hundred years, the authority of Delhi or its vassals increased sufficiently to open up east-west, north-south, and trans-Himalayan trading-cum-military routes. Thus began the first epochal transition in globalization. It was no doubt a slow process by modern standards, taking centuries to reveal its potential. Nevertheless, the conquest by Delhi's vassals of Malwa, Deccan, Gujarat, and Bengal was the foundation on which a more deep-rooted integration of roads, inland waterways, and the sea could advance during the Mughal Empire in the seventeenth century.

These developments had little effect on shipping technology. Nor did they change the basic dependence of the ports on river-borne access to the interior. Commerce in the Indian Ocean continued to be shaped by geography and local tradition. The Mughal Empire was interested in overseas trade, but it was much more interested in controlling and improving the land. The interest of the sultanate and the Mughal Empire in agriculture was furthered by the function of Islam as the state religion. Historians of medieval South India have observed that peripatetic Hindu merchants often made donations to temples as a symbolic gesture toward the state or fellow merchants. For Islam, in northern India, the economic meaning of religious sponsorship was of a somewhat different order. Islam notably supplied a cooperative principle among communities that colonized open land on the frontiers, cleared forests, and sometimes supplied soldiers to the state. In North India, it was a religion of the land rather than of the roads.

And yet, whether by design or otherwise, the Indo-Islamic empires did strengthen trading contacts between North and South India, connect eastern with western Deccan, integrate economic life across the Gangetic plains, bring Bengal and the Ganges delta into a closer relationship with the imperial core, and stimulate trade along the Ganges. The states extended their political authority over some of the ports, which now became centers of provincial administration, reflecting a closer integration of state and market than before, but the majority of the ports remained outside the northern empire. Nevertheless, when the Europeans started setting up warehouses in the Indian ports, some of the ports where they operated had recently come under the control of powerful states.

Indo-European trade

In no fewer than three places in his book *ReOrient*, André Gunder Frank states that the Europeans "bought a ticket" into the already flourishing Asian trade thanks to fortuitous access to American silver.[12] The silver helped, but the rise of European traders to a position of dominance in the Indian Ocean was not as much a matter of luck as Frank's language might suggest.

Whereas Asian trade had stayed confined within Asia, Europeans arrived in Asia with navigational experience acquired in the Atlantic. They held a more global understanding of the markets for Asian goods than did the Asians themselves. In 1600, Europeans built ships that on average were larger than Indian ships and had greater cargo capacity. The vessels were constructed differently from Indian ships, partly to accommodate a number of guns, and were less susceptible to variability in climatic and ocean conditions. It was not that the Indians did not know how to build large ships. But such constructions remained exceptional in a milieu that rarely extended farther than the Indian Ocean. In contrast, the Europeans used their shipbuilding knowledge to construct sturdy vessels that could make very long sea voyages. The result was the integration of the market on an interoceanic scale, something that South Asians had no experience with.

The increasing participation of the Western Europeans in the Indian Ocean was revolutionary on many fronts. The immediate manifestation of European participation was the exercise of raw violence, especially by the

---

[12] Frank, *ReOrient*, pp. xxv, 282, 356.

Portuguese, who were keen to establish a monopoly in the spice trade. But the Portuguese strategy did not cause any far-reaching changes in the physical and spatial structures of trade, and, once the Portuguese turned their attention to East Asia, their strategy became unsustainable just decades after it began. The European gunships served little long-term political or economic purpose.

More critical were the technological and institutional effects of the European arrival. From the seventeenth century onward, knowledge of shipbuilding in India began to change through the agency of the Indian artisans who worked in European shipyards, and regional ship designs began to converge. There may have been some decline in Indian shipping, but there was also considerable learning. When we reach the nineteenth century, Indian shipwrights dominate the industry in locations such as Bombay, Calcutta, and Surat. One source of comparative advantage for European shipping was the understanding of how to cast iron in large foundries. Because the states also wanted skilled cannon founders and good gunners, European mercenaries were in demand among the Indian courts.

Indo-European trade brought new institutions into the Asian trading world. The English and the Dutch East India Companies represented a mode of trade that was not indigenous to India. These joint-stock organizations were much larger in scale and better able to weather risks than were the family firms that ruled the Indian business world. They were also more specialized in specific goods, and being specialized, needed to make use of long-period contractual transactions. The fairground style of trading on the Indian coasts, therefore, was not consistent with the European mode of doing transoceanic business. Contractual transactions in turn carried their own hazards. In Indo-European trade, the transacting parties were neither protected by state law nor shared the same customary law. Conflicts over the terms and enforcement of contracts, therefore, were extremely common. Moreover, European powers were often in conflict with each other, as well as with the territorial states. These disputes imparted an air of instability to the Indo-European trade. The English East India Company responded to the instability by setting up ports in which the sovereign authority rested with the foreigners.

The three port cities that the English East India Company established and ruled in India were much more than new urban centers. They were qualitatively different from a Mughal city or a commercial center in the interior. Bombay, Madras, and Calcutta were not fairgrounds or emporia in the way that other Indian ports still were. Instead, they represented occupationally specialized sites with an overwhelming interest in commissioning textile production, the precursors of a nineteenth-century model of urban-ization. Bombay and Madras were set up in territories beyond the empire. And as the empire began to crumble in the eighteenth century, these well-defended company towns rose as safe havens for Indian merchants and artisans.

These three ports, furthermore, redefined the relationship between geography and commerce. With the exception of Calcutta, and perhaps of Portuguese Goa, the ports were located on sites that did *not* rely on river-borne trade to access the interior. They were not even located on rivers of any significance. Even Calcutta, which was situated on a river, did not greatly rely on the river in conducting its main businesses. Instead, these ports looked toward the ocean; in turn, they attracted the migration of merchants and artisans. They drew in skilled workers and capital, along with goods, from the interior. For the first time in Indian history, the ports were not dependent on the hinterlands, and the hinterlands came to the ports. The fortunes of Indian businesses were often tied to the fortunes of the local state. That factor did not change in the port cities. But then, in these cities, the state belonged to the merchants.

I would define the early modern epochal change, then, in terms of four characteristics – a new geography of trade that was less dependent than before on climate and terrain, a new model of urbanization that drew in mobile capital and skills, a new institutional regime more dependent on long-period contracts, and a new kind of empire founded by traders rather than by warlords. And yet, in significant ways, the new regime of inte-gration retained continuity with the past. The technology of overland transactions changed little; geography continued to be a paramount factor in facilitating or hindering road transportation.

Empire and beyond

The rise of the British colonial empire in India made little difference in the costs of carrying out trade. What did matter were the technological and institutional changes that it enabled. The railways and the steamships affected the integration of the land and the sea to an unprecedented degree. The Indian railways and overseas trade attracted capital from London, and new currency systems reduced the risks for overseas investment. The abolition of slavery encouraged plantations in the tropics and the New World to import Asian labor. The empire was readier than any previous regime had been to institute laws encompassing commercial, financial, and labor transactions. The British Empire also represented a diverse collection of world regions with a shared language and law. The imperial umbrella brought down the transaction costs in exchanges between parts of the empire.

The Indian entrepreneurships that had grown to maturity in the colonial cities shared a more cosmopolitan culture than their counterparts in the interior, formed unorthodox partnerships, and were readier to make unusual commitments. For them, the empire reduced a variety of trade costs, including the costs of accessing machinery and skilled labor from Britain. The factories, banks, insurance companies, trading firms, shipping firms, schools, colleges, charities, and associations that developed in Bombay, Calcutta, and Madras, all of which were dependent on imported knowledge and services, represented a break from Indian tradition in many ways. And yet none of this would be intelligible without reference to the readiness with which the Indian merchants made use of the imperial network.

By late in the interwar period (1920–39), much of this dynamism was gone. In the difficult global economic conditions of the late-interwar period, the interests of the British Empire and of Indian business were not as well aligned as they had been. The imperial umbrella was in tatters, even as politicians in Britain wanted more than ever for India to stay under that umbrella. Economic nationalism in India was dominated by the increasingly acrimonious disputes that this divergence of interest generated. The reduced attraction of the colonial connection for Indian businesses gave rise to India's demand for a less empire-oriented trade regime. Indian business became more inward looking in its search for markets and materials. The dynamics of globalization, therefore, broke down during decolonization, and decolonization happened partly because of this breakdown.

When the disruptions of the mid-twentieth century had subsided, a new nation and nationalist spirit rose from the ashes of foreign rule. An earnest attempt to develop the Indian nation began, and a choice was made quite early to reduce the role of the market in India's engagement with the world economy. Foreign aid took the role of commodity exports in funding domestic investments, which were now managed by the state. The decision to shift the mode of international contact from the market to the state was compatible with a parallel decision to make the state the main vehicle for industrialization. Domestic businesses welcomed this regime, having received protection from foreign competition in the bargain.

From a historian's perspective, the statist-autarkic regime was no more than an experiment, indeed, an aberration, in the millennia-old history of India's engagement with the world economy. Why and exactly when it retreated remain something of a mystery, though. Insofar as an endogenous rethinking of economic policy played any role behind the retraction of autarkic policy, the rethinking could have resulted from the contradictions created by the policy regime. National development had run into unsustainable costs in the form of fiscal and balance-of-payments problems. Beyond such short-term crises, autarky was simply not consistent with Indian history. Too many politically influential commercial actors were aware of the forgone profits from dealing with the world economy. No matter the underlying reason, it is understood that India's return to the world market began in a small and surreptitious way in the 1980s, before it became an accomplished fact. Thereafter, interaction again encompassed trade, investment, and remittance reminiscent of the nineteenth-century pattern of integration. And global contacts began to produce revolutionary effects on the capability of Indian actors to supply marketable goods and services to the world. The dramatic illustration of this capability was the growth of a knowledge economy in India.

Arguments and hypotheses

In this long-range narrative of Indian trade, migration, and investment, there are local and global elements. The distinctively local elements are the enabling and constraining role of geography, and the Indians' irrepressible "disposition to truck, barter, and exchange," to borrow a phrase from Adam Smith. That disposition should not be seen as a cultural attribute; rather, it was a reflection of the low costs of trade that geographical positioning could offer to some communities and regions. The constraining influence of geography has diminished today compared to the situation in past centuries, but it has not disappeared. The harshest environments and areas distant from the coasts remain even today the areas least affected by the enormous changes that are transforming India.

On top of these long-binding internal constraints, external circumstances also shape patterns of interactions. States deeply affected the process of spatial and market integration. Improvements in transportation and communication technology eased geographical constraints. To each such external circumstance, merchants, workers, professionals, and artisans in India responded resourcefully. In the eighteenth century, their response involved fine cloth; in the nineteenth century, indentured labor; and in the late twentieth century, knowledge goods. How they responded depended on externally induced changes in the costs of trade and on what goods and services the world wanted to buy from the Indians.

If we must distinguish the modern from the premodern form of market integration in India, we should include in our definition of the modern, three nineteenth-century concepts: the railway, the imperial umbrella of language and law, and institutional change. The railways influenced trade costs precisely because geography had made the costs prohibitively high in land-and-sea trade. The imperial umbrella was crucial in expanding the axes of interaction from commodities to encompass capital, labor, and technology. Finally, economic laws, especially in the sphere of commercial exchanges, broadened the scope of impersonal contracts.

Chapter outline

Following this introduction are nine narrative chapters set out in a chronological sequence beginning with commerce before the Islamic empires (Chapter 2), proceeding to state formation between 1200 and 1700 (Chapter 3), Indo-European trade (Chapter 4), commodity and factor markets in the nineteenth century (Chapters 5 and 6), the relationship between colonialism and development (Chapter 7), decolonization (Chapter 8), the statist experiment (Chapter 9), and return to the world market (Chapter 10). A last chapter (Chapter 11) summarizes the two-thousand-year story into five propositions.

This journey should begin with a time when geographical conditions were especially binding on trade.

2 Ports and Hinterlands to 1200

What we know about Indian long-distance exchange before the Common Era began is perhaps not enough to offer systematic conclusions about trade and merchants. We do know that a few regional nodes of commerce emerged and that the sites where these nodes appeared possessed both unique and shared geographical characteristics. Trading zones did not appear randomly along the extensive coastline, but formed in the deltas of major rivers, with the river providing access to towns and villages inland. Although little can be said about commercial organization beyond the existence of guilds, we do know that the merchants who traversed these zones were major benefactors of religious institutions. Indeed, religion was one of the enduring cultural exports of these times.

The capitals of the major states were located inland; the mainstay of the states was land, not trade. Formally, statecraft recognized the kingly duty to protect merchants, but not enough is known about how that principle was practiced. Commercial law received legitimacy from its links with both the state and religion. Some of these political, spatial, and cultural markers of commercial activity in the subcontinent were to prove remarkably long lasting.

This chapter considers what we can reasonably infer about the broad patterns of long-distance economic exchanges in the first millennium of the Common Era.

Formation of routes and ports

Evidence of long-distance trade in the South Asian subcontinent goes back to the Indus Valley civilization, which was roughly contemporary to the Early Dynastic Sumerians. The Indus Valley settlements started around 3000 BCE in the Punjab interfluvial tracts as agricultural communities. They later covered a wide geographical area in the Indus basin, appearing as small or large urban settlements and villages. The presence of many towns among them, some located sufficiently close to the sea, points to systematic urban-rural contact and maritime trade. The absence of ritual and political structures also suggests a pattern of corporate or elite control consistent with strong mercantile activity.[1]

Beyond these indications, little is known of trading activity directly. Based on a few of the artifacts that have been discovered so far, "one is almost irresistibly drawn to the acceptance of a strong cultural and/or commercial liaison, between Mesopotamia and the Indus Valley."[2] How systematic the contacts were and how extensive remain to be studied. The settlement of Lothal, one of the sites that often comes up in discussions of trade contact, was too small to carry out much trade. Nevertheless, the antiquity of the trade between West Asia and Gujarat, more precisely between the Gulf of Khambhat or Cambay, is amply illustrated. Notwithstanding an ongoing debate over whether references in Sumerian sources to trading sites refer to South Asia, the pattern of integration between local and long-distance trade in the Indus Valley civilization cannot be precisely identified.[3] Toward the end of the Indus Valley time scale, pastoralist nomads from Central Asia migrated to the Gangetic plains. Whether or not the decline of the Indus settlements was owed to this invasion or to Indus floods, the two groups had different livelihood profiles.

In the second half of the first millennium BCE, towns that matched the size of some of the larger Indus Valley settlements had begun to appear in the middle-Gangetic plains. Forests were being cleared to make way for kingdoms and city-states. Sixteen of these sites became collectively known as the *mahajanapada*, or great settlements (Table 2.1). They were engaged in a fierce competition for control over land and livestock and, partly induced by these political and economic issues, they became sites of an assertive form of Brahmanism. The *Mahabharata* epic illustrates these livelihood struggles and the potent mixture of politics and religion especially well. In turn, the aggressive version of Hinduism drew a reaction in the form of two religions of peace, Buddhism and Jainism (c. 500 BCE). The popularity of both religions depended on the sponsorship of wealthy

[1] M. Kenoyer, "Trade and Technology of the Indus Valley: New Insights from Harappa, Pakistan," *World Archaeology* 29(2), 1997, pp. 262–80.

[2] Elisabeth C. L. During Caspers, "Sumer, Coastal Arabia and the Indus Valley in Protoliterate and Early Dynastic Eras: Supporting Evidence for a Cultural Linkage," *Journal of the Economic and Social History of the Orient* 22(2), 1979, pp. 122–35 (quote on p. 135).

[3] On the debate, see the useful survey by Hermann Kulke, " 'A Passage to India': Temples, Merchants and the Ocean," *Journal of the Economic and Social History of the Orient* 36(2), 1993, pp. 154–80.

2.1. Lothal. A port town and a settlement of the Indus Valley civilization, located in Gujarat, India. In the second millennium BCE, Lothal had easy access to the sea via a river. *Source*: Dinodia

urban merchants for whom the message of peace had a stronger appeal than the latent violence of Brahmanism. Early Buddhist parables suggest Buddhism's ties to merchants, whereas Brahmanism remained tied to landlords, peasants, and pastoralists.

Although the early kingdoms were often at war with one another, river and road communication brought these territories into increasing contact. During the Mauryan Empire (320–185 BCE), the major states, having been either subdued or co-opted, joined the empire. Although the empire was centered in Pataliputra, or modern Patna, on the Ganges, it succeeded in opening access to the two maritime trading zones nearest to it. In the southwest, the powerful dependency Avanti enabled road traffic to reach Bharukacchha, or Broach. Traversing Satavahana territory, road communication also reached southward to the Konkan and eastward to the Krishna Valley. In the east, the semiautonomous Tamralipti in Bengal served as the access to the Bay of Bengal.

These highways and ports may not have been used much for overseas trading. References to overseas traders and oceangoing merchants remain

Table 2.1. *Dynasties and states, c. 500 BCE–1200 CE.*

	North and Central	South	East	West
500 BCE–0 CE	Pre-300 BCE: Mahajanapada or a cluster of settlements. 320–185 BCE: Mauryan Empire. 200 BCE to early CE: Indo-Greeks or Bactrians rule the upper Indus valley and eastern Afghanistan	To 230 BCE: Mauryan Empire. 230 BCE–second century CE: Former Mauryan vassals Satavahanas or Satkarnis establish an empire in northern Deccan; major centers Amaravati in the Krishna Valley and Pratisthan (Paithan).	320–185 BCE: Mauryan Empire, capital Pataliputra (present Patna in Bihar). 185–73 BCE: Sunga.	320–185 BCE: Mauryan Empire. Post-185 BCE: Satavahana control in present Maharashtra.
0–500 CE	c. 50–400 CE: Kusanas, a northwest-Persian tribe, establish a state in Bactria, followed by an empire ruling the western part of North India. c. 250–550 CE: Gupta Empire, main center Ujjain in central India; controls the Gangetic plains.	Vakatakas rule in northern Deccan and central India (the creation of the Ajanta caves); Chera and Ay kingdoms in Malabar and present-day southern Tamil Nadu; Pallavas in northern Tamil Nadu.	Kharabelas control Orissa coasts including coastal commerce and establish statehood over parts of eastern and central India; followed by Gupta conquest.	Kadambas and other local kings establish control in the western coastal areas.
500–1200 CE	606–47 CE: Harshavardhan, based in Kanyakubja (Kanau) in the middle Gangetic plains.	To 850 CE: Later Pallavas, early Pandyas, and the Cholas share or compete for hegemony.	550–750 CE: Fragmentation into Banga, Samatata, Harikela, Poundra, and other domains.	Chalukyas and Rashtrakuta dynasties rule the western side of the Deccan plateau

Table 2.1. (*cont.*)

North and Central	South	East	West
650–1200 CE: Invasion from Central Asia and political fragmentation. Dominant tribes include the Gurjar Pratihara and Rajputs clans.	850–1280 CE: Chola Empire based in the Kaveri delta. Eleventh–twelfth century: Pandyan revival; later Chera rule in Malabar and adjoining regions; Kakatiya and Hoysala dynasties in southern part of the Deccan plateau.	c. 750–1100: Palas, Senas, eastern Gangas on the Orissa coast in the eleventh–twelfth century. c. 1200: Bands of soldiers in Ghori's army raid the Sena capital.	and parts of western India.
c. 660–740 CE: Occasional battles between Caliphate armies and Rajputs.			
c. 1000–1187 CE: Ghaznavid rule in present northern Pakistan.			
1187–1200 CE: Muhammad Ghori captures Ghazni, defeats northern Rajputs, and establishes a state based in Delhi; inherited by a Mamluk general in 1206.			

rare in the early Buddhist literature. What we do know, however, is that Buddhist monks and the merchants who were their principal sponsors passed along these highways. Suvarnabhumi, the name by which lower Burma was known in the Buddhist *jataka* tales, sent merchants and monks to Bengal and Bihar, the earliest mission having occurred while Buddha was still living. Urbanization gathered pace along the Ganges, the Jumna, the Narmada, the Godavari, and the Krishna. Along these river highways, or what one author has called "corridors," the first discernible attempts to integrate the land with the sea, and the Deccan uplands with the Gangetic plains, were taking shape.[4] If commerce played any role as an integrative force, it was inseparable from that played by Buddhism and Jainism.

Nearer the start of the Common Era, the movement of goods and people over long distances occurred mainly within six regional systems. All of these systems owed their particular advantage in conducting trade to having at least two of three localized geographical resources: location near a navigable river, the prospect of a safe port at an estuary or a transition zone between a river system and an ocean, and access to mountain passes. The relatively small size of ships made it possible to negotiate the rivers and move goods and people inland. Moreover, the estuary location and in some cases the inland river port sheltered ships from the violence of monsoon winds, storm waves, and pirates.

Three of the six systems had access to the Indian Ocean. These three were trade with West Asia and the Mediterranean from the Malabar coast, trade with Sri Lanka and Cambodia from Coromandel, and trade with Burma and Thailand from Bengal. The Indus and the Ganges rivers, along which the fourth and the fifth systems were formed, enabled goods to be carried over long distances along the two great fertile plains of South Asia. Both rivers fed into the sixth regional system, overland trade with Central Asia, China, and Eastern Europe from the upper Indus plains.

South Asia was almost completely encircled by the Himalayas and its branches. Roads leading out of the region that did not require climbing the mountains and locating a suitable crossing point were almost non-existent. The only known route that did not involve a mountain pass instead crossed the desert in western India and connected Gujarat with the Makran coast in Sind. Some of the invading armies from Persia and

---

[4] William Kirk, "The Role of India in the Diffusion of Early Cultures," *Geographical Journal* 141(1), 1975, pp. 19–34.

Afghanistan came this way, but its importance as a conduit for goods traffic was probably not large.

By comparison, some of the trans-Himalayan routes were very important commercially and politically. The trans-Himalayan trade was a complex combination of intersecting routes. In the early nineteenth century, the British Indian civilians, frontier customs officers, and European travelers who produced the first systematic body of knowledge about the Himalayan commercial world found that the plains of the Indus and the Ganges were linked with Persia, Central Asia, Tibet, and China via a cluster of mountain passes. Perhaps the six most critical clusters were (1) in the west, a road that started at the shores of the Indus (Dera Ghazi Khan), reached Quetta, and proceeded through the Bolan Pass to Kandahar and Persia; (2) in the north, a road that entered Afghanistan through the Khyber Pass, and turning northeast, went via Gilgit to Central Asia; (3) a road that proceeded from the Punjab plains via Ladakh through the Karakoram Pass to Central Asia; (4) in the Kumaon-Garhwal region, a road that went from the plains along the valley of the Kali River that demarcates the present border between India and Nepal, and reached Tibet, Mansarovar, and the Sutlej Valley through the Lipu Lekh Pass, (5) in the eastern Himalayas, a road that connected Tibet and India via the Nathu La in Sikkim; and (6) in northeastern Assam, a road that went along the river Brahmaputra to the Zayul Valley and bifurcated to reach Tibet to the north, China to the east, and Burma to the south.

These roads, and especially the western Himalayan ones, were used for conquest and trade for centuries and kept the northwestern parts of the subcontinent autonomous from the great empires that ruled riparian northern India. It is likely that the Indus Valley civilization had been connected to the Mediterranean not only by sea but also via the Bolan Pass. The Karakorum Pass and Khyber Pass routes were used by traders and pilgrims from China; both led to the Silk Road, joining it in Khotan. Because all of these roads were unsuitable for wheeled traffic, except, to a limited extent, for the Khyber Pass route, cargo was carried by sheep, ponies, and camels. Some of the mountain passes were so high as to cause severe stress to the animals. Usually, it was necessary to change animals several times, so that the local populations needed to conduct a part of the trade. The strong presence of local elements and the harsh geography of mountain trade further distanced this segment from the trade of the plains.

Still, caravan trade and sea trade may have joined each other in certain locations. The region of present Punjab, towns along the Ganges, ports in the Indus and Ganges deltas, and ports on the Gujarat coast may have received goods by land and river together. Coastal trade, also called by archaeologists "looping," or port-to-port, trade, added another possibile way to combine maritime trade and overland caravan traffic. For example, one of the overland routes from China to India started at Yunnan and reached the river Irrawaddy; it then followed the river to Pegu, with which Bengal had an ancient maritime link. Despite such possibilities, there is little evidence that the trans-Himalayan traffic was connected systematically with the commercial world of the plains. Most seaports functioned autonomously, that is, they were served by distinct "hinterlands" along different systems of rivers. The main trading groups and the trading infrastructure varied significantly among the systems in question. For example, seminomadic breeders of horse and sheep dominated the trans-Himalayan trade, cattle breeders occupied the Deccan pathways, and boatmen and their sponsors controlled the river traffic in the plains.

That this pattern of trading was extraordinarily stable in the long run can be easily verified. Major archaeological sites on the seaboard were located on the estuaries of rivers, suggesting simultaneous access to the sea and to the interior by boats. Investigation in the Ganges and Indus plains also shows the dependence of prehistoric trade on the rivers. In other words, the major arteries of commerce, external and internal, developed along the rivers and at the points where the rivers met the ocean. There were exceptions, however; for example, the occurrence of deposits of valuable minerals in the Deccan plateau supported trade routes that were much too costly in time and money to sustain any other trade. But these exceptions proved the rule. All of these systems, moreover, survived well into modern times. Not until the end of the seventeenth century, when the English East India Company had established trading stations in Bombay and Madras, did the pattern finally begin to change. All of these older trading systems became less important after Indo-European trade began. In the eighteenth century, when the advantage began to tilt toward sites of trade that did not conform to the old geographical norms of location, the millennial pattern of commerce started to recast itself.

Not only was the regional pattern enduring, so also was the composition of trade. Through almost two thousand years, ships brought gold and horses into India and took away textiles and spices. Other goods figuring as imports and exports had, by comparison, shorter and more fluctuating careers. Great upheavals did take place in the volumes carried, in the destinations, and also in the patterns of sponsorship and consumption.

Time and again the participants, that is, the communities engaged in building ships, in trading, and, possibly, in financing trade, saw a reshuffling. A moderately strong correlation seemed to exist between state formation, especially the formation of empires, and the fortunes of trade. In this way, the long decades during which once stable and powerful empires, such as the Maurya, Gupta, Kusana, and Harsha, decayed, yield fewer artifacts pointing to a thriving long-distance trade. Through it all, the principal highways of traffic, the core merchandise, even the basic structure of ships, changed relatively little until the European era.

The earliest identifiable rise of commerce, albeit a gradual one, appears to have taken place in the middle of the first millennium BCE. This period is noted for three important changes. One change was the rise of religions that advocated nonviolence, thereby reducing sacrifices and expensive rituals. The emphasis on a frugal lifestyle and peaceful neighborly relations suited the mercantile temperament. Not surprisingly, merchants were the principal sponsors of these religions. Settlement sites have been found in the middle-Ganges plains for this earliest period of known commerce that indicate the presence of long-distance trade. A second change was the introduction of coinage in the sixth century BCE, which promoted regional monetary integration. The third change was the increasing use of writing, which may have indirectly helped long-distance and complex economic transactions.[5] This process of change was centered in the eastern Gangetic plains, where settled agriculture had given rise to powerful landed communities yet where access to the sea and to river-borne trade remained the principal means of procuring precious metals and consumption goods. States, therefore, chose to sponsor merchants and the religion of the merchants, Buddhism.

The Mauryan Empire revealed a combination of all of these elements – commerce, religion, agriculture, and coinage. The connection between religion and commerce was clearer in the northern part of the Deccan plateau, where a cluster of rockcut Buddhist caves received the patronage of not only kings but also subcastes, merchant guilds, and families.[6] Pilgrims, caravans, and soldiers all used the same roads in the plateau. Along these roads, or situated close to them, were some of the great marvels of Buddhist art, such as the cave paintings of Ajanta, believed to be commissioned by a Saivite Vakataka king in the fifth century CE.

---

[5] Himanshu Prabha Ray, "Trade in the Western Deccan under the Satavahanas," *Studies in History* 1(1), 1985, pp. 15–35.

[6] See Romila Thapar, "Patronage and Community," in Barbara S. Miller, ed., *The Powers of Art: Patronage in Indian Culture*, Delhi: Oxford University Press, 1992, pp. 19–34.

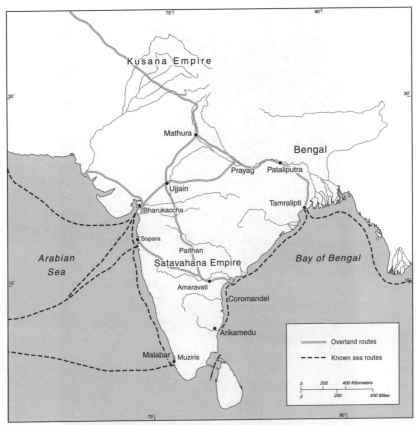

2.2. Trade routes, early Common Era.

Although these roads did lead to the sea, the standard sources on the great land-based empires, whose capitals were located deep inland, do not offer detailed accounts of maritime trade. There was a connection between the interior and the littoral, but the connection was a limited and intermittent one. The most famous episode of growth in maritime commerce happened for some parts of the coast that remained poorly integrated with the land-based states. This was the trade with the Roman world that developed from the first century onward. Roman trade achieved a limited integration of the hinterland accessible by the river, the ports, and the coast. The effect of Indo-Roman trade, therefore, was confined to parts of the peninsular region.

2.3. Bolan Pass. The corridor between the plains of the Indus and
Afghanistan and Persia, the pass was used for centuries by traders and
armies. This sketch was made in 1842. From the author's collection.

Indo-Roman trade

When in the eighteenth and nineteenth centuries, European orientalists
initiated research on early Indian history, their interests were in language
and culture. Economic history began in the twentieth century and continued to be influenced by the broad generalizations advanced by imperialist
historians, principally James Mill. In this interpretation, Indian history
displayed economic stagnation, insularity, and a hierarchy of which the
most politically visible form was despotism. In the early twentieth century,
H. G. Rawlinson, using numismatic evidence, and E. H. Warmington,

relying on Greek and Latin sources, readjusted the picture significantly and showed the presence of considerable Indo-European trade at the beginning of the Christian era.[7] In the mid-twentieth century, archaeological explorations in South India fleshed out the story of Indo-Roman trade.

Many aspects of that story, however, remain insufficiently known. One of the fundamental concerns is the identity of the traders. Were they mainly West Asians, Europeans, or Indians? There is scant reference to Indian agency in Indo-Roman trade. But the initial inference that the trade was conducted by outsiders has been challenged, although not conclusively dispelled, in writings that use Indian sources regarding merchants. Indo-Roman trade was once thought to be operated by "Roman" traders, which category likely included Arab and Persian communities as well, but the discovery of Tamil-Brahmi inscriptions in pottery found at Egyptian coastal sites suggests the presence of contemporary South Indian merchants in the Arabian Sea.[8]

More recent scholarship has done much to reposition Indo-Roman trade as a chapter in the story of economic change in India and the tradition of seafaring in the Arabian Sea rather than as a story set in classical Europe. R. Champakalakshmi contends that during the early historical period (300 BCE–300 CE), South India's cities were usually port cities and were closely connected with Indo-Roman trade.[9] The significance of Roman trade in the context of trade along the Indian Ocean coast is a debated issue, however. The Indo-Roman trade is slightly better documented than the world of which it was a part. The states that controlled the southern and western Indian coasts were clearly interested in the goods that came in from the oceanic trade, as well as in the customs revenues to be had from it. Still, these states were primarily reliant on revenue from land and had their nerve centers located in the interior of the Deccan plateau. Consequently, a political and economic cleavage continued to exist between the interior and the littoral.

Archaeological evidence shows the duration and dynamism of the Indian Ocean trade network linking the Roman Empire with India, East Africa, Iran, and Sri Lanka via the Red Sea. Literary evidence comes from a variety

---

[7] R. S. Sharma and D. N. Jha, "The Economic History of India Up to AD 1200: Trends and Prospects," *Journal of the Economic and Social History of the Orient* 17(1), 1974, pp. 48–80.

[8] Vimala Begley, "Arikamedu Reconsidered," *American Journal of Archaeology* 87(4), 1983, pp. 461–81.

[9] R. Champakalakshmi. *Trade Ideology and Urbanization: South India, 300 BC to AD 1300*, New York: Oxford University Press, 1996.

of sources, both Indian Puranic and Greco-Roman, but the preeminent place among the sources is occupied by the *Periplus of Erythraean Sea*. According to this source, Roman, Arabian, and Persian ships crossing the Arabian Sea reached three destinations in India: Broach on the Gujarat coast (Barygaza of Periplus), Muziris (Pattanam) and Nelkynda on the Malabar coast, and a cluster of ports on the Coromandel coast, of which the principal one was Arikamedu. Consistent with historical sources like the *Periplus*, archaeological findings at sites such as Pattanam indicate that a considerable and regular trade existed between West Asian and Mediterranean merchants and Indian traders and artisans.

Along these routes, Roman coins, amphorae, ceramics, especially red polished ware, and bronzes, and Indian cotton textiles have been found dated between the first and the fourth centuries CE. The Mediterranean market for these goods influenced the production of particular styles and types. One local industry known to have been significantly influenced by Roman technology was the manufacture of glass beads.[10] Other than gold, amphorae constituted the main article of import. A question of great interest is what an amphora represented in India. Was it a utility good? Was it an intermediate good, that is, an object for use in industries such as fish processing, alcohol distillation, or oil extraction? Was it an item symbolizing wealth and used mainly in palaces? Were amphorae in demand as containers for luxuries such as wine or for the other liquids they may have carried? It is even possible that the amphorae were imported mainly for the use of the Roman settlers on the coasts. So far, the evidence suggesting the amphorae's use and consumers is too fragmentary to settle the issue.

The pattern of distribution of "rouletted ware" and "russet-coated painted ware" suggests that the ports on the Coromandel coast may have been linked by trade among themselves and with Sri Lanka. But evidence of a direct link between the east and the west coasts by sea or over land, once thought to have been organized by Roman merchants, is scarce. Of the maritime ports, Arikamedu, on the eastern coast, has been the best researched. As a trade center, it functioned from the third century BCE until the first or the second century CE. Throughout this long period, parts of the site may have been lost to inundation, as indeed happened after it ceased to function as a port, destroying evidence of

---

[10] C. Margabandhu, "Trade Contacts between Western India and the Graeco-Roman World in the Early Centuries of the Christian Era," *Journal of the Economic and Social History of the Orient* 8(3), 1965, pp. 316–22.

2.4. Arikamedu. The site contains an eighteenth-century French building (shown here). Contemporary French travellers noted the significance of the place. *Source*: Arul Jegadeesh

any links between the Coromandel and Malabar coasts. The absence of a regular link between the two coasts can be inferred from the fact that the *Periplus* mentions only ports on the western coast. The estimated items of export from Arikamedu were beads, gemstones, shell bangles, ivory articles, textiles, spices, incense, and leather articles. The presence of some of these items is inferred rather than proved.

The original excavation of Arikamedu identified the rouletted ware as Roman, a thesis that now stands questioned but perhaps not discarded. More recent analysis of ceramic designs and dating confirm Vimala Begley's hypothesis that, though influenced by Roman designs, pottery was a local industry and evolved within an Asian tradition of ceramic production and decoration.[11] In particular, the evidence points to the existence of considerable commercial and technological exchange between Bengal and

---

[11] Vimla Begley, "Rouletted Ware at Arikamedu: A New Approach," *American Journal of Archaeology* 92(4), 1988, pp. 427–40. See also Osmund Bopearachch, "New Archaeological Evidence on Cultural and Commercial Relationships between Ancient Sri Lanka and Tamil Nadu," *Journal of Interdisciplinary Studies in History and Archaeology* 1(1), 2004, pp. 60–72.

Tamil Nadu. Material that was Roman in origin turns up in some of the other eastern port settlements as well.

It has been suggested that the Roman traders held a special advantage in crossing the Arabian Sea, for although monsoon winds were used for navigation, the dangers of the monsoon demanded the larger and sturdier ships built in Rome. Communities located on the Arab-Persian Gulf, the Gerrheans, the Characenians, and the Palmyrenians, among others, performed the role of middlemen in connecting India with the Mediterranean.[12] The ships used by Indian, Persian, and Arabian sailors were of a different construction from those used by the Romans. *Periplus* calls these "small vessels, sailing close around the shores of the gulfs."[13] Roman colonies existed in some locations in West Asia and on the western Indian coast, and Greco-Roman donations to Buddhist sites and monasteries suggest a pattern of sponsorship that had Indian and commercial antecedents. The Indian princes employed Roman shipwrights and Greco-Roman soldiers, and presents were made of European slaves. "Singing boys and beautiful maidens for the harem" find mention in the *Periplus*.[14]

Whereas Roman ships called on western India once a year, the trade that they encouraged or participated in continued throughout the year. The principal western Indian ports, Sopara (a northern suburb of Mumbai) and Broach, or Barygaza, on the south Gujarat coast, were connected by mountain passes to cities located in the interior of the Satavahana domain and that of its vassals. Bengal muslins were transported overland to these sites for export. The *Periplus* states that "[i]nland from this place [Barygaza] and to the east, is the city called Ozene [Ujjain], formerly a royal capital; from this place are brought down all things needed for the welfare of the country about Barygaza, and many things for our trade: agate and carnelian, Indian muslins and mallow cloth, and much ordinary cloth."[15] Similar remarks are made about Paithan and Tagara, or Ter, in northern Konkan.

The existence of a regionally integrated Indian trading system would be reading too much from these references in the *Periplus*. The references to

---

[12] Vimala Begley and Richard Daniel de Puma, eds., *Rome and India: The Ancient Sea Trade*, Madison: University of Wisconsin Press, 1991.

[13] *The Periplus of the Erythraen Sea* (trans. Wilfred Schoff), London: Longmans Green, 1912, p. 45.

[14] *Periplus*, p. 42. See also Michael Vickers, "Nabataea, India, Gaul, and Carthage: Reflections on Hellenistic and Roman Gold Vessels and Red-Gloss Pottery," *American Journal of Archaeology* 98(2), 1994, pp. 231–48.

[15] *Periplus*, p. 42.

southern Deccan and northwestern India in the same source are of a general nature and suggest limited contact or obstructions of a natural or political kind. Bactria is mentioned as a source of silk traded in Gujarat ports, but the volume of the trade was stated to be limited. The Malabar port of Muziris was the principal source for pepper and pearls, but both these goods were produced in small areas located near the port. All in all, the references to backward regional linkages in the *Periplus* are sketchy indeed. As recent scholarship shows, based on Ptolemy's descriptions of India, which was more detailed on Bactria under Kusana rule than on the Deccan port cities, it is possible to reconstruct the Taxila-Ujjain trade route in the first or the second century CE quite plausibly, and it is even possible that the route stayed almost intact until the seventeenth century. Clearly, the Kusana rulers taxed trade on this route. But the links among the northern empires with coastal and maritime trade remains obscure.[16]

Determining the extent of Indo-Roman trade can be approached from the Roman end, of course. How frequent and significant are the references to Indian goods in Roman sources? There are indeed references in Roman literary sources to Indian spices and fine cloth and, in more generic terms, to the wealth of India. Still, too few objects identifiable with Indian trade have been found in the Mediterranean. This should be no surprise since spices and cloth are perishable over such a long period of time. It is nevertheless surprising that few or no crafted and manufactured goods other than textiles seem to have traveled from India to the Mediterranean, despite the antiquity of metallurgy in the South Asia region.[17]

The *Periplus* is almost silent on trading institutions and arrangements. Some suggestions on this dimension are available from literary texts like the *Jataka*, segments of the *Arthasastra*, which have been dated to the early first millennium CE, and the writings of the Sanskrit grammarian Panini, possibly the fifth century CE. Almost all of these sources pertain to the middle Gangetic plains. The wide usage of three distinct terms to refer to merchants, bankers, and caravan runners establishes the obvious point that long-distance trade allowed a division of labor among the capitalists it engaged, especially between the bankers, who were more sedentary, more politically connected, and wealthier, and the agents who were more peripatetic and poorer. The sources hint at the coexistence of a variety

---

[16] P. H. L. Eggermont, "The Murundas and the Ancient Trade-Route from Taxila to Ujjain," *Journal of the Economic and Social History of the Orient* 9(3), 1966, pp. 257–96.

[17] Grant Parker, "*Ex Oriente Luxuria*: Indian Commodities and Roman Experience," *Journal of the Economic and Social History of the Orient* 45(1), 2002, pp. 40–95.

of systems of sale, including that of artisans selling their wares to the final consumers, which was more common in the highly skilled crafts. The presence of some specialization among merchants may have been owing to artisans turning to trade. Alongside specialist merchants, there were others who would purchase shares in the mixed cargo of a ship.[18] Given that the cargo of most ships contained a highly variable mixture of goods, such merchants served a diverse clientele. Conspicuously rare in these descriptions are references to merchant contracts over long distances and long periods. One source, the Muziris papyrus, records a loan contract that was possibly drawn in Rome to be executed in India. But the details of the contracting parties are not known.[19] In contrast, writings that used Indian literary and epigraphic sources did indicate the extensive presence of guilds and corporate bodies. Hindu codes also recorded conspicuous references to corporate bodies, which tended to be based on the principles of caste, that is, founded on notions of purity maintained by endogamy, and juridical autonomy granted by the state to wealthy endogamous professional groups.[20]

The institutionalization of Buddhism, with its relatively urban character, is believed to have encouraged trade and the mobility of merchants in the classical era, both indirectly, by weakening barriers derived from proscriptions about food, marriage, or partnership between socially unequal agents that Hindus faced in conducting trade, and directly, by making monasteries a haven for traveling merchants. Proselytization over long distances inevitably created wider contacts that were exploited or created by the mobile traders.[21]

For about three centuries after the beginning of the Christian era, as Indo-Roman trade flourished on the western coast, an overland trade was conducted among India, Central Asia, and China along routes that carried merchants and Buddhist pilgrims alike. The silk cloth known from the Mauryan times as *chinamsuka* remained an article in Indo-Chinese trade for nearly two thousand years. The dating and provenance of this cloth can be debated. It has been suggested that the passages in the literary sources that refer to this cloth were later insertions and that the cloth may

---

[18] Ray, "Trade in the Western Deccan," p. 21.

[19] Parker, "*Ex Oriente Luxuria*," p. 64.

[20] P. V. Kane, *History of Dharmasastra (Ancient and Medieval Religious and Civil Law in India)*, Poona: Bhandarkar Oriental Research Institute, vols. 1–6, 1946, mainly vols. 3 and 4.

[21] See the useful review article, Kathleen D. Morrison, "Commerce and Culture in South Asia: Perspectives from Archaeology and History," *Annual Review of Anthropology* 26, 1997, pp. 87–108.

have entered India via migrants from Central Asia rather than from China itself.[22] Whereas Indian imports from China mainly consisted of silks, Indian exports included coral, pearls, glass vessels and beads, precious stones, lapis lazuli, incense, perfume, and myrrh. Clearly, the market for these goods would have been urban and wealthy consumers, possibly the court itself. It can be inferred, therefore, that a nexus between royal patronage (in this case the patronage of the Kusana court), the monastery, and trade had developed on the northern borders of India.[23] Recent research suggests the presence of two other articles as well, both possibly exported from Bengal to China by sea, namely, cotton cloth and horses.[24]

Western Indian Ocean in late antiquity

From the fourth century on, Roman coins and goods in India become scarce. The impetus for what one historian of South India has called "early Indian urbanism" weakened.[25] Other scholars characterize the post-Gupta political fragmentation and climate of uneasy coexistence in North India as "early medieval" on the ground that it represented the absence of hegemonic empires. These characterizations imply that, compared to in the imperial states, there was weaker integration of the interior with the ports. At the same time, there was hardly any stoppage of trade. Most likely, the coastal regions continued to trade, if less vigorously than before, but with a new set of partners and with a larger number of itinerant merchants connecting the ports with a more limited set of supply zones.

One of the goods that survived the turmoil in West Asia, and may even have experienced "a definite increase in demand," was horses. Ranabir Chakravarti's research on the horse trade in the subcontinent suggests the trade's antiquity and stability.[26] The rise and fall of empires affected

---

[22] Lallanji Gopal, "Textiles in Ancient India," *Journal of the Economic and Social History of the Orient* 4(1), 1961, pp. 53–69.

[23] Xinru Liu, *Ancient India and Ancient China: Trade and Religious Exchanges, A.D. 1–600*, New York: Oxford University Press, 1988.

[24] Stephen F. Dale, "Silk Road, Cotton Road or ... Indo-Chinese Trade in Pre-European Times," *Modern Asian Studies* 43(1), 2009, pp. 79–88.

[25] James Heitzman, "Temple Urbanism in Medieval South India," *Journal of Asian Studies* 46(4), 1987, pp. 791–826.

[26] Ranabir Chakravarti, "Horse Trade and Piracy at Tana (Thana, Maharashtra, India): Gleanings from Marco Polo," *Journal of the Economic and Social History of the Orient* 34(3), 1991, pp. 159–82; "Early Medieval Bengal and the Trade in Horses: A Note," *Journal of the Economic and Social History of the Orient* 42(2), 1999, pp. 194–211.

the demand for horses in the same direction. Horses came into the subcontinent from Persia by the Arabian Sea, from Central Asia over mountain passes in the western Himalayas, and possibly from Yunnan across the eastern Himalayas. The northern overland route was sponsored by the Kusanas in the early centuries CE, and Chakravarti shows that some of the horses that entered by this route may have been exported by sea from Bengal to the Coromandel ports. Conspicuously rare in accounts of the horse trade is any mention of the regular transport of horses overland across the Deccan plateau, whether in a north-south or an east-west direction, which is not surprising given the scarcity of pasture and water in parts of the plateau. For the same reason, the horse trade stimulated maritime ports and led to the development of new ports on the Konkan littoral. The period between the ninth century and the twelfth is seen to have witnessed a considerable increase in horse trading between the Persian Gulf and Aden and western India. In turn, because horses were a tool of warfare, regional states tried constantly to control and divert the trade, making such commerce riskier than before.

Disputing an older view that there was an overall retraction of trade in late antiquity and particularly a decline in Indo-Mediterranean trade thereafter, recent scholarship on West Asia finds that trade split in the western part of the Indian Ocean. The Indian and West Asian link came to be dominated by a number of new merchant communities, mainly Sasanians and Ethiopians. Sasanian occupation of Yemen contributed to this reshuffling, and Byzantine shipping in the Red Sea declined. New entrepôts emerged consistent with the pattern of political control in West Asia.[27] Arab and Persian groups, in partnership with Indians and East Africans, began to control the Arabian Sea trade, setting a pattern that was to last long into the future. Indian Ocean cities on the Arab peninsula served a middleman function until well into the European entry into the Indian Ocean. The middleman role of the peninsula encouraged the reexport trade between India and Africa, as the presence in coastal regions of Indian red-polished ware testifies. Coastal trade flourished and, in South Asia, shifted northward, away from Malabar and Coromandel, as the increasing importance of the Sind port of Daybul suggests.

It is impossible to conjecture about the rise or fall in volume of trade between India and the Mediterranean from the fifth century to the tenth century. Reading the Indian historical literature, it would appear that the end of the Gupta Empire in the fifth century, and increasing political

[27] Michael G. Morony, "Economic Boundaries? Late Antiquity and Early Islam," *Journal of the Economic and Social History of the Orient* 47(2), 2004, pp. 166–94.

fragmentation of India thereafter, led to a disintegration of trade and in turn to a weakening of the link between overland and maritime trades. The fall in the occurrence of foreign coins in India suggests a similar trend. On the other hand, Indian trade remained important to West Asia, North Africa, and the Mediterranean. The presence of powerful merchant diasporas in managing India trade in North Africa and West Asia is reaffirmed in the cluster of material available from Geniza sources.[28]

Although research on the documents collected from the Fustat Geniza began early in the twentieth century, if not earlier, the research was first applied to the history of the Maghribi Jewish community in the city rather than to the history of regional trade.[29] The research of S. D. Goitein in the second half of the twentieth century changed this orientation.[30] Goitein concentrated on a subset of the Geniza material dealing with mercantile transactions, helping to contextualize this material, or a significant part of it, within state formation and the Arabian Sea trade from the late eleventh century. His research established that prominent members of the Maghribi community, who were already part of Mediterranean trade, and who owned manufactories, shifted their attention eastward with the decline of the Abbasid Caliphate and the rise of the Fatimids in Egypt, and with the consequent emergence of Aden as a major entrepôt.[31]

According to Goitein, "Only at the very end of the eleventh century, when the overwhelming power of the Christian Mediterranean states reduced Muslim and Jewish seafaring, did other outlets for enterprising men have to be found."[32] It was then that some of these "enterprising men" "felt their way" over Yemen to the seacoast and eventually to India. One of the pioneers who initiated the India-Mediterranean textile trade was the maker of and dealer in purple cloth from Tunisia, 'Arus b. Joseph al-Arjawani al-Mahdawi. Much more is known of his nephew and

---

[28] The sources referred to were Hebrew manuscripts found in the Ben Ezra synagogue in Cairo in the nineteenth century, and later transported and stored in libraries around the world. The documents date from the ninth century CE and deal with, among other subjects, religious, juridical, and commercial ones.

[29] E.g., S. Schechter, "Geniza Specimens," *Jewish Quarterly Review* 13(1), 1901, pp. 218–21.

[30] S. D. Goitein, "From the Mediterranean to India: Documents on the Trade to India, South Arabia, and East Africa from the Eleventh and Twelfth Centuries," *Speculum* 29(2), 1954, pp. 181–97.

[31] Roxani Eleni Margariti, *Aden and the Indian Ocean Trade: 150 Years in the Life of a Medieval Arabian Port*, Chapel Hill: University of North Carolina Press, 2007.

[32] S. D. Goitein, "Portrait of a Medieval India Trader: Three Letters from the Cairo Geniza," *Bulletin of the School of Oriental and African Studies* 50(3), 1987, pp. 449–64.

son-in-law, ʿAllan b. Hassin, who was apprenticed early to his uncle and was often away on voyages, as was his father-in-law. ʿAllan's letters constitute an important source on how the India textile trade evolved and have often been used by Goitein in his reconstruction of the trade. It would appear that ʿAllan took clothing given him by his father-in-law for sale in Yemen. It would have been common for wealthy merchants to contribute money to voyages such as these. The next stage in the evolution of this trade must have taken place as individuals like ʿAllan set off from Aden to Malabar, following a route already familiar to traders from India. Under the best of conditions, the journey took between two and three weeks.

The letters that ʿAllan sent from India spoke repeatedly of his having to brave the dangers from the monsoon winds and, in less clear terms, from the government of the port city of Quilon. The risks of the voyage included a temporary breakdown in civil order in Aden, leading to rioting and bloodshed. The merchants did not own the ships on which they traveled; the ships were owned by sailors and carried a large number of passengers from other places. ʿAllan's letters suggest that ship captains often acted as the procurers of goods, but that seasoned merchants frowned on the practice because of the risk of buying poor quality that it carried. ʿAllan wrote the letters when he was an old man and in them he also expressed regret over having been away from home for the better part of his life, exhorting his sons to avoid a similar business style, perhaps by installing permanent agents in the distant ports.

The Geniza documents indicate the importance of textiles and dyes in the basket of regular imports from the subcontinent. In the eleventh century, the merchant house of Ibn ʿAwkal purchased "Sandani" (from Sanjan?) indigo and lac, which provided the major components for blue and red dyes. It also procured pepper from Malabar. These articles were destined for European markets. Other occasional products included sandalwood and aloe, and medicinal fruits and vegetables, especially myrobalan (*Terminalia chebula*, a textile-dye ingredient).[33] There is also a mention in at least one document of a considerable quantity of iron. In return, the Mediterranean products exported to India contained beads and corals, which, along with mats (carpets?), were sent as presents to various destinations.[34]

---

[33] Norman A. Stillman, "The Eleventh-Century Merchant House of Ibn ʿAwkal (A Geniza Study)," *Journal of the Economic and Social History of the Orient* 16(1), 1973, pp. 15–88.

[34] S. D. Goitein, "The Main Industries of the Mediterranean Area as Reflected in the Records of the Cairo Geniza," *Journal of the Economic and Social History of the Orient* 4(2), 1961, pp. 168–97.

As valuable as the Geniza sources are, they shed little light on the trading world of the Indians compared to what they say about the community or the commercial and political institutions of the Red Sea region. There are intriguing references to partnerships between foreign merchants and Indian agents, but little more than glimpses.

One recent attempt to reread Goitein in conjunction with local sources in the hope of gleaning more information on the Indians has had limited success. This work by Chakravarti suggests that port building was actively pursued by the coastal states, which were individually small and perhaps not strong polities fiscally but were interested in maritime trade precisely for those reasons. Indeed, some of these states, or their local arms, may even have been established by shipowners. But even when not shipowners themselves, these rulers maintained good relations with shipowners and merchants. The majority of the shipowners were West Asian Muslims, but a few Indian and Konkani participants could be found among this class. More controversially, the paper finds signs of friendly partnership between Hindu and Muslim maritime merchants on the Gujarat coast. A critical rereading of the political economy of the Arabian Sea, however, suggests that there was, in fact, a quite heightened degree of competition between these two groups of merchants, at times breaking into violence.[35]

As will be seen in the next section, while India's west coast reestablished trade links with the Mediterranean, an important new connection was being forged in the east.

Coromandel, or two deltas

There is a strong suggestion in the historical scholarship that the Chola state, which developed in the Kaveri delta spanning the Thanjavur, Tiruchirappalli, and Pudukottai districts of the Tamil Nadu state, and existed between c. 850 and c. 1280, achieved a reintegration of ports and hinterlands after the connection had seemed to weaken between the fourth and seventh centuries. The authority of the state extended over a much wider region, unified by activities such as ritual gift giving and

---

[35] Ranabir Chakravarti, "Nakhudas and Nauvittakas: Ship-Owning Merchants in the West Coast of India (c. AD 1000–1500)," *Journal of the Economic and Social History of the Orient* 43(1), 2000, pp. 34–64; Roxani Eleni Margariti, "Mercantile Networks, Port Cities, and 'Pirate' States: Conflict and Competition in the Indian Ocean World of Trade before the Sixteenth Century," *Journal of the Economic and Social History of the Orient* 51(4), 2008, 543–77.

temple sponsorship by both the state and the overlords. In this way, during the medieval and imperial periods (600–1300) temples supplied the institutional axis for the cities of South India.[36]

The fiscal system and integrative policies of the state strengthened the towns as points of trade. Transactions in grain, spices, and cloth were regular and large scale. Less regularly, there was trade also in elephants, horses, and precious stones. Burton Stein suggests that the consolidation of imperial power in this way "contributed to the decline of the established itinerant trade groups which had enjoyed prominence during the earlier Chola period, when nadu localities existed in a more isolated, self-sufficient manner."[37] Kenneth Hall makes a similar point in showing the emergence of regulated marketplaces against the backdrop of decaying local networks.[38] The authority of merchant guilds in these centers is well established and was cemented by the gifts the merchants made to the temples. The urbanization and rootedness of trade, scholars hypothesize, enabled or increased the practice of using consumption goods obtainable from trade as symbols of royal power, while also making the taxation of trade easier to achieve than before. In this way, trade, integrative state policies, merchant guilds, and fiscal authority were mutually enhanced. Even though this picture seems, on the whole, plausible, one must recognize that historians of medieval South India make quite liberal use of speculation in filling in the details. For example, there is little evidence as yet on just how important foreign trade was to the income of the Chola state. And the impression that trade was of marginal importance, while unproven, cannot be dismissed.

In any case, the rise of the Chola state shifted the direction of external trade toward the east and also revived the status of Coromandel as a regional trading system. Archaeological and epigraphic evidence points to the antiquity of sea trade between Southeast Asia and India. Indeed, recent scholarship suggests that "after the fourth century C.E., concurrent with a number of political and cultural changes in the subcontinent, ... growing Southeast Asian political entities widely adopt a common script, iconography and set of political terms derived from Indian models."[39]

[36] R. Champakalahsmi, "Urbanisation in South India: The Role of Ideology and Polity," *Social Scientist* 15(8/9), 1987, pp. 67–117.
[37] Burton Stein, "Circulation and the Historical Geography of Tamil Country," *Journal of Asian Studies* 37(1), 1977, pp. 7–26.
[38] Kenneth Hall, "Coinage, Trade and Economy in Early South India and Its Southeast Asian Neighbours," *Indian Economic Social History* Review 36(4), 1999, pp. 431–59.
[39] Monica L. Smith, " 'Indianization' from the Indian Point of View: Trade and Cultural Contacts with Southeast Asia in the Early First Millennium," *Journal of the Economic and Social History of the Orient* 42(1), 1999, pp. 1–26 (quote on p. 2).

The "political and cultural changes" in question refer to the Gupta Empire's reaching its apogee and to the sponsorship that Vedic culture received among many South Indian polities as a result. Merchants and religious personages in turn carried these ideas to Southeast Asia.

It is believed that contact became systematic and possibly larger in scale from the tenth century onward. The concurrent rise of imperial states in China (the Sung), Cambodia (the Khmer), Burma, Egypt (the Fatimids), and northern Vietnam (the Ly) consolidated intra-Asian trade during this time.[40] Two other factors that accounted for "the Asian trade boom" after the tenth century were the demand for textiles and the presence of two strong imperial states at the textiles' origin and destination, the Chola and the Khmer. These factors were mutually reinforcing, for some of the textiles being shipped from South India were destined for consumption by the elite. Thus it was possibly consumption rather than the fiscal motivation that led the Khmer local administration to monitor the textile trade. Moreover, because this market was so secure and profitable, and India so far away, the trade encouraged import substitution, mainly in Cambodia and Java.[41]

It was not only knowledge about textile production that was exported to Southeast Asia during the peak period of Chola political and economic expansion. Spices such as pepper and important sources of dyes, such as safflower and indigo, journeyed from South India across the sea, just as cotton had more than a thousand years before, to take root in Java.[42] Ceramic styles traveled too. Metal casting and jewelry styles were also incorporated into Javanese crafts. As had happened with textiles, Javanese production substituted for South Indian imports of pepper and dyes too after the twelfth century.

Who were the agents in these transactions? There is no epigraphic evidence of Tamil merchants among the merchants whose presence in Southeast Asia was noted. Most identifiable groups came either from the Telugu-speaking regions in the northern Deccan or from Konkan, the leading group being represented by the trade guild known as the Ayyavole. It is also curious that the merchants maintained only a weak institutional

---

[40] Kenneth Hall, "International Trade and Foreign Diplomacy in Early Medieval South India," *Journal of the Economic and Social History of the Orient* 21(1), 1978, pp. 75–98.

[41] Gillian Green, "Indic Impetus? Innovations in Textile Usage in Angkorian Period Cambodia," *Journal of the Economic and Social History of the Orient* 43(3), 2000, pp. 277–313.

[42] Jan Wisseman Christie, "Javanese Markets and the Asian Sea Trade Boom of the Tenth to Thirteenth Centuries," *Journal of the Economic and Social History of the Orient* 41(3), 1998, pp. 344–81.

identity in the Javanese ports. Little trace of a guild or of extension of the guild form can be found in Southeast Asia. From the eighth century, references to cooperatives of itinerant merchants, the most important group being the Ayyavole, begin to appear in Andhra and Tamil regions. They were usually identified in connection to a territory, village, or town, and sometimes to the principal commodity traded. The composition of these groups was quite diverse. Their constitutions and rules remain obscure, and the range of services that they offered cannot be completely ascertained. After Chola ascendance, these associations progressively urbanized and became less mobile than before, eventually becoming a different kind of group altogether (see also Chapter 3).

The fertile delta of the Krishna, with its easy access to the Bay of Bengal, became the site for a contest for control in the fifth to seventh centuries. The Chalukyas, who eventually came to rule this segment of coastal Andhra (c. 620), received the support of the artisans and the Teliki (extractor of oil from oilseeds) merchants of the delta, which was crucial to political stabilization, not the least because these well-organized merchant associations could also supply the Chalukyas with soldiers.[43] Further north of the delta, on the borders of Orissa and Andhra Pradesh, a cluster of seaside commercial centers appear in inscriptions dated from about 1000 CE, suggesting the presence of Bay of Bengal merchants. The most important market in the region was possibly Bhogapura, but little is known about the trade of this region beyond what we can guess from the presence of royal patronage and merchant sponsors of temples.[44] Comparatively more is known about the Bengal delta.

Bengal

The delta of the Ganges River system, which forms a part of Bengal, had served subcontinental trade in four distinct ways: as a point for the reexport of northern imports (such as horses) via the Bay of Bengal, as a source for fine cotton textiles exported to western and northern India, as a point of contact with trade across the eastern Himalayas, and as a link between South Asia and East Asia by sea. It is possible to show the antiquity of all of these routes but impossible to track the trade volumes and changes therein.

[43] P. S. Kanaka Durga, "Identity and Symbols of Sustenance: Explorations in Social Mobility of Medieval South India," *Journal of the Economic and Social History of the Orient* 44(2), 2001, pp. 141–74.

[44] K. C. Dash, "Economic Life of Orissa under the Imperial Gangas," in N. R. Patnaik, ed., *Economic History of Orissa*, New Delhi: Indus, 1997, pp. 49–61.

From the early centuries CE, lower Bengal traded with Burma, selling textiles for gold and silver. The small hoards of gold coins found near Chittagong indicate the conversion of the metal into regional coins. However, the numismatic evidence is far too slight to construct a detailed history. The preeminent trading post in Bengal was Tamralipti, which, according to one account, was located on the main channel of the Ganges early in the Common Era. The port had contacts with the major inland river ports, Varanasi and Pataliputra on the one side, and with Southeast Asia and Sri Lanka on the other. "The exports," writes H. G. Rawlinson, "were various kinds of birds and beasts, including ... the valuable Sind horses, ivory, cotton goods, jewels, gold, and silver."[45] It was through the Ganges-Bengal corridor that Buddhism was exported from India to Sri Lanka. The decline of Tamralipti early in the second half of the millennium remains unexplained. The shifting of the river was a plausible cause. But the advent of strongly land-based states may also have deurbanized and decommer-cialized lower Bengal to some extent.

Marshaling an impressive range of evidence, V. K. Thakur concludes that "the foreign trade of Bengal which was prospering up to the beginning of [the] 7th century A.D. began to shrink considerably by the middle of this century; and all commercial activities declined towards its end."[46] In this view, the retreat from trade continued well into the beginning of Islamic states in Bengal, that is, the thirteenth century. However, such accounts need to be qualified. An anomaly acknowledged by Thakur is the urban-ization along the banks of the river Bhagirathi. Attributed to temple building, the riverine location of the new towns almost certainly benefited from their geographical position being advantageous to trade. It was this urban flourish from the tenth century onward that served as a foundation for the revival of maritime trade and its growth in later centuries. The possibility of shift strengthens the inference that Tamralipti did not decline because of a general decommercialization, but for specific geo-graphical causes. A second anomalous factor was that the trade in horses continued on.

Following on the decline of the Gupta Empire in north India, Bengal experienced rule by three powerful states – the Shashanka, the Pala, and the Sena dynasties – punctuated by periods of weak kings and

---

[45] H. G. Rawlinson, *Intercourse between India and the Western World*, Cambridge: Cambridge University Press, 1916, p. 5.

[46] V. K. Thakur, "Trade and Towns in Early Medieval Bengal (c. A.D. 600–1200)," *Journal of the Economic and Social History of the Orient* 30(2), 1987, pp. 196–220 (quote on p. 206).

anarchy. The strength of the rule is gauged as usual from records of conquests, suggesting an extraordinary capability for military buildup. There was, however, a logistical problem with such a buildup. The main-stay of the army, the cavalry, needed a reliable supply of horses. Pala inscriptions point to the systematic participation of royal agents in the fairs and markets of present Haryana, where horses had been available for purchase for a very long time. There is also mention of the tributary northern princes giving horses as gifts. The origins of the horses remain uncertain, however. It appears that it was after the tenth century and the advent of the Senas that the horse trade and itinerant horse traders moved into Bengal. This inference is drawn from the fact that Muhammad Bakhtiyar Khilji, whose small cavalry overran Nadia, the abode of the Sena king, in c. 1205, was mistaken for a Turkish or Arab horse dealer. The only chronicle of the invasion (*Tabaqat-i-nasiri*, by the Indo-Persian judge and historian Minhaj-i-Siraj) also mentions an unidentifiable market where horses were brought for sale from across the eastern Himalayas.

Limited contact between Bengal and China via the export of Persian horses and the exchange of religious missions continued in the first millennium. Two overland routes of much antiquity have been identified. One of these started from Yunnan, went west towards Assam and Manipur, and ended in Chittagong or the Arakan coast on the Bay of Bengal. These coasts had maritime links with Bengal. The other started from Yunnan and took a long southward detour through the Pagan Empire in medieval Burma before joining the Bay of Bengal ports. Both routes made use of the valleys of major rivers – the Salween and the Irrawaddy – to negotiate difficult and in places almost impassable terrains. That China traded with India via these routes, and sent Buddhist monks to the courts in India, is known. However, toward the end of our period, the India-Burma link was more visible than the India-China one. The Pyu city-states in lower Burma in the ninth century consolidated the India-Burma connection. Although disrupted by the Nanchao conquest, the link was reestablished during the rule of Anawrahta Minsaw (1014–77) in the Irrawaddy delta.[47]

The visit of Cheng Ho's fleet to Bengal in the fourteenth century seemed to confirm the continued interest in Bengal from the Chinese side. But the economic significance of these exchanges must be qualified

---

[47] Janice Stargardt, "Burma's Economic and Diplomatic Relations with India and China from Early Medieval Sources," *Journal of the Economic and Social History of the Orient* 14(1), 1971, pp. 38–62.

2.5. Terracotta panel on a Bengal temple (Darhatwa) showing a ship, possibly of Indian construction. *Source*: Rangan Datta

in view of the skepticism expressed by historians about the absence of significant archaeological, numismatic, and historical evidence suggesting sustained interest. There is no sign so far that trade between Bengal and China before European entry in the Bay of Bengal was anything more than intermittent and marginal.

Conclusion

With such patchy knowledge as we now have about long-distance and overseas trade from India, it would be exceedingly difficult to reconstruct the long-term patterns of change in the scale of maritime trade between South Asia and either West Asia or East Asia. The risk is too great that discussion on the subject would end up as either singularly static or agreeing by default with the view that toward the end of the period the volume of long-distance trade had begun to fall.

Nevertheless, one intriguing clue to the long-term pattern is suggested by shipping technology. The remains of boats actually used in the Arabian Sea and constructed either in India or in West Asia are frustratingly hard to come by. Analysis of wood fragments shows conclusively that the ships plying between the Red Sea ports and western coastal India were mainly of Indian construction. The limited material so far discovered suggest that the size, design (square sail), material (teak), and technology (sewn construction) changed little from the early historic times to the seventeenth century.[48] An acceptable reading of the evidence for economic history is that shipping technology was rigidly constrained by climate and local resources. The scale of trade may well have increased but not reached a volume that would have induced merchants to sponsor larger ships and riskier trips.

The big debate in ancient economic history, conducted mainly in the 1970s, bypassed the issue of trade, focusing instead on land control and on the origins of hierarchy in private property on land. The Marxist historian D. D. Kosambi offered the first major statement, which was disputed by other historians who followed. Kosambi's thesis carried the implication that consolidation of landed power, or "feudalism," happened at the expense of commercialization. His statement of the thesis was attractive because it had a cultural dimension attached to it. Buddhism, and to a more limited extent Jainism, had been religions patronized by the mobile merchant. The monasteries, in turn, may have helped the states collect taxes on trade. But the monastic order undermined hierarchy, which made it "useless" for an empire that wanted to raise money from land and needed a docile and exploited peasantry. The Brahmins, on the other hand, "were a valuable support to the new state mechanism." They had the ritual authority to sanction kingship, and they ritually fused class with caste, making it possible for new "self-sufficient" agrarian settlements

---

[48] Roberta Tomber, Lucy Blue, and Shinu Abraham, *Migration, Trade and Peoples*, London: British Association of South Asian Studies, 2009, p. 6.

to emerge. Hinduism was the religion of the Gupta kings, and many of the new villages arose via land grants made out to the Brahmins.[49]

Inspired by the nineteenth-century assumption of early Indian inertia, carried over into Karl Marx's concept of the Asiatic mode of production, a later reading contended that the Gupta conquests, which resulted in the creation of many feudatory powers in the empire, eventually led to "the emergence of a self-sufficient local economy, the paucity of coins, the retrogression of trade, and decentralization in administration on account of grants of revenues to brahmanas and later to officials."[50] Regardless of whether an actual fall in trade took place, it is plausible that maritime trade remained a distinct sphere of activity, with only an occasional connection, which was neither sustained nor deep, to regional state formation. However, when Indo-Islamic empires consolidated their authority in northern India, the autonomy of the two spheres, inland states and long-distance trade from the coasts, began to weaken.

[49] D. D. Kosambi, "The Basis of Ancient Indian History," in two parts, *Journal of the American Oriental Society* 75(1), 1955, pp. 35–45, and 75(4), 1955, pp. 226–37.

[50] R. S. Sharma, "The Origins of Feudalism in India (c. A.D. 400–650)," *Journal of the Economic and Social History of the Orient* 1(3), 1958, pp. 297–328 (quote on p. 327).

3   Receding Land Frontiers, 1200–1700

The consolidation of empires in North and South India entailed serious attempts to integrate the ports in the Deccan and Bengal with the land-based empires and revived channels of communication with Central Asia along which commodities and skills moved more freely than before. The movement of armies on the long-distance routes secured the major arteries of goods traffic and even created a few new ones. The Mughal Empire took these integrative tendencies to new heights. The consolidation of the empires led to urbanization in the two great riparian plains. The cities along the Ganges and the Indus were home to garrisons, courts, traders, artisans, intellectuals, and artists, and maintained commercial links with cities in West and Central Asia. The relationship between trade and the state was mediated by the consumption of traded goods by the elite rather than by income earned from customs duties. The main income of the states came, as before, from land tax. Urbanization and increased consumption needs, therefore, necessitated expansion in culti-vation. In the words of Kosambi, "The inevitable counterpart of the caravan merchant ... was the new armed feudal landlord who squeezed a greater surplus from the land by force."[1] The consequence of the extension of the political and agrarian frontiers was far-reaching for Bengal, Deccan, and Gujarat.

These attempts to integrate the ports with the inland cities produced limited results on the coasts. The empires did not have a well-designed maritime policy, and the conquest of the ports was usually driven by military and political concerns rather than by commercial ones. In Bengal, for example, the joint expansion of Islam and the new states focused on agrarian settlements. The coasts and the ports continued to have a relatively autonomous character; they were populated by migrant merchants and were only loosely governed by a regional state. As urban centers they were small when compared to the capital cities of the interior.

---

[1] D. D. Kosambi, "The Basis of Ancient Indian History (II)," *Journal of the American Oriental Society* 75(4), 1955, pp. 226–37.

Underlying state formation, then, much remained unchanged in the 500 years covered in this chapter. The most important factor to remain unchanged was the geographical determination of the location of commercial hubs. The deltas and the estuaries continued to exert a deep influence on the pattern of integration of the land and the sea. Commodity composition continued to be dominated by low-bulk, high-value goods. Grain was only rarely mentioned in the list of tradable goods. All of these were symptoms of the limited extent to which landed occupations and maritime trade were integrated. The list of commodities traded was diverse, suggesting that the merchants rarely specialized in any one product. The seafaring merchants moved within the Indian Ocean and were not known to venture beyond. Significant economic transactions with other lands were confined to commodity trade, extended in the case of Mughal India also to an exchange of skills, and did not extend to labor and capital.

Nevertheless, a change had occurred, and general interpretations of the character of economic exchanges in this time have revolved around ideas about the changing role of trade in the larger economy. I begin with alternative perspectives on this theme.

Perspectives

The long interregnum between late antiquity and the beginning of a Mamluk dynasty in Delhi in the early thirteenth century falls into that category of time that historians of India once called feudalism, carrying the connotation of a retreat in long-distance trade (see Chapter 2). It is true that in much of western Uttar Pradesh and in Haryana, Rajput clans set up dynastic rules around agricultural resources and possibly trade was not the mainstay of any of these regimes. Yet it is not easy to discern any decisive change in the balance between commerce and agriculture in the subcontinent as a whole.

The onset of the so-called retreat in long-distance trade coincided with another of the great turning points in history, one with somewhat similar intonations, the increasing control of the Mediterranean in the seventh century by the Arab caliphate. According to the Belgian historian Henri Pirenne, the change in military balance in the region led to the withdrawal of Europe from overseas trade, turned Europe into a rural backwater after the once-thriving cities of the Roman Empire suffered a decline, and gave rise to the agrarian self-sufficient economic structure that became the foundation for a feudal system. The Pirenne thesis has been the subject of an unresolved debate: Was Islam the cause of European isolation? It has been argued that, on the contrary, the materially more advanced Arab world stimulated alternative trading worlds and trade routes in the eastern part of the continent, indirectly turning Europe into a productive periphery that had incentives to expand the supply of resource-based goods, including grain and slaves, in exchange for manufactures. This Islamic resurgence was weakened, however, by the Mongol invasion and by reliance on military structures that imposed high governance costs. One consequence of a divided world was the rise of Venice as the middleman between the two halves; indeed, Venice became a point of contact between Europe, the Islamic world, and distant China.[2]

How did Islamic resurgence affect South Asia? Was there growth? Was there more integration of networks? André Wink answers these last two questions with a positive, suggesting a progressively closer union between the disparate trading worlds of Asia from early in the second millennium. In his account, the economic integration was achieved by the spread of Islam as a political and cultural force.[3] The Islamic content of the integration and the systemic character of whatever form of integration took shape have been criticized.[4] But the possibility of growing contact between discrete networks early in the second millennium cannot be discarded. There is little disagreement that from the fourteenth century onward, the eastern and western Indian Ocean trades became more closely connected than before, as did the overland trade between Central Asia and India, and that population movements and diaspora settlements became more frequent. A comparative reading of Ibn Battuta's account of southern Asian commercial exchange and of Duarte Barbosa's account one hundred fifty years later suggests the same conclusion.[5]

---

[2] Henri Pirenne, *Medieval Cities: Their Origins and the Revival of Trade*, Princeton, NJ: Princeton University Press, 1969. For a useful discussion, see Ronald Findlay and Kevin H. O'Rourke, *Power and Plenty: Trade, War, and the World Economy in the Second Millennium*, Princeton, NJ, and Oxford: Princeton University Press, 2007, pp. 71–73.

[3] André Wink, *Al-Hind: The Making of the Indo-Islamic World*, vol. 1, *Early Medieval India and the Expansion of Islam, 7th–11th Centuries*, Leiden: E. J. Brill, 1991.

[4] Sanjay Subrahmanyam, "Of *Imarat* and *Tijarat*: Asian Merchants and State Power in the Western Indian Ocean, 1400 to 1750," *Comparative Study of Society and History* 37(4), 1995, pp. 750–80.

[5] Ibn Battuta, *Travels in Asia and Africa,1325–1354*, London: Routledge, 1929; Duarte Barbosa, *A Description of the Coasts of East Africa and Malabar*, London: Hakluyt Society, 1866.

Another critique of a decline in trade looks at the North Indian economic landscape itself. The careful reconstruction of the economic history of North India based on archaeological and numismatic data that John Deyell offers paints quite a different picture from that of growing agrarianization.[6] Deyell shows that coins were debased and became cruder copies of classical coins in the early medieval period, indirectly suggesting that states were weaker and poorer, as well as the high cost of procuring precious metals. Coinage was progressively centralized from the thirteenth century, as the Turkic rulers saw themselves as independent states rather than as an arm of Central or West Asian political centers that had been lost to the Mongols.

These revisionist views have been challenged in rejoinders from the feudalism school.[7] But the remaining point of the debate concerns the timing and agency of a new integrative tendency, rather than the fact of one. Most historians would accept a pre-European pattern of economic integration. It gathered force partly on the back of preexisting trade networks in the western Indian Ocean, partly on state formation that joined the Indus and the Ganges trades and Transoxania and Khorasan with Hindustan, and partly on the spread of the Delhi Sultanate into the Deccan and Bengal. It is also plausible that with this shift, which could be only a gradual one given the limited capacity of the early sultanate, the axis of commercial transactions, which had so far been the peninsular coastal regions, moved slightly north. Counteracting the pull of the north, state formation in the Deccan stimulated maritime links by increasing the demand for the horses brought in by the sea route. Nevertheless, it would be fair to say that beginning in the fourteenth century the northern overland and river-borne trade recovered an importance that it had lost during late antiquity.

Delhi sultanates

The trans-Himalayan connection predated the Indo-Islamic states by many centuries. The antiquity and strength of cultural and economic links between Central Asia and the Punjab in the classical era were

[6] John Deyell, *Living without Silver: The Monetary History of Early Medieval North India*, New Delhi: Oxford University Press, 1990.

[7] For such a criticism, see K. M. Shrimali, "Money, Market and Indian Feudalism: AD 600–1200," in Amiya Kumar Bagchi, ed., *Money and Credit in Indian History: From Early Medieval Times*, New Delhi: Tulika Books, 2002.

attributable to the Kusana state that straddled both and that owed its own fiscal might in this vast area of poor agriculture to the taxation of trade. From the twelfth century, a new empire harnessed the agrarian surplus of the Indus-Ganges Doab on a much larger scale than any classical state had, while restoring the transfrontier trade links.

The principal cities of the sultanate were located at the meeting point of the Vindhya Hills, which were largely forested and unsuitable for cultivation, and the fertile riparian plains of the north. Delhi was almost within sight of the hills. The image of a "fluid frontier" that combined the strengths of the arid zone, namely, pastoralism, caravan trade, horses and camels, and soldiery, with that of the agrarian zone, namely, taxation, characterized Delhi when it first became a capital.[8] Central Asian traders brought horses to the fairs and markets that developed near Delhi after the sultanate began. Over the next few centuries, the fiscal strength of the sultanates was consolidated by means of the establishment of a number of administrative-garrison-market towns in the Indus-Ganges Doab and by the transformation of some of these towns into semiautonomous polities as a result of the increasingly hereditary nature of large land-holding grants during the reign of Firozeshah Tughlak. Consolidation of local power made the local grantees more interested in diversifying their income bases, which favored their towns' emergence as commercial centers. The fiscal consolidation of the northern empire also possibly transformed the nature of the horse trade, as we shall see.

The travel accounts of Muslim nobles journeying from Delhi toward Gujarat and Deccan in the fourteenth century represent a progressive development of trade routes through the central Indian countryside. The north-south spread of Islamic state power surely secured these trade routes, while also reviving traffic between the Indus River valley and the Ganges plains via Nagaur in Rajasthan and Bayana in central India. More than to protect commercial interests, the strengthening of the road network resulted from a process of "provincialization" of the empire, which saw the progressive clearing of forests, founding of agricultural settlements, and erection of religious shrines along the old highways.

Perhaps the most significant example of this process from an economic-historical point of view was the eastward and southward spread of Islam. The eastward expansion brought the Ganges delta into closer contact with North India.

---

[8] Jos Gommans, "The Silent Frontier of South Asia, c. A.D. 1100–1800," *Journal of World History* 9(1), 1998, pp. 1–23.

The Deccan and the Bengal frontiers to 1500

The western-southern Deccan plateau – the vast region comprising the southern uplands of Maharashtra as well as parts of the Rayalaseema region straddling Andhra Pradesh and Karnataka – emerged as a site of state formation from the twelfth century on. Although mostly arid and providing only subsistence agriculture, this region contained fertile river valleys, fortified military settlements, and valuable minerals. The arid areas moreover formed a strategic frontier zone between the western seaboard and the irrigated river valleys. The importation of warhorses and camels, and the breeding of oxen and horses in the riparian plains, gave rise to settlements of pastoralists, nomadic traders, and soldiers. Agricultural resources in the region being limited, crucial to the states' success were trade with the coast and the enterprise of the nomadic traders who were also cattle breeders and herders.

According to Burton Stein, South India, from early in the second millennium CE experienced an agrarian expansion and a conversion of forests and pastures into farms, along with a conversion of forest-dependent and pastoralist peoples into settled plough-using cultivators.[9] Temples cemented the cultural coherence of the new economic units, the cultivating village. From the twelfth century, the processes of state formation were activated as a result partly of the southward expansion of Muslim power and partly of the northward expansion of trade and of the political centers located on the coastal deltas. Local tribal groups joined the soldiery or settled in the small cultivating communities that developed around temples and religious institutions or did both. The important trade in Abyssinian slaves, who were recruited directly into the sultanate courts, and who from the fourteenth century onward formed distinct communities in the capitals, added to the population movements into the Deccan. State formation, one account contends, helped expand the livelihoods that formed the frontier zone, a process of change in the Deccan that was "breathtaking" in scope.[10]

Such a narrative of the Deccan frontier from the twelfth century to the Mughal conquests can be misread as a picture of economic dynamism. If the history of state formation in the Deccan in this time shows anything, however, it shows that the region was caught up in a contestable political scenario, punctuated by warfare, cycles of violence, attempted

[9] Burton Stein, *Peasant State and Society in Medieval South India*, New York: Oxford University Press, 1980.

[10] Gommans, "The Silent Frontier of South Asia," pp. 1–23.

centralization, and the repeated failure of such attempts. Such turmoil may have been advantageous for certain service classes and the military labor market. It could not have been favorable for long-distance commerce, and it reveals, if anything, the tortuous way that the north-south corridor of trade evolved.

What such an unstable polity could mean for commerce and trade routes is amply illustrated by an almost contemporary source on the region's history, the Ferishta. Most major trade routes were described as very unsafe by this source. "The banditti of Dowlutabad," it reported, were "long famous for their daring robberies." In the period before Ibrahim Qutb Shah, "the country of Telingana [was] remarkable for its number of thieves and robbers."[11] Some exaggeration is likely, given that the Ferishta wanted to end with a story of the restoration of peace with the reign of Qutb Shah. But the description is plausible in view of the accounts of weak states living off the income from poor soil. The lack of safety on the roads also helps to explain the phenomenon of merchant associations like the Ayyavole taking part in the military labor market. One of the main services that these associations extended to their members was the sharing of hired mercenary guards.

A similar story of limited engagement and precarious state formation emerged from the other major frontier zone, Bengal. When the Turko-Afghan armies conquered Bengal in the fourteenth century, the center of commerce and industry was the western part of the delta through which the main channel of the Ganges then flowed. The ruling elite settled down in a few key towns in middle Bengal, of which one, Saptagram, or Satgaon, was a center of maritime trade. We can surmise that state formation thus facilitated a closer connection between riverine commercial traffic and maritime trade; the two joined at Saptagram. But that would be reading too much into the history of Saptagram. The main income of the state still came from land rather than from commerce. The peasants and landlords were mainly Hindus, and agriculture was poorly commercialized until the sixteenth century. The state merely consisted of a warlord superstructure over a fundamentally non-Islamic, agrarian, and subsistence-oriented foundation.

And yet, between 1300 and 1500, the trend was unmistakably toward both the consolidation of state power and attempts to create links between the land and the ocean. In the Deccan plateau, these trends matured in the emergence of the Vijayanagar Empire.

[11] Jonathan Scott, *Ferishta's History of the Dekkan*, London: Shrewsbury, vol. 1 of 2, 1794, pp. 352, 408.

Vijayanagar

Between the fourteenth and the early sixteenth century, an important state that emerged from the turmoil was the Vijayanagar Empire, with its capital located in the Tungabhadra Valley. Little is known of the economic history of this empire. That it sponsored and was dependent on long-distance trade is, however, well known. The existence of a powerful and wealthy empire across the Western Ghats created new politically protected outlets to the sea on the Konkan.

The Vijayanagar Empire was critically dependent on trade but possessed only a precarious access to the coast. Given its land-locked nature, the Vijayanagar state, throughout its existence, tried to retain access to the port settlements in the Konkan. Apart from its revenue motivation, Vijayanagar policy to control the coast had much to do with who controlled the import of horses from Persia. In the last fifty years of its rule, the Vijayanagar state succeeded in maintaining cooperative relations with its neighbor, a newly formed Portuguese settlement, and thus access to the seacoast.

Inscriptions and literary sources indicate the presence of merchants allied to the Vijayanagar state who no doubt dealt in the two most important items of long-distance trade at this time, textiles and horses. The diamond trade also engaged wealthy groups of people. Partly reflecting the nature of the sources, the little we know about them invariably hint at state-business links. For example, the *Haravilasam* of the Telugu poet Srinatha described a rich merchant of Nellore port, Avachi Tippaya Setti, who had a monopoly license to import goods for the court, including the strategically valuable cargo, horses from Hormuz. Interestingly, Setti, being based in a region over which the empire had little control, had access to a number of courts, of both friends and foes of Vijayanagar, including the courts of Gajapati of Orissa, the Bahmani sultan Feroze Shah, and Harihararaya of Vijayanagar.

Most contemporary accounts of Vijayanagar suggest a flourishing of nonagricultural production in the imperial realms. But these accounts must be read with a great deal of caution. Almost all of them concentrate on conditions in the capital city and are so taken up by the pomp and paraphernalia of the royal palace that a reliable measure of trade remains hard to construct. The Italian traveler Ludovico di Varthema's account (1504) of the Vijayanagar capital (also Vijayanagar) stated that the city had a circumference of seven miles, or an area of three square miles. If we take the density of population to be as high as 10,000 per square mile, the city should still be quite small in population size and overwhelmingly a garrison town, since the resident cavalry numbered between 20,000 (Duarte Barbosa) and 40,000 (Varthema).[12] Arriving in the city in 1514, when the empire had already lost considerable land to the Deccan sultanates and was engaged in debilitating conflicts with many of its own vassals, Duarte Barbosa stated that the city had "infinite trade." This unhelpful phrase is followed by a description of export and import items that was devoted to precious stones and horses.[13] This description again indicates a palace-dominated trading regime. It is safer to conclude that whatever trade integration the state did achieve was a tenuous one in the best of times and was in decline by the sixteenth century.

Late in the sixteenth century, the Qutb Shahi regime in Golkonda opened an eastern corridor between the Deccan and the coast, known as Masulipatnam. This port town, which had earlier been a small source for textiles, now became a major link with Sumatra, Arakan, Pegu, and Bengal.[14] Many of the Persians who were invited to settle in the Bijapur and Golkonda territories were merchants. In turn, traders traveled overland from Masulipatnam to Surat or Cambay to join the West Asian trade with the East and Southeast Asian ones. That link notwithstanding, the two trading complexes remained largely unconnected. In fact, until the entry of Western European trading companies in the Bay of Bengal, the east coast trade was distinctly smaller in scale than the western coastal one.

Outside the Vijayanagar capital, the sketchy economic history of the crumbling empire paints a picture of the increasing dominance of vassals, who lived in fortified settlements and subsisted on income from land. Such a degree of decentralization of power could not have been good for market integration; among other reasons, it made roads unsafe to travel on. And it was indeed quite damaging to merchants, as the late history of the Ayyavole guild shows.

South of Vijayanagar

Who were the Ayyavole? Considerable scholarship exists on the merchant guilds of South India early in the second millennium. Epigraphic evidence

[12] Robert Sewell, *A Forgotten Empire (Vijayanagar): A Contribution to the History of India*, London: Swan Sonnenschein, 1900, p. 118.

[13] Barbosa, *Description of the Coasts of East Africa and Malabar*, p. 85.

[14] Sanjay Subrahmanyam, "Persians, Pilgrims and Portuguese: The Travails of Masulipatnam Shipping in the Western Indian Ocean, 1590–1665," *Modern Asian Studies* 22(3), 1988, pp. 503–30.

from 1050 CE described the Ayyavole as "wandering merchants" whose commercial and family networks extended to many countries and regions. They owned caravans. Their merchandise was quite varied, and included grain and elephants, but the longest list of articles they traded in consisted of precious stones. Although not enough is known about the internal organization of these groups, frequent references to "dharma" as a composite of personal and professional law suggest that their sense of commercial law was well-developed and often received royal sanction. This emphasis on law was supported by a strong and seemingly well-defined internal hierarchy. The Ayyavole's sponsorship of warlords and mercenaries is also clear in some inscriptions.[15]

Perhaps the most comprehensive body of research on South Indian guilds deals with temple sponsorship by the Ayyavole. The merchants were not the only sponsors of temples, but they were of a particular kind. They patronized major pilgrimage sites, which one historian argues is evidence of the mobile merchants' presence in locations where trading networks intersected.[16] The mobile merchant groups that we know about were present in maritime trade networks as well, but their main field of activity was in overland, interregional, and interurban transactions.

The later evolution of the medieval South Indian guilds remains somewhat obscure. "Sometime between the thirteenth and the sixteenth century," writes one historian, "references to medieval mercantile assemblies and guilds died out and was replaced after the sixteenth century by reference to mercantile castes similar to those we know today."[17] The transformation is attributed to increasing political imposition and interference in the affairs of local merchants leading to a decline in the more cosmopolitan cross-regional forms of assembly and a consolidation of more insular, perhaps caste-based, forms of network. In the sixteenth century, warlords affiliated with Vijayanagar attempted "to convert the area [they] held into an isolated self-sufficient economic unit.... This tendency carried with it various consequences the most immediate of which was to improve the position of local merchant groups and to hasten the demise of the regional merchants groups."[18] Interestingly, the

[15] V. Rajamani, "Trade Guilds," *Journal of Tamil Studies*, 1989, pp. 1–11.

[16] Cynthia Talbot, "Temples, Donors, and Gifts: Patterns of Patronage in Thirteenth-Century South India," *Journal of Asian Studies* 50(2), 1991, pp. 308–40.

[17] David West Rudner, "Religious Gifting and Inland Commerce in Seventeenth-Century South India," *Journal of Asian Studies* 46(2), 1987, pp. 361–79 (quote on p. 362).

[18] Richard Frasca, "Weavers in Pre-Modern South India," *Economic and Political Weekly* 10 (30), 1975, pp. 1119–23 (quote on p. 1120).

withdrawal from interregional trade coincided with, if it was not caused by, the appearance of European traders in Coromandel.

North India under the Mughals

The Mughal conquest did not usher in any disruption in the pattern of spatial integration already taking shape for three hundred years. But the formation of a new state in the north strengthened urbanization and interurban contact in riparian northern India.

The core economic region of the Mughal Empire was located at the meeting point of the upper Indus and the western Gangetic plains, where fertile land, large rivers, and, especially, proximity to roads going to Central Asia, Persia, and Kabul led to the rapid growth of towns. Delhi, Hisar, Lahore, and Firozabad joined the older set of trading towns in the eastern and southern reaches of the plains, including Bayana, Badaun, Sambhal, Kalpi, Mathura, Kanauj, Etawah, Bahraich, and Lucknow.[19] Further to the east, the eastern Gangetic plains continued to be less urbanized; the major centers, Benares and Patna, being located further apart than comparable settlements in the west. However, this was to change in the seventeenth century, and especially after the Mughal conquest of Bengal.

One of the cities established late in the sultanate period was Agra. The phenomenal growth of this town even before it was chosen as a capital was owed to its favorable location on the Jumna and its rapid emergence as a commercial transit point and market. Despite active road building, the river remained the primary means of commercial traffic. In the seventeenth century, the river connected Hindustan with Benares, Bihar, and Bengal. The river brought grain, silk, and cotton from Bengal and Bihar; indigo and sugar from Awadh; and cotton from Punjab. Agra also became a center of banking and finance, and housed firms that discounted and issued bills.[20]

Inside northern India, the mobility of capital and enterprise was encouraged. The enormous scale of revenue transactions, and with it of grain dealing, led to a proliferation of market towns that became home to

[19] Hameeda Khatoon Naqvi, "Progress of Urbanization in United Provinces, 1550–1800," *Journal of the Economic and Social History of the Orient* 10(1), 1967, pp. 81–101.

[20] K. K. Trivedi, "The Emergence of Agra as a Capital and a City: A Note on Its Spatial and Historical Background during the Sixteenth and Seventeenth Centuries," *Journal of the Economic and Social History of the Orient* 37(2), 1994, pp. 147–70.

merchants, bankers, money changers, and brokers. The administration's preference for receiving revenue in the imperial currency indirectly encouraged the monetary integration of a territory that had been fragmented before the Mughals. Almost without exception, the largest and the most successful firms belonged to a network of branches that operated in a number of towns. The spatial extension of firms was necessary for the movement of goods and money and was helped by the relatively safe passage to and easier residence in a number of cities. It is interesting that even this traffic of capital occurred mainly along the major rivers, where the principal business centers and transit ports were located.

A good example of the effects of Mughal integration of commercial spaces is the house of the Jagatseths of Bengal. The founder of the firm, Hiranand Sahu, hailed from Nagaur, located on the east-west trade artery, and in 1652 migrated to Patna, again a city that owed its commercial importance to the eastward spread of the empire. His sons continued to look after the North Indian branches of the family banking business, the eldest, Manik Chand, having taken over the Bengal branch. In the early eighteenth century, when the Jagatseths emerged as effectively the state banker, Manik Chand relocated from the capital Dhaka, another city that drew its importance from Mughal conquest, to the newly established residence and capital of the provincial governor Murshid Quli Khan.[21]

In a similar way, the empire also stimulated trade along the two external routes that had long existed, the Persia-India maritime trade, and the India-Transoxania overland trade. Ships went by sea from Gujarat and Goa to Persia and met caravan traffic coming overland across Khorasan. The simultaneous existence in India and Iran of two friendly and powerful empires not only integrated them culturally and politically through an exchange of administrators, artists, and artisans but also created a shared interest in trade. Cambay and Surat, ports in Mughal-controlled Gujarat, experienced a great expansion due to this joint interest. Between them and the Persian port Hormuz, they supported large caravans in Persia and in India. Portuguese traders from Goa joined the sea trade, and before the Mughal conquest of the Deccan, they formed a bridge between the Deccan sultanate territories, which produced diamonds for export, and coastal commerce.[22]

[21] J. H. Little, "The House of Jagatseth," *Bengal Past and Present* 20, 1920, pp. 1–200, and 22, 1921, pp. 1–119.

[22] Muzaffar Alam and Sanjay Subrahmanyam, "The Deccan Frontier and Mughal Expansion, ca. 1600: Contemporary Perspectives," *Journal of the Economic and Social History of the Orient* 47(3), 2004, pp. 357–89.

Increasing traffic of goods and increasing mobility of merchants between India and Central Asia were among the effects of the transition.[23] As we have seen, the trans-Himalayan trade routes using the Karakorum Pass, the Khyber Pass, and the Lipu Lekh converged in the cities of Central Asia (see Chapter 2). The rivers Indus and Ganges fed these networks with goods from Gujarat and Bengal. Overland trade not only served the urban markets and fairs in the plains but also met the need for consumption goods of the populations living in the hills. Subsistence, survival, and commerce were intertwined in the hills. At Samarkand, belonging to the territory of the Uzbek khanates, trade from Turkish territories and trade from India met. That these routes were traversed by merchants in the fourteenth and fifteenth centuries was remarked on by Arab and European travelers in Central Asia.[24] As one of these accounts stated, merchants maintained warehouses in a variety of locations, including Gujarat. The frequency of travel and the scale of business increased in the seventeenth century. Indians who settled in Central Asia were described sometimes as merchants and sometimes as bankers, and nearly all were agents of family businesses based in India, mainly in Multan.

The principal articles of import from India were textiles, which were available in wide variety and from different regions of India. Hindu communities of traders and bankers resided in the market towns and supervised the movement of goods. Some of them oversaw the local production of textiles in Indian styles, having brought with them master artisans to train local weavers. Artisans were prominent among the slaves who were part of the reexport items of trade. The main import into India was horses, along with a number of semiluxury goods. Although the states that shared control over these trade routes understood the economic value of these routes, they rarely cooperated in sharing the gains. The land routes remained dangerous, partly because of state-sponsored predation, as with piracy on the sea route. Commercial enterprise, therefore, was heavily dependent on community cooperation, for example, in forming large caravans or in securing the mutual trust necessary for credit relations to function smoothly. In addition to the overland route, Mughal dominion stimulated trade on the maritime route to Persia, and a similar effect could be seen in the mobility of merchants and in the

---

[23] Muzaffar Alam, "Trade, State Policy and Regional Change: Aspects of Mughal-Uzbek Commercial Relations, c. 1550–1750," *Journal of the Economic and Social History of the Orient* 37(3), 1994, pp. 202–27.

[24] Scott Levi, "The Indian Merchant Diaspora in Early Modern Central Asia and Iran," *Iranian Studies* 32(4), 1999, pp. 483–512.

growth of manufacturing in port towns along the way. The commercial significance of the Sind littoral, for example, grew considerably in the seventeenth century.

Historians have noted an increasing overlap of commerce with the imperial court in this period. Some of the merchant houses were close to the court, and, in turn, courtiers took part in maritime trade and shared in its profits. The broader significance of this overlap remains to be explored. The phrase used to characterize such enterprise, "portfolio capitalist," suggests an entrepreneurial flourish.[25] In present-day terms, such participation in private businesses by powerful politicians holding state office would be called corruption. Be that as it may, the proximity of political power and commercial power shows the difficulty of making a sharp distinction between them. Their connection is also evident in the principal articles of commerce.

The main import to India from Central Asia, horses, did have a connection with state formation.[26] Horses came into India from Central Asia via the overland routes; once in India, the horses were sold at the major fairs. The horse was a peculiar form of cargo. It was valuable, it did not need to be carried but could walk across the mountain passes, and, by and large, it was able to withstand the high elevation. The horse was thus a particularly convenient item of merchandise in overland trade, which was an expensive mode of transportation at the best of times. Horses also came by sea from West Asia into the Indian port cities. Jos Gommans estimates, on the assumption that the volume of import constituted roughly 10 percent of the existing stock (considered to number 600,000 in the early eighteenth century), the import value of horses at about Rs. 20 million, which exceeded the value of Bengal exports to all the European East India Companies combined. The comparison is slightly misleading, however, because horses and cotton cloth served different kinds of need. The horse was an expensive instrument of warfare, paid for with taxpayers' money; cloth was an emerging mass consumer good. A larger horse trade did not indicate greater consumer welfare, possibly the opposite. It is nevertheless striking how large the scale of the horse trade was at its peak.

The regional states, not least the East India Company after it became the ruler of Bengal, tried both to breed horses and to control the horse

---

[25] Sanjay Subrahmanyam and C. A. Bayly, "Portfolio Capitalists and the Political Economy of Early Modern India," *Indian Economic and Social History Review* 25(4), 1988, pp. 401–24.

[26] Jos Gommans, "The Horse Trade in Eighteenth-Century South Asia," *Journal of the Economic and Social History of the Orient* 37(3), 1994, pp. 228–50.

trade in order to secure supply. Neither course of action was remarkably successful. The foreign horse merchant was too elusive an agent to be regulated, and regions like Bihar did not have suitable ecological conditions for successful breeding. At its peak, the horse trade sustained states and merchant communities along the Indo-Afghan frontier. Gommans follows up his study of the horse trade to frame an argument about state making on the border.[27] The Mughal Empire was strategically centered in geographical zones that were bordered on one side by fertile floodplains populated with settled peasantry and on the other side by steppes. The steppes supplied the army with cavalry soldiers and provided pastures for the horses and other animals on which livelihoods as well as military pursuits depended. In a later time, the English East India Company, with its reliance on infantry and artillery rather than on cavalry, made the western steppes less important to the company's political and military aims, recasting the relationship between these arid zones and the Mughal Empire.

Opening up of Bengal

From about 1550, the eastward shift of the main channel of water in the Ganges delta enabled extensive clearing and settlement of the eastern delta. Rice cultivation increased. Like the Buddhism carried by the mobile merchants, Islam in the Ganges delta defined the identity of mobile peasants. As Richard Eaton has shown, the expansion of the agrarian frontier from the west to the east was reinforced by an expansion also of the political frontier and the spread of Islam as a cementing force in the new agrarian communities.[28] Islam symbolized how "preliterate peoples on the ecological and political frontier of an expanding agrarian society became absorbed into the religious ideology of that society."[29] The significance of this expansion was the encouragement that it gave to exports. The eastern seaboard became relatively more important than before. Chittagong (also Chattagram, or Mughal

---

[27] Jos Gommans, *Mughal Warfare: Indian Frontiers and High Roads to Empire, 1500–1700*, London: Routledge, 2002.

[28] Richard M. Eaton, *The Rise of Islam and the Bengal Frontier, 1204–1760*, Berkeley: University of California Press, 1993. See also Atis Dasgupta, "Islam in Bengal: Formative Period," *Social Scientist* 32(3/4), 2004, pp. 30–41.

[29] Richard M. Eaton, "Approaches to the Study of Conversion to Islam in India," in R. C. Martin, ed., *Approaches to Islam in Religious Studies*, Tucson: University of Arizona Press, 1985, pp. 107–23 (quote on p. 11).

Islamabad), in particular, expanded as a port. The loosely organized maritime trade in which the smaller and interior river ports such as Bakla, Sripur, and Sonargaon took part gained from commercial efflorescence in Southeast Asia. Burma, Arakan, and Bengal traded more than before and consolidated the network in the eastern Bay of Bengal that the Mughals tried, without much success, to bring under their control.

Mughal conquest of Bengal in the 1590s was driven by Bengal's enhanced economic value. In turn, the conquest secured a preexisting tendency of economic integration with the north. But Mughal administrative or military presence did not extend further than a few miles from the major navigable rivers.

The eastward spread of Islam, settlement, agriculture, and state power did not, however, shift the axis of long-distance trade completely to the east. Although Bengal rice was now a visible product in the coastal trade, the eastern seaboard was a treacherous and unstable stretch of water for the development of large ports. The daily tides in Meghna on the seaboard could become murderous for boats. Each day during the ebb tide, the rivers exposed sandbanks in their middle, and these sandbanks shifted position. Even seasoned mariners did not always know the routes through this maze. The rivers in the Sundarbans opened out to snake-infested no-man's-lands. The main river in the central part of the delta, Brahmaputra, was notorious for whirlpools. Even in the nineteenth century, transportation between the interior towns and the major river ports was much too hazardous, time taking, and expensive to sustain any significant market integration. In this landscape, the Mughal capital Dhaka emerged as a major manufacturing and commercial center. But the real center of urban-commercial-intellectual activity remained in the west, along the now much-depleted channel called Bhagirathi.

The sixteenth century experienced a cultural efflorescence in this western zone, led by the Vaishnavite movement in the early sixteenth century.[30] Saptagram was one of the minor centers of the movement. If Islam cemented the eastward expansion of the land frontiers, the devotional movement, partly in reaction to Islam, revived Hindu merchant identity in the western delta and strengthened Saptagram's position as the primary commercial center in Bengal.

---

[30] The Vaishnavites belonged in a set of devotional movements that emerged in India between the fourteenth and the seventeenth centuries. The movements developed usually around mystic figures, in this case, Chaitanya (1486–1534).

Saptagram was the leading port of Bengal for possibly more than two hundred years, from the early thirteenth century until the mid-sixteenth century.[31] Located on a channel off the Bhagirathi, the port became unusable in the sixteenth century when the channel dried up. There is a speculation that the Bhagirathi during this time carried the main body of the Ganges southward, but the precise timing of the history of the river cannot be established. Although the western delta had been a center of Buddhism, which hinted at merchant sponsorship, its engagement in overseas trade was limited before the rise of Saptagram. In turn, the rise resulted from the consolidation of a state in Bengal.

As an urban center, Saptagram reached its zenith about 1500. In medieval Bengali literature, representations of the seafaring merchant tend to be dominated by the figure of Chand Sadagar of Manasamangal. The numerous versions of the verse more or less all describe in some detail a business trip that Chand made to Saptagram. In the most famous version, composed about 1497, Chand visited the temples on the banks of the Bhagirathi. He also went to see the town and was duly impressed by the wealth and opulence in every home, by the erudition and radiance of the Brahmins, and by the might of Saptagram's Muslim rulers and generals. At its peak, the crescent riverfront received ships from Malaya, China, Java, Ceylon, Maldives, Persia, Chola territory, and Egypt. Early in the fourteenth century, the port town had a royal mint. Coins that can be traced to Saptagram are dated from roughly 1320 to 1540 CE and bear the names of the sultans of Bengal. That the town was the home of a rich, courtly elite is evident from the ruins of mosques and large buildings. Apart from exporting Bengal textiles to Southeast Asia and China, the port was vital to the regional economy, indeed, to the entire North Indian economy, as a source for specie that came in from Burma.[32]

A similar cluster of Bengali ballads and poetic narratives were produced between 1495 and 1595 by poets who were located near the eastern seaboard where Chittagong was the main seaport.[33] These works contain descriptions of sea voyages, as well as of cities and coasts that have been identified as the Arakan, the Andaman Islands, Sri Lanka, and possibly

---

[31] Aniruddha Ray, "The Rise and Fall of Satgaon: An Overseas Port of Medieval Bengal," in S. Jeyaseela Stephen, ed., *Indian Trade at the Asian Frontier*, Delhi: Gyan Publishing, 2008, pp. 69–102.

[32] John Deyell, "The China Connection: Problems of Silver Supply in Medieval Bengal," in Sanjay Subrahmanyam, ed., *Money and the Market in India, 1100–1700*, Delhi: Oxford University Press, 1994.

[33] Pandit Haraprasad Sastri, "Reminiscences of Sea-voyage in Ancient Bengali Literature," *Journal of the Asiatic Society of Bengal*, 1893, pp. 20–24.

the western coast of India. They also offer glimpses of the hierarchy among boatmen, the goods that were traded, the uncertainty about the kind of reception a merchant fleet could get in foreign ports, and the fears and risks that constantly accompanied a voyage. Whereas many of these voyages must have sometimes encountered unknown perils, too much should not be made of the anxiety that pervades these accounts. Fear was, after all, a literary device and an excuse for invoking the deity in whose honor the work was written. One could, however, argue that the deity was so necessary because of the unusual risks. Be that as it may, despite the many difficulties in fixing the geography and history of these voyages, there is no question that oceangoing merchants supplied extensive patronage for and protection to these poets, who represented a mainly rural and agricultural literati.

Some later manuscripts (mid-sixteenth century) make plentiful references to a historically specific risk, the Portuguese pirates who inhabited the islands off the eastern seaboard. About 1530, Portuguese traders first visited Saptagram and started trading there. In little more than a decade, it became impossible for them to maneuver their large ships to the port. They formed a settlement at Betore, located further south on the west bank of the Bhagirathi, and brought smaller boats up to Saptagram. Eventually Betore, though only a seasonal fairground, took away a considerable part of the foreign trade of the old port. In one account, the Portuguese destroyed competition by force, which did not help the trade of Saptagram.[34] In fact, the end of Saptagram began when a number of wealthy Hindu textile merchants resettled on the east bank of Bhagirathi, that is, across the river from Betore. These merchants were the first well-to-do Indian citizens of what was to become Calcutta in 1690. This migration cannot be dated precisely, but may not have happened before 1600. Betore was an intermediary station. The Portuguese move away from Saptagram was complete when the Mughal Empire granted them permission to set up a port in Hooghly (1579).

According to one reading, the shift of the river did not begin to be a problem until the 1570s. For, as the Venetian merchant Cesare Federici testified in 1567, Saptagram remained a considerable trading center and a home of wealthy merchants for some time after large ships stopped

---

[34] Rakhal Das Bandopadhyay, "Saptagram" (in Bengali), *Bangiya Sahityaparishatpatrika*, 1908, pp. 34–35. A slightly different account of the site was presented by another archaeologist who surveyed it, D. G. Crawford, "Satgaon or Triveni," *Bengal Past and Present* 3(1), 1908, pp. 18–26.

visiting the port.[35] The attraction of the town remained its considerable but short-lived importance as a Vaishnava center. Between 1520 and 1540, the great Vaishnava saint and leading disciple of Chaitanya, Nityananda, lived in Saptagram. He and his entourage were the guests of the Hindu merchants of the town, thereby earning the town and its wealthy Subarnabanik merchants numerous references in the versified biographies of Chaitanya. Almost certainly, the composers of some of these works were also supported by the merchants. According to one of these, the *Chaitanyabhagavat*, Nityananda came to Tribeni, located near Saptagram and already a major pilgrimage town, to bless the merchants of Saptagram.

As we will see, the significance of the Bhagirathi-based commercialization would become apparent a century later, when the European merchant companies set up trading stations along this river bank. The move tilted the balance of commerce away almost completely from the eastern to the western segment of the Bay of Bengal.

Gujarat and Konkan in transition

In the western Indian Ocean, starting in the thirteenth century, there emerged an early modern "world system."[36] The Mamluk sultans of Egypt successfully played a mediating role in the trade between Asia and Europe in the fourteenth and fifteenth centuries, with the result that the volume of traffic on the Red Sea grew significantly, if at the expense of alternative routes.[37] The Venetians and the Genoese merchants operated a smaller alternative bridge via the Black Sea and overland across Persia. Ports on the Konkan and Malabar, notably Cambay, connected the Red Sea on the western side with other subregional commercial networks, East Africa, South Arabia, the Persian Gulf, and most importantly, South east Asia.[38] A huge variety of commodities were traded. The single most

---

[35] Samuel Purchas, *Hukluytus Posthumus or Purchas His Pilgrimes*, Glasgow: James MacLehose, vol. 10 of 20 vols., p. 136.

[36] Janet Abu-Lughod, *Before European Hegemony: The World System, A.D. 1250–1350*, New York: Oxford University Press, 1991.

[37] John L. Meloy, "Imperial Strategy and Political Exigency: The Red Sea Spice Trade and the Mamluk Sultanate in the Fifteenth Century," *Journal of the American Oriental Society* 123(1), 2003, pp. 1–19; Richard Mortel, "Aspects of Mamluk Relations with Jedda during the Fifteenth Century," *Journal of Islamic Studies* 6(1), 1995, pp. 1–13.

[38] Archibald Lewis, "Maritime Skills in the Indian Ocean, 1368–1500," *Journal of the Economic and Social History of the Orient* 16(2/3), 1973, pp. 238–64.

important commodity group was possibly spices. Minerals and a few agricultural goods were added later, but they did not form either a regular item of trade or a large one.

The Red Sea trade was carried from India in vessels of 300–400 tons, which were bigger than the ships that were standard in the Bay of Bengal and the eastern Indian Ocean. The abundance of teak in Malabar was of considerable advantage to the ship-building industry. In the wider context of the peninsular coastline, however, the larger sizes were exceptional rather than the norm. The usual ships made in and floated off India were much smaller in size, and seemed to belong to maritime traditions that borrowed little from one another. As far can be told from archaeological and historical evidence, the size and mode of construction of ships changed relatively little in the first millennium, though this point remains somewhat controversial.[39] A similar scenario seems to emerge for the first half of the second millennium as well.

Based partly on Portuguese sources and partly on inscriptions on the mosques that dotted the landscape, it is possible to date the peak period of Cambay to between the fourteenth and the mid-sixteenth century. During this time, Cambay served the same function that Surat was to assume later and that Broach had served earlier. It was the terminus of land routes from the north, and a trading post where caravans met the ships.[40] Substantial merchants in Cambay could aspire to political eminence and social leadership, as the mosques testify. A good example of political patronage comes from a cluster of mid-seventeenth-century sources that shed some light on an Iranian horse and jewel merchant, Ali Akbar, who received from the emperor Shah Jahan the office of ports administrator, with dual charge for Cambay and Surat. The grant was a mutually beneficial one; Shah Jahan got access to the horse market of Busra, and Ali Akbar received political backing for some of his private ventures.[41] In the closely situated port of Diu, maritime traders likewise developed close ties to regional politics in Gujarat. Individuals moved between trade and administration, though it is not clear whether this interdependence had a fiscal basis.

[39] Himanshu Prabha Ray, "Seafaring and Maritime Contacts: An Agenda for Historical Analysis," *Journal of the Economic and Social History of the Orient* 39(4), 1996, pp. 422–31.

[40] Sinnapah Arasaratnam and Aniruddha Ray, *Masulipatnam and Cambay: A History of Two Port Towns, 1500–1800*, New Delhi: Munshiram Manoharlal, 1994.

[41] Elizabeth Lambourn, "Of Jewels and Horses: The Career and Patronage of an Iranian Merchant under Shah Jahan," *Iranian Studies* 36(2), 2003, pp. 213–41, 243–58.

3.1. Trade in the Gulf of Cambay, India, by the Boucicaut Master (1390–1430) from the *Livre des Merveilles du Monde*, c. 1410–12. The *Livre* by John Mandeville of Liège was an account of travel to the Holy Land, India, and other parts of the world. The Indian scenes were probably appropriated from the accounts of fourteenth-century travelers, especially that of the Franciscan friar Odoric. Boucicaut Master of Paris was the most famous manuscript painter of his time. *Source:* The Bridgeman Art Library

Such mutual dependence weakened in the early sixteenth century in Diu, an end sought by the Portuguese control of the waters. Portuguese entry into these waters early in the 1500s and especially their attempt to impose a tax on merchant marines complicated the local political rivalry. In the end, Cambay declined, and Diu became a Portuguese port (1535), but the sultanate in Gujarat compensated for the loss by fortifying a southern port in Surat.[42] When, in 1570, the Mughal Empire conquered Gujarat, Surat began its career as the principal point of access for the empire to the western seaboard. The significance of the conquest was soon apparent. In the second half of the sixteenth century, much of

---

[42] Sanjay Subrahmanyam, "A Note on the Rise of Surat in the Sixteenth Century," *Journal of the Economic and Social History of the Orient* 43(1), 2000, pp. 23–33.

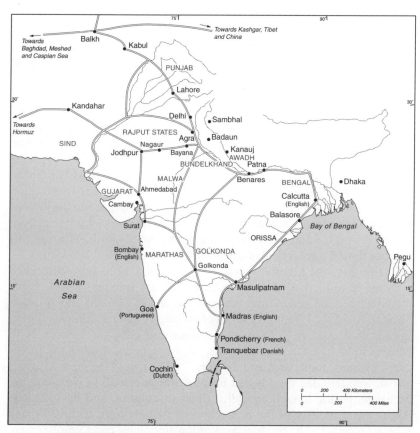

3.2. Trade routes, c. 1650.

the Indian shipping connecting the Red Sea and Southeast Asian commercial networks and converging in a port in Konkan bypassed the
Portuguese by using Surat.[43] And by early in the seventeenth century,
Surat was also connected by secure overland links to the heart of the
empire. Thus Surat became firmly integrated with the internal economy
of Mughal North India.[44]

[43] C. R. Boxer, "A Note on Portuguese Reactions to the Revival of the Red Sea Spice Trade
and the Rise of Atjeh, 1540–1600," *Journal of Southeast Asian History* 10(3), 1969, pp.
415–28.

[44] M. N. Pearson, *Merchants and Rulers in Gujarat: The Response to the Portuguese in the
Sixteenth Century*, Berkeley and Los Angeles: University of California Press, 1976.

Transactions in knowledge

Although a "market" for labor or capital was still absent, the consolidation of empires across Islamic Asia created firm conduits over which many talented individuals traveled back and forth between the richest cities. These movements had a sponsored character and almost always involved people with special rather than generic skills. The courts sought to legitimize their symbolic authority by means of gift exchanges, conspicuous consumption, and sponsorship of temples and mosques. They therefore held experts in a variety of practical fields in high honor. The "tripartite Muslim Asia" consisting of Iran, Turan (Central Asia), and Hindustan was bound together by a shared elite culture.[45] A nonmilitary motivation behind these movements was the need for legal scholars to run the judicial system. The sultanate and Mughal courts of India received scholars from Persia, Egypt, Central Asia, and, more rarely, the Maghrib. Through this conduit flowed a great deal of scientific and technological knowledge.

In this way, the Ghorian conquests of around 1200 were associated with the introduction of the Persian wheel, the spinning wheel, paper manufacture, and sericulture, whereas the use of cannons and muskets became established through a series of exchanges and experiments during the fifteenth century.[46] Through pensions and gifts, the aristocracy in Mughal India sponsored accountants, "scholars, poets, theologians, physicians, painters, musicians, and dancers."[47] The first of the great Mughals Babar, who founded the Mughal Empire, was interested in cross-cultural exchange, having himself straddled different cultures, and his grandson Akbar was a sponsor of the practical arts. Akbar's court gathered many scholars together. The predominant group among his court scholars were "masters of the spirit," or theologians.[48] In some instances, three kinds of

---

[45] See particularly Richard C. Foltz, *Mughal India and Central Asia*, Oxford and Karachi: Oxford University Press, 1998.

[46] I. A. Khan, "Early Use of Cannon and Musket in India: A.D. 1442–1526," *Journal of the Economic and Social History of the Orient* 24(2), 1981, pp. 146–64.

[47] Irfan Habib, "Potentialities of Capitalistic Development in the Economy of Mughal India," *Journal of Economic History* 29(1), 1969, pp. 32–78. See also by Irfan Habib, "The Peasant in Indian History," *Social Scientist* 11(3), 1983, pp. 21–64; "Pursuing the History of Indian Technology: Pre-modern Modes of Transmission of Power," *Social Scientist* 20(3/4), 1992, pp. 1–22; "Akbar and Technology," *Social Scientist* 20(9/10), 1992, pp. 3–15; and "Technology and Economy of Mughal India," *Indian Economic and Social History Review* 17(1), 1980, pp. 1–34.

[48] Shireen Moosvi, "The Mughal Encounter with Vedanta: Recovering the Biography of 'Jadrup,'" *Social Scientist* 30(7/8), 2002, pp. 13–23.

expertise – theological, medical, and inventive – were combined in one person, such as the Persian scholar Fathullah Shirazi.

Another motivation behind these cross-cultural exchanges was the need for skilled artisans to supply urban consumers and to work on construction projects. The large surpluses and thriving towns led to extensive commodity production. A union of consumption and power sustained the town economies. The Mughal court and nobles consumed a very large quantity of craft goods. Power was affirmed by generosity and display. The mansions of princes and nobles, modeled after the imperial palace-fortress, "dominated social, economic, and political activity" in the cities of Mughal India.[49] Consumption expressed dominance. The aristocracy maintained manufactories, or "karkhanas," for the production of both consumer goods and military supplies.

The migration of experts and master artisans was variously induced by famine, trade, military campaigns, the attraction of protected urban settlements, and the spread of religion. But a more long-standing influence on migration was the direct or indirect patronage offered to skilled artisans to induce them to settle in the cities. The master artisans who were at top of the skill ladder in the cities of Mughal India were either employed by the political elite or received special privileges from the rulers. In South India, similarly, an additional sponsor of the artisanate was the great temple, though temple power and state power were usually indistinguishable. Almost all of the highly skilled groups were outsiders who settled in the capital cities. The South Indian groups moved between northern and southern parts of the Deccan, whereas many of the North Indian groups came from Kashmir and Central Asia.

The Mughal imperial channel of knowledge exchange took on a new meaning between 1600 and 1650 with the growth of the Indian Ocean trade and the introduction of Jesuit missionaries to the court. These new channels brought into India cartography and navigational techniques.[50] Again by way of the Europeans, two new world crops, tobacco and maize, were introduced from the Americas, and sericulture expanded in Bengal. Map making was another sphere in which technological change proceeded from contact between indigenous and Western practices. In the seventeenth century, the measurement of distances was connected to the need to estimate the distances marched by armies. Cadastral surveys

---

[49] Stephen Blake, *Shahjahanabad: The Sovereign City in Mughal India, 1639–1739*, Cambridge: Cambridge University Press, 1991, p. 203.

[50] Kapil Raj, "Colonial Encounters and the Forging of New Knowledge and National Identities: Great Britain and India, 1760–1850," *Osiris* 15(2), 2000, pp. 119–34.

were a developed system and used to establish property rights. In India, from 1700, these practices borrowed from Western knowledge techniques of representing space. Significantly, Jesuit visitors found the globe to be a particularly successful gift in the Mughal court. A wide range of manufactured consumer goods were also brought to India in the seventeenth century by the Europeans. These goods included glassware such as telescopes and spectacles, mechanical clocks, and swords. Western artillery, seamanship, and naval warfare techniques evoked particular admiration. Western goods were purchased by officials and governors of port cities such as Surat and then sent on to Agra and Lahore; in some cases, their local manufacture was sponsored.[51]

Not all technological transactions in this period happened through the court. An important form of exchange had begun on the coastal regions via the operations of the merchant marine, as we shall see in the next chapter.

Conclusion

During the 500 years discussed in the chapter, political integration helped market integration between the north and the east, between the north and the south, and between the uplands and the coasts in the south. Its effects were hardly revolutionary, however.

The composition of trade did not change much. Factor markets integrated little. The only tractable quantitative measure of market integration at the end of this period is the average interest rates charged for business loans. Early in the seventeenth century, the averages were considerably smaller in Agra, the heart of the Mughal Empire and a leading center of internal trade. They were also relatively small in Ahmedabad, closer to the maritime trading hubs of the Gujarat coast than anywhere in the Deccan.[52] Deccan rates were double or more those of North Indian. The gap remained wide as far as we can measure.

By and large, the new states that unleashed integrative tendencies treated agriculture and the peasantry as their priorities, leaving foreign trade more or less alone. The major exceptions to this policy, represented by the emergence of Surat as a Mughal port on India's western coast, were motivated not by fiscal interests but by interests of defense. State

---

[51] Ahsan Jan Qaisar, *The Indian Response to European Technology and Culture (A.D. 1498–1707)*, Delhi: Oxford University Press, 1982, pp. 10–13.

[52] Irfan Habib, "Usury in Medieval India," *Comparative Studies in Society and History* 6(4), 1964, pp. 393–419.

Table 3.1. *Dynasties and states, 1200–1765.*

	North and Central	South	East	West
1200–1525	1206–1526: The Delhi sultanates – Mamluk (1206–90); Khilji (1290–1320); Tughlaq (1320–1413); Sayyid (1414–51); and Lodi (1451–1526) – based in Delhi and control of the western Gangetic plains.	Northern half of the Deccan plateau receives armies from the north in 1294, 1307, and 1338. Kakatiyas lose to a Tughlaq army in 1323. 1347–c. 1550: Bahamani sultanate (1347–1527), based in Gulbarga, controls the northern Deccan plateau, and Vijayanagar Empire, based in Hampi (1336–1565), controls the southern part. c. 1490–1520 CE: Bahamani sultanate fragments into Bijapur, Golkonda, Ahmadnagar, Bidar, and Berar.	To 1342: Loosely under the control of Delhi; independent rule by Shamsuddin Ilyas Shah (1342–58), minor sultans, and Alauddin Husain Shah (1494–1519). Assam under autonomous Ahom (a Shan Burmese clan), Koch, and Chutiya rulers; Orissa under the eastern Gangas.	Gujarat annexed to the Delhi sultanate c. 1300; independent sultans after 1400. The Deccan sultanates control present Maharashtra. 1510–1539: Portuguese defeat Bijapur sultans to establish colony in Goa (1510), and from Gujarat sultans wrest Daman and Diu (1535–39).
1526–1680	Mughal conquest of Delhi (1526) and Malwa (1562); Rajput states, including Bundelkhand, owe allegiance.	The five sultanates progressively subdued by the Mughals in the seventeenth century. Vassals or *nayakas* of Vijayanagar (Mysore, Madurai, Gingee, Tanjore, and others) establish independent dominions, challenged from time to time by the Deccan sultanates.	Mughal conquest of Bengal and Orissa, c. 1575–85. Assam campaign fails.	Mughal conquest of Gujarat, 1572. In present-day Maharashtra, Deccan sultanates come under Mughal dominion.

Table 3.1. (cont.)

	North and Central	South	East	West
1680–1765	Maratha conquest of Malwa, Berar, Bundelkhand, c. 1700–1705. Independent kingdoms continue in Rajput territories in western India. The Mughal Empire breaks up in the middle Gangetic plains into Awadh, Rohilkhand, Punjab, and Benares, among others. Struggle for control of the western Gangetic erupts between Afghans and Marathas, c. 1750–61, ending in Maratha defeat.	Maratha dynasty in Tanjore from c. 1675. Nizam ul-Mulk establishes independent state in Hyderabad (Golkonda) in 1724, cedes the Andhra coast to the East India Company in 1765. Independent states continue in Mysore and Kerala (Travancore).	The Mughal viceroy of Bengal, Bihar, and Orissa, Murshid Quli Khan, establishes independent rule, c. 1717. Parts of Orissa ceded to Marathas in 1751. In 1765, the East India Company assumes charge of the revenues of Bengal, Bihar, and Orissa.	Maratha forces (formerly soldiers in command of hill forts under the Bijapur sultans) establish state in western Maharashtra, c. 1680. Maratha conquest of Gujarat, c. 1700–1705.

formation, the growing European presence, and the migration and reset-
tlement of artisans and merchants contributed indirectly to the diffusion
of innovations. But little change can be seen in the organization of
commerce.

In an indirect way, the limits of political authority over the littoral were
evident also in the pattern of early European intrusion into this system, if
so fluid a situation can be called a system. The entry of the Portuguese, the
English, and the Dutch changed little. The only visible difference was a
political one, and it stemmed from Portuguese attempts in the sixteenth
century to impose a monopoly by bombarding the leading ports on the
Arabian Sea littoral. These moves did not affect trade vitally, but did
increase the costs of protecting property and lives. By the mid-seventeenth
century, however, the European factor had begun to alter the institutional
basis of long-distance trade. Chapter 4 deals with this transformation.

4   The Indian Ocean Trade, 1500–1800

Indo-European trade laid the foundation for a new economic order in Asia and in Europe. Asian goods created new consumer markets in Europe. Asian trade had a formative effect on the world's money markets. In the eighteenth century, the European desire to maintain the supply of Asian goods contributed to the motivation to colonize. Indo-European trade was also the medium of transmission of new technological knowledge in both directions. There was so much two-way traffic that it would be hard to characterize the effects in terms of a model of European influence on India or an Indian "incorporation" into a European world economy. In any case, the hybrid technological, institutional, and political order that followed had momentous consequences for India. This chapter explores the evolution of Indo-European trade. The discussion leads to larger questions about the meaning of the trade for Indian history.

The Indian Ocean world at 1500

Situated in the middle of the "great arc" of Asian trade, India is geographically well placed to trade with both sides of the Indian Ocean.[1] It was not usual for any one merchant group to connect the extremities of the arc. Direct trade between West Asia and China was not unknown but, always rare, it declined after 1400. One consequence of that decline was the relative expansion of India's ports as points where cargo could change ships and ships could be restocked with food and water. This development strengthened the segments within the Indian Ocean and brought the West Asian and African ports of Aden, Hormuz, and Kilwa into closer contact with Malacca in Southeast Asia; at the same time, the middleman position of India grew. The Indian ports were more than transit points, however.

---

[1] I borrow the phrase from Om Prakash, *European Commercial Enterprise in Pre-colonial India*, Cambridge: Cambridge University Press, 1998.

They were also markets themselves. The extent of India's land and the diversity of its resources made the ports sources for a variety of textiles, including silk and muslin, and for raw products like rice, sugar, oil, cotton, and indigo. India imported for its own consumption gold and silver, specialized consumer goods, horses, and, for the reexport business, a variety of spices. The spices came from the Indonesian islands to Cambay, to be forwarded to West Asia, and then onward to Europe.

Goods bound for Europe left the Indian shores (from Cambay or Calicut) to reach either Aden at the mouth of the Red Sea or Hormuz Island at the entry to the Persian Gulf. Arab merchants would convey the goods to either Suez or Tor at the northern end of the Red Sea, or Persian merchants would take them to Basra at the northwestern end of the Gulf. From Suez, caravans picked up the merchandise to carry it to Cairo or Alexandria. From Basra, likewise, caravans picked up goods to take to either Aleppo or Tripoli (Lebanon). At these Mediterranean ports, merchants from the European mainland would take charge of the goods. The Venetians dominated this part of the transaction, but there were many others besides them who were engaged in the trade under separate treaties with the Ottoman and Egyptian rulers. Turks, Muslims, Ragusans of Dubrovnik, Armenians, and Greeks each had a share in the business. Southern Europeans dominated shipping and worked as mercenaries in the Mamluk army. The relationship of the southern Europeans with the major states was sufficiently secure for the Europeans to consider collaborative projects to dig a Suez Canal c. 1500.[2] Had they succeeded in that endeavor, the history of the world might have been different.

Distinct communities of merchant-mariners operated the ships and formed the main component of the Indian port towns – in Cambay, the Gujarati Muslims; in Malabar, the Mapilla Muslims; in Coromandel, the Chulia merchants and the Telugu Chettis of the Balija and Komati communities, and in eastern India, the Oriyas and Bengalis. Some of these were mainly merchants, others mainly shipowners and merchants on the side. In each case, mercantile enterprise was linked to a local ship-building tradition as well. Of these groups, the Gujarati may have experienced a significant expansion in the scale of their business in the fifteenth century because of the cessation of direct Arab-China trade. They were sufficiently mobile to make use of the opportunity, settling themselves in Malacca and Aden, and forging closer ties between West Asia and Cambay. The Coromandel and Bengal trade was comparatively smaller

[2] Nicholas Mirkovich, "Ragusa and the Portuguese Spice Trade," *Slavonic and East European Review* 2(1), 1943, pp. 174–87.

in size and less affected. The main Coromandel port was Pulicat, which was one of the principal connectors between the Vijayanagar Empire and the eastern Indian Ocean. In Bengal, Saptagram and Chittagong conducted trade with Burma, Indonesia, and China. All of these ports, moreover, participated actively in the port-to-port coastal trade. Ships from Bengal bound for the Red Sea would routinely halt at Konkan or at Cambay or in the Maldives.

None of these ports was firmly linked to an inland empire. The states that earned an income from them were relatively small and only locally influential. The Samudri king ruled a small state from Calicut, Cambay had its own king, and many small ports along the Konkan coast were ruled by chieftains. In the east, the authority of the sultan of Gaud on the Chittagong port was substantial, but the authority of his court became shaky in the 1530s after Mughal and Afghan expansion in the west. One consequence of this change was the struggle for control over Chittagong among the Portuguese, the Arakanese, and, later, the Mughals. The commercial operators in these ports, therefore, needed to adapt to pan-regional economic or political tendencies rather than try to control and shape these forces.

The equilibrium was upset with the growth of two ports. One of these, Masulipatnam, was in Coromandel, and its rise was associated with the power of the Qutb Shahi rule in Golkonda. Conveniently located, the port could serve Southeast Asia, Bengal, and the Gulf trades, and it quickly became home to Persian merchants. Located on the estuary of the Krishna in a fertile cultivated plain, it could become a victualing stop. Ship building and repair as well as skilled artisanal production were also attracted to the region. The second port of importance in the early seventeenth century was Surat, in Gujarat. Surat had shared in the improved fortunes of Gujarati trading enterprises in the fifteenth century but had remained overshadowed by Cambay. Surat's status as a competing hub was a threat to Portuguese designs to control West Asian trade, and, therefore, the Portuguese sacked the port city in 1530. A slow consolidation of trade began again in the second half of the sixteenth century, but it was only after the annexation of Gujarat by the Mughal Empire in 1576 that Surat came to be treated as a vital asset. A strong yet semi-independent administration was set up to manage the port's commercial policy and taxation.

In the sixteenth century, the Portuguese enterprise operated from Goa, Cambay, Cochin, and Bengal. A century later, the Dutch and the English avoided sites where the chance of a direct confrontation with the Portuguese was increased. Initially, the Dutch and the English operated from Surat and Masulipatnam. Their pattern of shifting the sites of their ports to safer and more secure port towns was taken to new heights in the second half of the seventeenth century, when the English moved their base to Bombay, Madras, and Calcutta.

The Portuguese enterprise

On August 14, 1415, Ceuta, a port city located on the northwestern corner of the African continent, fell to a Portuguese navy of forty-five thousand men. The Portuguese expedition had been more religious than economic in intent. Nevertheless, Ceuta, "the key of the Mediterranean," as well as a key to the West African littoral, was a valuable commercial asset. Ceuta's capture made it feasible for the Portuguese to launch more ambitious expeditions down the Atlantic in search of mythical Christian lands, as well as gold, silver, and spices.

In a curious way, the Portuguese situation created the will to and the capability for undertaking long-distance maritime voyages of uncertain prospects. The exact combination of events, conditions, and preparations that led to such expeditions form the subject of endless discussion. So does the question of exactly when these voyages had began. Portugal was one of the poorest nations in Europe. And yet, its people had strong navigation skills. Some of the early raiding parties were already equipped so that they could leave sight of the coast. Royal patronage also contributed to this naval capability. Moreover, the poverty of the nobility and the high mortality of the population made maritime expedition a feasible way to make a living. This drive to find secure livelihoods partly explains why the early fifteenth-century expeditions were short-distance ones. Settlements of colonist farmers, fishermen, traders, and slavers were established in each new place before the next move happened. In each instance, the regular exchange of information between those in charge of the naval missions and the sailors who had already ventured beyond the known limits of the sea meant that the next exploration would go further. The vessels' small size – even Vasco da Gama's India trip included ships that were barely 200–250 tons – helped longer expeditions by requiring frequent stops. In this fashion, the Portuguese extended their presence from Ceuta to Tangier, Madeira, Cape Verde, Guinea, Senegal, and Ghana between 1415 and 1480.

In the 1480s, an adventurous overland private journey to Sofala, a port town on the Mozambique coast, and the expedition of Bartholomew Diaz, which circumnavigated Africa to a little beyond the Cape of Good Hope, created sufficient knowledge of the western Indian Ocean to make a trip to India look both promising and possible to undertake. Commercial interest in India at the time was almost monopolized by Venetian merchants. The main traffic in Indian goods made the relatively short journey across the Arabian Sea to reach the Persian Gulf, where caravans would take the cargo to a Mediterranean port, and onward to Europe. Although the Portuguese court was not in complete agreement on the wisdom of cutting out the Venetian traders in the event that a sea route to Asia could be found, the group that wanted to press the advantage given Portugal by the Diaz voyage prevailed. The nobleman Vasco da Gama was named leader of the India mission. Da Gama had battle and navigational experience, but he was probably chosen more for his political skills. The mission was to be partly diplomatic in nature, rather than a crusade. After more than three months at sea, followed by a series of stops, the fleet reached the east coast of Africa, which had an established trade with India. During the several months that the fleet explored the east coast harbors, friendly contacts were established with many local kings, but the first stirrings of religious hostility also occurred. A Gujarati pilot picked up in Mombasa steered the fleet to Calicut in May 1498.

The fleet's experience on the Malabar coast was a mixed one. Its attempt to trade was not very successful, which da Gama attributed to the resistance of Muslim merchants. But he did return to Portugal, after a voyage that saw many sailors die in transit, with a consignment of cinnamon, cloves, pepper, nutmeg, and precious stones. More valuable than the cargo was the knowledge of navigating the Arabian Sea that da Gama brought back with him. However, it was really da Gama's second visit to Calicut, in 1502–3, that defined the pattern of Portuguese expansion to follow. That voyage resulted in a number of treaties giving the Portuguese permission to trade, but it also left in its wake horrific excesses that included the bombardment of Calicut and the massacre of passengers on a ship bound for Mecca.

When the expedition by Afonso de Albuquerque took place the next year, the aim was to create dominions and colonies rather than diplomatic missions. In little more than a decade, settlements were established in Ceylon and Goa; Cochin and Cannanore became friendly states, and Malacca and Hormuz were subdued into treaty ports. Martaban in Burma opened its doors, and a powerful allied fleet commanded by the Mamluks was routed in Diu. This last challenge was more or less engineered by the Venetian merchants who had been worried about the competition from the Cape route and had been working toward a military solution for some time. Aden held out, but only just. Portugal's longer-term objective, redirecting the Asian spice trade from the Mediterranean route to the Cape route, was within reach.

In the first half of the sixteenth century, Portuguese maritime trade focused on the western Indian littoral. Although the capture of Malacca had broadened the sphere of trading operations and, especially, had made it easier for the Portuguese to explore the eastern Indian Ocean, Bengal and Orissa were not an official priority for them as much as was the spice route. The Crown took a great interest in the trade and made the trade by the Cape route a monopoly of Casa da India, a Crown trading firm. The Estado da India, which was based in Goa, was the Crown's representative in the second half of the century. The main interest of the Casa da India was in trading as much Indonesian spices as possible without mediation. Simultaneously, the state tried to obstruct the West Asia trade route – destroying some Arab shipping in the process and collecting protection money from the other Arab firms – and to redirect Indonesian trade to the Cape route. To exert its control, the Estado da India, in exchange for a small fee, issued passes to any ship that wanted to ply the Indian Ocean. It was obligatory for the pass holder to pay customs at a port under Portuguese control. The authority of Goa was represented in the waters by the captains of the vessels that belonged to the king. But the business of collecting protection money was also informally carried out by sea captains and private traders, and not only on this route.

Why was the Portuguese enterprise especially prone to use of force? In the rather special circumstances of the early sixteenth century, when the Portuguese wanted to oust the Muslim merchants in the spice trade of Malabar and Sumatra, violence became a necessary weapon. A crusading impulse may have made the conflict worse. When that phase had passed, the strategy of firing one's way into the Indian Ocean was no longer either necessary or successful. But in the first half of the century, the violent attempts paid off. The Portuguese intervention saw pepper prices stabilize in Europe after a fall in the late 1400s.[3] Profits were sustained at high levels, possibly several hundred percent. Lisbon almost became an entrepôt, although the city was hardly ready for that honor. Because of the limitations of Lisbon, much wholesale trade was diverted to the Flemish free port of Antwerp. Though the Netherlands was located in the thick of the European spice trade, dependence on Portugal was odious to the Dutch provinces, which were at war with Spain and Portugal. This situation

---

[3] Frederic C. Lane, "Pepper Prices before Da Gama," *Journal of Economic History* 28(4), 1968, pp. 590–97.

eventually supplied one of the motivations for the formation of the Dutch East India Company in 1602.

The first half of the 1500s saw some disturbance in the Persian Gulf trade. The Portuguese controlled Hormuz, taking a commanding position in the Gulf route. A series of diplomatic and naval expeditions had established the Portuguese as the most powerful players in Malacca on the Malaysian coast, Nagasaki in Japan, Macau off China, Goa and Diu in Konkan, and Cochin in Malabar. With this ring of fortified settlements in place, and their partners, the Spanish, stationed in Manila, the Iberians could think of a system for the command and control of the Indian Ocean. In the short-term, the affected parties were the West Asian traders. In the long run, the situation led to European conflicts that spilled over from the Atlantic into the Indian Ocean, as we shall see. The political situation turned murky when the Turks invaded territories of the Mamluk sultans (1516–17) and when the Venetians fought with the Turks in 1537–40. On the whole, however, local participants seemed to reconcile themselves to Portuguese power in the region, paid taxes, and carried on as before. In the second half of the century, the Levantine route, especially the shorter and easier one over Mesopotamia, revived. Politics apart, an overland journey was safer than a sea one. And Portuguese attempts at enforcing the monopoly had begun to fail.

The Portuguese Crown began to farm out its authority to private merchants and sea captains early in the second half of the sixteenth century. This was a time when the attempts to control long-distance maritime routes along these routes faced serious challenges from rivals and were being given up. Southeast Asian supplies of pepper slipped through Portuguese controls into Venetian hands from as early as the 1560s. Interestingly, shipping volumes via the Cape did not immediately respond to this failure. The data show that the number of ships plying the route between Lisbon and India fell continuously in the sixteenth century, whereas the average tonnage carried increased. In the end, the total annual volume held steady in 1500–1600 (4,000–5,000 tons Lisbon departures), increased somewhat in 1600–1620 (6,000–7,700 tons), and declined steadily and sharply thereafter.[4] By 1650, annual volume leaving Lisbon for Asia was less than two thousand tons.

During the earlier part of this trajectory, the Crown's involvement in the trade was in retreat, but private Portuguese traders increased their participation. The work of James Boyajian supplies "evidence of the riches and

---

[4] Cited in Prakash, *European Commercial Enterprise*, p. 32.

sophistication of private Portuguese trade within Asia."[5] On the long-distance route, the private actors included members of the so-called New Christian community, Jewish groups who had converted to Christianity. Along with these people, *casados*, or settlers, also entered private coast-to-coast trade. Based in Bengal and Goa, they carried bulk goods such as sugar or rice, connecting Bengal with the Orissa coast, where Pipli had emerged to become a port of call, and eastern India with southern India, Ceylon, and Hormuz.

After 1640, the forces of decline seemed to prevail in Portuguese commerce more generally. The territorial empire in South Asia ended up as a small, impoverished, and economically insignificant settlement based in Goa, leaving the Dutch and the English East India Companies in command of the commercial heights. Historians have debated whether the failure of the Portuguese enterprise was economic or political. In one view, the ultimate failure was due to the "redistributive" and "precapitalist" nature of the enterprise. It lived off the profits of others rather than make its own activities profitable.[6] In another view, the Portuguese commercial empire ended not because of its own premodern outlook but because of external factors, including the resistance of strong territorial states such as those under the Mughals, Ottomans, Japanese, and Persians.[7] By the time later European actors displayed a propensity to colonize land in India, some of these territorial states had become weaker.

The Bengal seaboard presents conditions quite different from those of the western coast of India. By the middle decades of the sixteenth century, a substantial number of Portuguese were present in Bengal as private traders, mercenaries, artillerymen, and shipwrights.[8] The fragmented political authority after the Mughal invasion in 1595, as well as the rising ambitions of Arakan, created a whole new political prospect in the region. The Bengal story revolves around two towns, Hooghly and Sandwip. In

---

[5] James Boyajian, *Portuguese Trade in Asia under the Habsburgs, 1580–1640*, Baltimore: Johns Hopkins University Press, 2007, p. xiii.

[6] Niels Steensgaard, *The Asian Trade Revolution of the Seventeenth Century: The East India Companies and the Decline of the Caravan Trade*, Chicago: University of Chicago Press, 1974.

[7] For a discussion, see M. N. Pearson, *The Portuguese in India*, Cambridge: Cambridge University Press, 1987; Sanjay Subrahmanyam, *The Portuguese Empire in Asia, 1500–1700: A Political and Economic History*, London and New York: Longman, 1993; and Sanjay Subrahmanyam, *The Career and Legend of Vasco da Gama*, Cambridge: Cambridge University Press. 1997.

[8] Sanjay Subrahmanyam, "Notes on the Sixteenth-Century Bengal Trade," *Indian Economic Social History* Review 24(3), 1987, pp. 265–89.

both places, the Mughal provincial administration suspected the Portuguese of river piracy. Although for a long time the Mughals were not strong enough to oust or suppress the Portuguese in Sandwip, they did succeed in doing so in Hooghly.

Sebastiao Gonzales was the most famous example of the opportunism and ambition exhibited by members of the loosely constituted community on the Bengal seaboard. A salt trader, Gonzales was in the company of a small band of refugees from Arakan who had rearmed themselves and befriended the king of Bakla, a seacoast state, in the last decade of the fifteenth century. Gonzales was their commander. Buttressed by boats and horses from Bakla, and with timely help from a Spanish fleet as well as some subterfuge, Gonzales captured Sandwip from the Mughals in 1607. He thereupon reneged on his promises to Bakla to share the Sandwip revenues, established a customshouse, and received respectful mention in Mughal sources. When the threat of a Mughal counterattack materialized after a few years, Gonzales planned a joint campaign with the Arakan king but withdrew from it, leaving the Arakan navy to face a rout. The Arakans retaliated, and Gonzales sought help from the viceroy at Goa. The viceroy sent a symbolic fleet in aid of an unreliable ally. Eventually, Portuguese mismanagement of the campaign, the death of the commander of the Goa fleet, the sudden appearance of a Dutch fleet that used the Portuguese fleet for target practice, and the appearance of a large ebb tide that cut the Portuguese fleet in half combined to bring about a Portuguese defeat. The Goa fleet refused to engage further, and in 1616, the Arakan king captured Sandwip. The Portuguese commercial presence in the Indian Ocean rapidly declined shortly after this episode. Although this decline was in the main caused by other factors, Portuguese misadventures in the Bay of Bengal played no small part in it. In the meantime, the English and the Dutch East India Companies had entrenched themselves on the western Indian Ocean.

East India Companies: Origins

A number of circumstances induced the merchants of the City of London to form an overseas trading company in the last years of the 1500s. The sixteenth century had ended in England in a curious combination of static trade and rising ambitions. Almost all of the shipping engaged in the European trade was foreign owned. Joint-stock companies were in existence, for example, the Levant Company and the Venice Company; neither

4.1. Wall hanging (cotton) showing early traders to India, late sixteenth century. *Source*: The Bridgeman Art Library

of these did much business, however, and, on the whole, the joint-stock companies failed to break the stranglehold that southern European merchants maintained over the overland traffic with Asia. The destruction of Antwerp in 1576 by Spanish forces led to a redirection of trade, but, according to Lawrence Stone, no great change in trade volumes.[9] Nevertheless, English shipping did see an expansion and reorganization after this event, and it acquired more flexibility in the last half of Elizabeth's reign. The other event in the commercial arena that contributed to a reorganization was the end to the long-festering conflict between the English merchants operating in Central Europe and the Hanseatic League merchants operating in London who enjoyed preferential trading rights in England but resisted extending reciprocal privileges to the English

[9] Lawrence Stone, "Elizabethan Overseas Trade," *Economic History Review* 2(1), 1949, pp. 30–58.

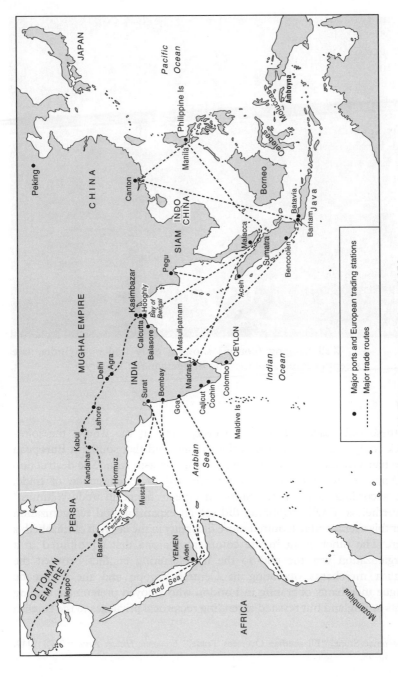

4.2. Maritime routes and ports with European presence, c. 1650.

in Europe. The suspension of immunities or withdrawal of special privileges (1578) and the eventual expulsion of the league by Elizabeth (1597) encouraged company formation in the City.

More than these external events, Elizabethan London developed a set of conditions that made ambitious overseas exploration more feasible than before. Spices from Malabar and Indonesia were known to Europe in the sixteenth century but had to be procured either from the Portuguese or from Genoese and Venetian merchants and their allies in the Ottoman and Persian Empires. Early overland journeys, such as that made by the Englishman Ralph Fitch, recorded the goods that Europe could buy from India. The predatory expeditions of Francis Drake and Thomas Cavendish exposed the weaknesses of Spanish and Portuguese defenses in the Atlantic and the Pacific. Exploration by Walter Raleigh, Humphrey Gilbert, John Hawkins, and Martin Frobisher increased English knowledge of navigation, brought the existing maps within reach, and created much interest in navigation for commercial purposes. Among the sailors, ship captains, and explorers who attended the meeting at Founders' Hall (Sept. 22, 1599) in London that led to the formation of the English East India Company were both individuals who had acquired their reputations in Atlantic exploration and merchants whose interests straddled the Atlantic Ocean, Africa, and the Levant. Prominent members of the Levant Company were willing to spend money on shipping over the Cape route in order to bypass the Levant route.

These developments bore fruit in 1599–1600. The City merchants, town notables, and members of the fleet of Drake and Frobisher came together to form the Company of the Merchants of London Trading to the East Indies and obtained a royal charter granting them a monopoly in the trade east of the Cape. The terms of the monopoly obliged the company to pay taxes to the Crown, allowed the company to take out bullion but regulated the amount, and made unauthorized trade in the goods that formed the company's staple business punishable by law. In effect, the company held the right to farm out the trade to its shareholders or to "factors" engaged by them, while also hiring employees to conduct its own trade.

The Dutch East India Company followed formation of the English company two years later. In the Dutch provinces, after the fall of Antwerp, the authority of the monarchy was relatively weak and the authority of the city guilds strong. A "deviant medieval heritage" had led to relatively weak seignorial powers, secure and saleable private property in land, and powerful corporate capitalist bodies long before Amsterdam emerged as a leading financial center of the world.[10] Much of the Dutch capital and the organization was devoted to shipping, and this field was expanding because of difficulties in obtaining traded goods from southern Europe.

In the late sixteenth century, Dutch ships made relatively short-haul commercial expeditions into the Atlantic. One convoy called on the Cape Verde Islands to procure salt, which was becoming hard to get because of an Iberian blockade. Dutch ships and sailors were also hired by the Portuguese as transporters between Brazil and Europe. Over the next ten years, the pattern of Dutch maritime and commercial journeys was established, with ships going regularly to the West Indies and the Cape of Good Hope and dealing in a more or less fixed set of goods. At least one voyage made it to the Strait of Magellan and the eastern Pacific. Salt hauling continued to be an important aim, but gold, silver, pepper, and possibly slaves joined the cargo.

The Dutch decision to pool capital and consolidate the number of small East India companies into the United Company in 1602, with a monopoly charter, was partly a response to the formation of the English East India Company and partly a response to the problems of securing spices overland. Although it was a joint-stock company representing merchants, the Dutch East India Company was a different kind of firm from its English counterpart, being in the nature of a shipping cartel. In one view, the cartel was less dependent on royal patronage than was the English company; however, a different reading attributes Dutch commercial success in Asian waters to the occasional but critical intervention of state naval power.[11]

Shortly after the formation of the company, Dutch shipping, consisting of large armed vessels of 500–1,000 tons, established itself as a formidable power off the western coast of India and the Indonesian Islands. In the early 1600s, the contest for control of trade in the Atlantic and in Indonesia between the Dutch and the Spanish was fierce and only occasionally contained by diplomatic efforts. By 1630, Dutch power was the main factor behind the disarray that beset Portuguese trade in India and Indonesia. Dutch power in Indonesia was also the factor that led the English to concentrate on India and to use diplomatic missions to the Mughal court to obtain trade treaties. In this enterprise, the English went further than the other western Europeans.

---

[10] Jan de Vries, "On the Modernity of the Dutch Republic," *Journal of Economic History* 33(1), 1973, pp. 191–202.

[11] Jonathan I. Israel, *Dutch Primacy in World Trade, 1585–1740*, Oxford: Clarendon Press, 1989.

Of the major maritime nations in Western Europe, the French were the last to enter the race for the East Indies. An early French enterprise set up in 1604 for this purpose and protected by a royal monopoly dissipated its energies in infighting. Inevitably, rivals offered their services to the court, and a new enterprise formed in 1615. The first voyage of this firm to Java ended in a failure. Nothing more happened in the next twenty years except for an attempt to set up a trading station and settlement in Madagascar. When La Compagnie des Indes was reconstituted in 1642, its first missions were to explore Madagascar. India became a priority much later.

In 1661, Jean-Baptiste Colbert took over the reins of the French treasury. A merchant and banker by family background and training, Colbert immediately set out to expand the French navy and acquire and develop ports. Along with meeting his nation's defense needs, Colbert had his eyes on strengthening overseas commercial exploration. In 1664, a new *compagnie* formed under his initiative. When missions to India were again organized, the French could use their existing bases in Madagascar quite effectively. However, conflict with the Dutch during the Nine Years' War (1688–97) in Europe made French presence in the Indian region shaky again. It was not until 1700 that the French established a secure foothold in India. Thereafter, even as France was engulfed in a financial crisis and the French company underwent many changes at home, the Indian mission survived and was consistently profitable.

The company form and its problems

English and Dutch overseas trading was organized quite differently from the state-sponsored Portuguese ventures. The joint-stock form of both companies reduced the danger of bankruptcy. The monopoly charter that the English East India Company carried reduced its risk of competition from other Englishmen. But perhaps the most important effect of the representation of trade by a single firm was that the company could send credible diplomatic missions to the courts in India seeking a license to trade. These peaceful missions might not have succeeded without a series of victories that the English scored over the Portuguese off the Konkan between 1610 and 1640. Still, the element of diplomacy did set the English apart from the Portuguese in the manner in which both powers earned concessions to trade in India. Nevertheless, neither of these organizational innovations – the company form and the diplomatic embassy – was an effective solution to three problems that plagued the English East

India Company almost from its beginning in 1600 until the end of its trading career in India in 1813.

First, the monopoly charter was difficult to enforce with the company's resources. This was because of competition from City merchants who envied the success of the company and tried to form rival firms. The joint-stock concept did succeed in pulling in private capital from a large number of investors, but the management of the company was restricted to an oligarchy of big shareholders. The opaque management and the constant attacks on monopoly, which took on ideological overtones in the eighteenth century, made the English East India Company's career controversial and mired the firm in numerous allegations of corruption. The outsiders sought to create a lobby within Parliament to seek an end to the company's monopoly, and both sides made use of the stormy relationship between the Crown and Parliament in the middle decades of the seventeenth century. On two occasions the Crown granted charters to rival East India Companies, which did not survive. Even when the company's charter was not under threat, entrepreneurial figures like the merchant Thomas Pitt managed to establish their own trading empires in India in open defiance of the company. In distant India, private trade was a source of irritation between the company and the local kings. To catch the private traders and prosecute them, the company needed the help of the local police. But the kings were loath to be seen to favor the company over the other European traders in their realms. Bribes, therefore, were generously paid to preempt competition from interlopers. By the second half of the eighteenth century, as the Mughal Empire fragmented into a number of regional states, only a semblance of an agreement between the English East India Company and the Mughal court was still working.

Second, the company faced a threat of encroachment from within the establishment. This threat came from the private trading of company employees. The whole enterprise of overseas voyages succeeded by allowing the peripatetic employees some freedom to carry out private trade, but it was impossible to restrain them from overstepping the limits and poaching on the employers' interests. The fact that many of the employees were drawn from among mariners and soldiers whereas company principals were sedentary merchants made their mutual suspicion even more likely. Private trade created a host of complications in the overseas branches of the East India Company. Conflicts of interest were so rife as to be beyond any means of regulation. The officers spied on each other, engaged the company's Indian agents to serve the officers' private interests, and appropriated common resources for their own profit. The more powerful and capable the officer, the greater was the conflict of interest. Consequently, the more powerful and capable the officer was, the greater was the likelihood of a disciplinary proceeding against him.

Third, the diplomatic embassies that the English East India Company sent to India were not totally effective. Their effectiveness was limited because the writ from the Mughals did not cover South India and an agreement with a Mughal emperor could be obstructed, if not challenged, by the local administrators of Surat or Hooghly. Also quite serious were two issues that would crop up regularly in the relationship between a local king and company officers. The agreement stipulated the payment of customs based on trade volume. The company head office, however, indicated to the officers that they could try to bribe officials to escape paying the full amount of the taxes. But bribery raised the perennial difficulty that with every change of administrator a fresh agreement had to be made. In addition to taxation, a field of potential dispute was seignorial right, or the right to have a mint on Indian soil. The company imported gold and silver for the payment of Indian goods, but it did not have the right to convert these metals into coins. Conversion was expensive and entailed a dependence on Indian bankers.[12] Despite these difficulties, however, the trade remained exceedingly profitable, and its scale became larger in the 1700s compared to the 1600s.

Scale of trade, 1600–1800

Across two hundred years, the commodities prominent in the basket of imports and the volumes traded did not remain static. The changes reflected the consumer boom in Western Europe that moved from one good to another, the shifting advantages of the overseas branches, and the growing interdependence between the European conquest and the settlement of America, the African slave trade, and the importation of Asian luxuries. Asian import into Europe was dominated by spices in the first half of the seventeenth century; by Indian cotton textiles, saltpeter, and Chinese silk and porcelain in the next one hundred years; and by Chinese tea in the second half of the eighteenth century. The major article in the English East India Company's imports of about 1700 was cotton cloth.

---

[12] These points are more fully elaborated in Tirthankar Roy, *The East India Company: The World's Most Powerful Corporation*, New Delhi: Allen Lane, 2012.

Saltpeter, an ingredient in gunpowder, was also in great demand in war-
ridden Europe.[13]

Although plain cotton was initially a means of payment in Indian Ocean
trade, colored cottons from India were wanted for fashionable clothing
and even began to define design standards in apparel.[14] Chinese tea had
been introduced into Europe early in the seventeenth century, but it was
still an expensive article. Imports increased rapidly in the eighteenth
century when supplies steadied. By then, tea was the leading Asian consumer good in the markets of Europe and North America, and the main
business interest of the English company. However, this picture neglects
commodity flows within the Indian Ocean region that facilitated the
Europe-Asia trade. Thus for a brief period in the seventeenth century,
Persian horses went to India to balance the trade. Moreover, the Dutch
had discovered that Indian cottons were a handy means of payment for
spices in Indonesia. One article that sold well in exchange for slaves was,
again, Indian cotton cloth.

Among the other Indian goods traded, silk was of some importance in
the mid-eighteenth century. The English and the Dutch companies conducted the most business in Bengal in the eighteenth century, at the cost
of all other settlements in India. One of the attractions of Bengal was
the availability of a portfolio of valuable exports – cotton cloth, opium,
saltpeter, sugar, and silk. Bengal was long the major producer in India of
raw silk and silk manufactures. From the middle decades of the century,
silk occupied a critical part of the English company's exports.[15] The
Dutch had been selling Bengal silk in Japan in the seventeenth century,
and that market having become uncertain, they found an alternative
market in Europe. The new opportunity, however, was frustrated by

---

[13] On the history of the English and the Dutch companies, see K. N. Chaudhuri, *The Trading
World of Asia and the English East India Company, 1660–1760*, Cambridge: Cambridge
University Press, 1978; Holden Furber, *John Company at Work: A Study of European
Expansion in India in the Late Eighteenth Century*, Cambridge, MA: Harvard University
Press, 1948; Tapan Raychaudhuri, *Jan Company in Coromandel, 1605–1690: A Study in the
Interrelations of European Commerce and Traditional Economies*, The Hague: Martinus
Nijhoff, 1962; Om Prakash, *European Commercial Enterprise in Pre-colonial India*,
Cambridge: Cambridge University Press, 1998.

[14] On Indian textiles especially, essays in two recent collections are state of the art: Giorgio
Riello and Prasannan Parthasarathi, eds., *The Spinning World: A Global History of
Cotton Textiles, 1200–1850*, Oxford: Oxford University Press, 2010; Giorgio Riello and
Tirthankar Roy, eds., *How India Clothed the World: The World of South Asian Textiles,
1500–1850*, Leiden: Brill, 2010.

[15] Chaudhuri, *Trading World of Asia and the English East India Company*, pp. 343–58.

protectionist moves at home, and the Dutch company never quite regained the ground it had lost in Japan.[16]

Interestingly, the volume of European trade in Bengal silk was relatively small in the total business in goods; exports of Bengal silk by the English and the Dutch did not exceed 150 tons annually in the 1730s. By comparison, in the 1750s, Asian merchants exported by land five times as much as the volume that the Europeans carried.[17] Indeed, the dominance of North Indian merchants was so strong that the Europeans could never gain an advantageous position in this trade. The volume of the trade was in decline in the second half of the century because of political uncertainty in northern India and disease that attacked the silkworms. By 1820, when Asian silk export to Europe exceeded 500 tons, Bengal occupied a negligible share.

The New World contributed to the Asian trades indirectly by strengthening the European consumer boom. Virginia tobacco in the middle decades of the seventeenth century and Caribbean sugar in the eighteenth century were the most important American goods shaping consumption demand. Furthermore, profits from the sugar trade were reinvested in building ports, docks, banks, and insurance in London, and in the slave trade in West Africa. Indian textiles were used as means of payment in Africa for slaves, in turn feeding into production for export to the Americas. But more than anything else, it was silver from the Americas that contributed to the making of Asian trade. The Spanish conquest had made silver progressively cheaper in Europe than in China and India. These circumstances, together with the almost inexhaustible demand for silver as a private asset in India, made it possible to continue the purchases of Asian goods until the mid-eighteenth century.[18]

The success of silver as a means of payment was not owed just to the metal's elastic supply. Money was more expensive in Asia than in Europe, a difference that derived from the structure of the respective financial systems. The sustained dependence of the trade on liquid rather than on borrowed capital as soon as the traders reached Asian shores stemmed from the exorbitant real interest rates that borrowing in Asia entailed.

---

[16] Els M. Jacobs, *Merchant in Asia: The Trade of the Dutch East India Company during the Eighteenth Century*, Leiden: Brill, 2006, pp. 109–15.

[17] Sushil Chaudhury, "International Trade in Bengal Silk and the Comparative Role of Asians and Europeans, circa.1700–1757," *Modern Asian Studies* 29(2), 1995, pp. 373–86.

[18] André Gunder Frank, *ReOrient: Global Economy in the Asian Age*, Berkeley and Los Angeles: University of California Press, 1998; Dennis O. Flynn and Arturo Giráldez, "Cycles of Silver: Global Economic Unity through the Mid-Eighteenth Century," *Journal of World History* 13(2), 2002, pp. 391–427.

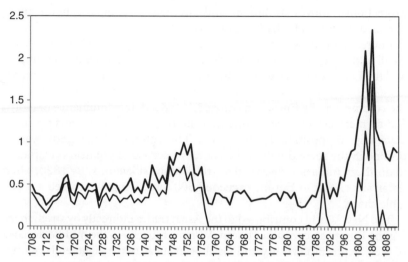

4.3. Import of bullion and goods (m £) by the English East India
Company into India, 1708–1810. *Source*: British Parliamentary
Papers, 1812–13 (152), *An account of Bullion and Merchandize*.

Only late in the eighteenth century did English irons and iron goods like
cannons and guns begin to sell well in India, reducing the dependence on
silver somewhat. Again from late in the eighteenth century, Indian opium
was found to be a convenient means of payment for Chinese tea, freeing
the Europe-India trade, if fitfully, from the bonds of silver.

Given the overwhelming dependence on silver, a rough measure of the
volume of the business would be the total value of silver and of goods
imported into India. The relevant data for the English East India
Company are presented in Figure 4.3. The real volume of the textile
trade did not in fact change much between 1700 and 1800. The slow rise
in the value largely reflects the rising prices of textiles in the first sixty years
of the time series. There was a structural break point in the middle of the
century. Trade dropped abruptly, and silver inflow stopped almost completely. This break was a result of the political developments of the time, to
which I will return. In the mid-eighteenth century, the English East India
Company was the leader of the market, with roughly 50 percent market
share in textiles; the French and the Dutch shared the remaining half. The
English, however, were a smaller player in the Coromandel, though they
were dominant in Bengal. The late eighteenth-century decline in fortunes
was experienced by all of them. One common unfavorable factor was the

rise of private traders and American competition. But political and military rivalry in India also drained the resources of the competing powers. While the French and the Dutch East India Companies ended their careers, the English company continued, but only by reinventing itself as a colonial power.

Partners, employees, agents

How much did European trade depend on Indian institutions and agents? By the benchmarks of premodern trade, the Asian trading organization was efficient, dynamic, adaptive, and capable of responding to opportunity. In the beginning, as the trade historian Om Prakash points out, "the Europeans had no option but to operate within the given organizational structure."[19] This "given organizational structure" included accommodation by bankers and money changers, partnerships with local merchants, and the services of artisans and shipwrights. The Indian employees of the European companies deserve little comment, for the major part of the business was conducted with the help of merchants who worked on commission. Nevertheless, in the eighteenth century, some individuals engaged on salary did perform a politically useful service for the company, namely, spying on the affairs of and on occasion negotiating with the princely courts. Also, as we will see, the reliance on salaried employees tended to increase in the late eighteenth century, partly on account of long-standing problems in contract enforcement.

It is useful to remind ourselves how dependent Indo-European trade was on Asian traders. The latter retained control over almost all aspects of Indo-European business except the final sale and shipment by sea. They functioned not only as agents and middlemen for the Europeans inside India but also as the principal actors in overland trade, in transactions between Indian regions, and in transactions between Indian Ocean regions. All forms of caravan trade and the markets where caravan goods came to be sold were dominated by the Indians. River-borne trade likewise was controlled by the Indians. Pedro Machado has recently pointed to "the resourcefulness and dynamism of indigenous merchants and capital in exploiting markets in the Indian Ocean." Machado's work shows how the Gujarati traders supplied cotton textiles

---

[19] Prakash, *European Commercial Enterprise*, p. 4.

produced in Gujarat to Portuguese Mozambique in the last quarter of
the eighteenth century and established an import trade in African ivory in
the process.[20] In this scenario, there could be no question of Europeans'
achieving dominance over trading institutions. Their goal was rather to
build stable and productive partnerships. As this section will show, the
road to such partnerships was not an easy one.

Of the individuals who supplied useful services to the European companies in India, a rough distinction can be made between those who sold
services for one-off payments and those who were engaged under a more
or less permanent contract. Bankers were the principal members of the
first group. Interest rates were higher than in Europe even for reliable
clients. The terms of duration for loans were shorter on average, which is
evident from the many interest rates quoted by the month. The major
component in the demand for money was financing revenue payments
and the grain trade after harvests, so that interest rates varied greatly by the
season. To finance the purchase of manufactures, therefore, a company
needed to choose the lender and the time of borrowing carefully. The
major reason for depending on the banker, however, was to convert silver
bullion into coins with high silver content. So lucrative was this business
that occasionally local rulers and princes joined in. Using their legal
monopoly on coinage, they could try to increase the profits from minting
coins or exchanging currency.

As the Mughal dominion shrank in the eighteenth century, and new
powers emerged, the business of the conversion of one local currency into
another increased in importance. Money changing entailed risks. Since
almost all currencies were metallic, the exchange rate between them was
related to the intrinsic value of the currencies' metal content. Bankers
ascertained the intrinsic value and decided the fair exchange rate. The
greater the diversity of the coins, the more information and trust was
needed in this exchange. But information was not always adequate, and
trust could fail, with the result that sometimes bankers refused to accept a
coin from another region, or they released money that was debased
and that the bazaar refused to accept. When this problem became serious
in the eighteenth century, the East India Company moved to solve it.
Payments of money from one of its branches to another were effected by
means of promissory notes purchased from one branch of a banking firm

[20] Pedro Machado, "A Regional Market in a Globalised Economy: East Central and South
Eastern Africans, Gujarati Merchants and the Indian Textile Industry in the Eighteenth
and Nineteenth Centuries," in Riello and Roy, *How India Clothed the World*, pp. 53–84
(quote on p. 83).

and redeemable at another branch or in another town. The dependence on bankers continued, if in a different form.

After the English company assumed power in Bengal, the great banking firms of northern India suffered a mixed fate. Some of them, such as the Jagatseths of Bengal, were no longer necessary to the new regime, which centralized its main monetary functions. The company's custom in the remittance business was a source of prosperity for other firms, however, such as Gopaldas of Benares and Arjunji Nathji of Surat. As borrowing was often used in the late eighteenth century to finance war, the indigenous bankers who were allied with the English company were regarded as friends of the regime. These houses had agents in nearly all major commercial towns of northern and western India. They were connected through a system of intelligence unmatched by the government in efficiency. Therefore, bankers were often relied on for military intelligence.

Indian maritime trading communities were entrenched in the coastal trade. In Gujarat, Malabar, and Coromandel, they owned boats and conducted trade. Although owning their capital, sometimes the coastal communities also hired their services to ship-owning merchants of Bombay. One of the main businesses of these communities was to load cargo and food on ships that sailed from Bombay for Europe. At Calicut, pepper was a common cargo, and timber from Canara was loaded on ships that took it to the East India Company naval yard at Trincomalee. Dhows, which were medium-sized boats of 50–250 tons fitted with a mast and lateen sails, carried coconut and copra from Malabar to Bombay. From the late eighteenth century or a little later, the dhows also carried European manufactures from Bombay to the southern Arabian ports, bringing back on their return dates, wine, and horses. On the Coromandel coast a similar mid-sized boat plied the route between Madras and Ceylon. These boats, called dhoni, could navigate the shallow waters of the Palk Strait that heavier ships could not negotiate.

Although useful to it, some coastal communities had an uneasy relationship with the East India Company. Those with a base in the islands off the main coast were often engaged in piracy. In the 1660s, the Malabar community Mappilahs was described by Jean-Baptiste Tavernier as made up of ruthless pirates and enemies of Christians. When they arrived on the Arab coast, some of the dhows of the Konkan coast were hired to conduct piracy on the Red Sea. They were usually fitted for armed combat, although whether mainly for attack or for defense is not always clear. In the Coromandel, navigators had less to fear from predators but did have to adapt to the treacherous postmonsoon climate and sudden shifts in ocean currents in the Bay of Bengal by building smaller and flatter boats. Much coastal trade, therefore, was left to local interests.[21]

The purchase of goods depended essentially on the Indian contracting merchants. They procured cloth and other supplies from the producers and the bazaars, usually after receiving advances from the company. The typical system in the late seventeenth century was for the merchants to bring samples of cloth to the factories, and then to receive orders and collect the advances. In the early eighteenth century, knowledge about cloth types was sufficiently stable and advanced for the factories to wait for samples. Orders were then placed directly via chief agents or brokers.

Between 1650 and 1750, then, the commercial relationship between the Indian agents and the European factors underwent a change. There was a tendency to expand the scale of contractual purchases and a preference for elevating a few men as the principal contractors or brokers above the others. Based on available biographies, it seems that in the seventeenth century, the principal brokers tended to be military and political men, whereas in the eighteenth century their counterparts were more often indigenous merchants. The transformation was a result of the concentration of contracting in the port cities, obviating the need to rely on local armed men to enforce contracts. In part, the change also reflected the much larger scale of the business in the eighteenth century, which needed the help of specialist merchants rather than merely people in possession of military or political power.

The principal brokers of the English, the Dutch, and the French companies administered the distribution of the contracts to an army of under-contractors. As a result, they commanded prestige, power, and credit in the bazaar. The brokers held an information advantage over their principals in knowing where the sources of supply were located. They could speak the local language, and sometimes they colluded with the under-contractors to cheat the companies on quality. Indeed, the brokers were under some pressure to cheat their principals.

As the chief broker for the French in the 1740s, Anandaranga Pillai explained that the broker's job was not an easy one and did not even carry

[21] John Edye, "Description of the Various Classes of Vessels Constructed and Employed by the Natives of the Coasts of Coromandel, Malabar, and Ceylon," *Journal of the Royal Asiatic Society of Great Britain and Ireland*, London: W. Parker, 1834, pp. 1–15.

enough profit.[22] The broker faced enormous difficulties in keeping his own empire of undercontractors intact and running. Whenever relations soured between the local state and the merchant firms, the broker was in the line of fire from both. Because the European factors neither knew nor wanted to have anything to do with the undercontractors and artisans, the broker's excuses for nonperformance of contracts could never be verified, and therefore could never be believed. For this reason, a relationship of dependence and distrust developed between the indigenous brokers and the European factors. Their unstable relationship also derived from a conflict of interest that was intrinsic to the business of the companies. The brokers were expected to serve both the companies and the private trade of senior employees. But serving the private interests of a company official exposed a broker to unwanted attention from the company directors and rival officers.

The business relationship between the Europeans and their closest Indian partners was, therefore, ridden with contradictions. These could be manifested in suspected or real fraud, oppression, threats, imprisonment, or invective directed at the Indian merchants. Almost all the major Indian brokers we know of seemed to suffer on this account.

Early in the second half of the seventeenth century, the chief broker of the English East India Company in Coromandel was Kasi Viranna, whose help was indispensable to the company in matters of transportation, procurement, and taxation in Madras. And yet, the appointment letter for Streynsham Master, the chief of Coromandel, expressly urged Master to avoid any situation in which "Verona" was entrusted with exclusive contracting powers, "for from thence many inconveniences may arise."[23] A similarly difficult relationship existed between the factors at Balasore and the chief broker in 1670, Khem Chand Shah. Shah found himself squeezed between two masters who were at times hostile to each other, the Mughal governor and the company, and, as a result, his principals questioned his loyalty to the firm. In 1678–79, the broker in Masulipatnam, Kola Venkadri, secretly negotiated with the king of Golkonda; the broker was imprisoned by the English in retaliation. In the 1730s, in Surat, disputes between leading Parsi and Hindu merchants over the brokerage of the company damaged the relationship between the principals and the agents. And, in 1756, Amirchand, the leading broker for the English company in Bengal, conspired to dethrone the reigning nawab, Siraj ud

---

[22] H. Dodwell, ed., *The Private Diary of Ananda Ranga Pillai*, vols. 1–8, Madras, 1922, vol. 2, p. 156.
[23] Richard Temple, ed., *The Diaries of Streynsham Master, 1675–1680*, London: John Murray, 1911, p. 211.

Daula. He was suspected by Robert Clive of double-crossing the English and penalized rather than rewarded for his efforts.

In the English East India Company's correspondence, the business relationship between Indians and Europeans was called a "contract" or a "compact," and sometimes disputes that arose between the parties to it was called "breach of contract." These terms had no known Indian counterparts in the context of the sale of goods. Neither the Hindu nor the Islamic code of law recognized contracts and agreements; they dealt mainly with debt rather than with sales. These codes were also too closely tied to religious identity to function as the law of the land (*lex loci*). Indeed, there is no historical evidence that religious strictures were used in an actual court of law. For all we know, the word "contract" was introduced by the Europeans, for the large-scale purchase of a commodity based on an advanced agreement was a form of exchange that had been unknown in India before the arrival of the company. As established by the company, the system of ordering and receiving cloth involved elaborate written contracts between the chiefs of Bombay, Madras, and Calcutta and the merchants and master weavers with whom they worked. These contracts specified quantity, price, dimension, quality, advances, and wages. When goods were delivered to the factory, senior officers examined the cargo, satisfying themselves that the terms of the contract had been fulfilled. In later years, the word "contract" was extended to cover a wide variety of exchanges, such as the promises made by Banjara caravan runners to supply the company's army with grain.

The insistence on a written contract might be surprising given that there was no law in India to deal with breach of contract. What good did a contract do then? In part, the contract made bookkeeping easier. Moreover, the contract served as a kind of moral obligation. Breaking a sales contract, if not exactly punishable under the Islamic law that was in force, was nonetheless condemned as sinful.

In their territorial acquisitions, however, the English company could moderate these transaction costs by introducing different laws. The next section explores how the company acquired its land.

From merchants to landlords: The port towns

With European wars spilling over into the Indian Ocean, all of the merchant companies wanted to construct fortified settlements. The Portuguese had shown the way with a string of forts that combined trade and naval

4.4. Terracotta panel from an eighteenth-century Bengali temple showing a group of Europeans carrying guns. The temple, the Radha Gobinda temple of Aatpur, is located twenty miles northwest of Calcutta. *Source*: Rangan Datta

command. In the seventeenth century, the Portuguese lost their hold in Persia, Ceylon, and Bengal. The English, in their turn, had been more or less driven from the Indonesian pepper trade by the Dutch and were keen to strengthen their hold in India. One outcome of this turmoil was the emergence of three small territories that the English East India Company found themselves in secure possession of: Madras (c. 1640), Bombay (c. 1660), and Calcutta (c. 1690).

The purchase of these territories involved potentially violent disputes with local states. Each site came to the English separately, through a process of threatened or actual warfare. And yet, once the threats subsided, each territory emerged not only as a little colony of the company with its own laws and administration but also as a commercial center, a port, and a destination for migrant Indian artisans and merchants. Each site started small, with a tiny European population, a port without a harbor, and a sliver of coastal land where farmers, fishermen, and artisans lived in villages. In each case, a fort and its walls enclosed the factory and the European population; the villages formed a kind of suburb from which supplies of goods and workers came into the fort town. These two worlds transacted their business at arm's length well into the eighteenth century, when a convergence began to take place. In port towns such as Surat, Hooghly, and Masulipatnam, where trading was concentrated, the English merely had the right to live and conduct trade and had to share this right with other European merchant companies and private traders. But in Bombay, Calcutta, and Madras the English were the landlords. This new identity worked in curious ways on both the company's policies in India and the Indian regimes that were warily watching the rise of the company.

The new fort towns represented a growing schism within the East India Company between its London directors, who were City merchants, and the factors, sea captains, and soldiers who managed the affairs of the Indian branches. As we have seen, the company carried out its trading operations by offering to its salaried employees the incentive of conducting trade on their own private accounts. Individuals who had completed indentures would also sometimes join in private trading, as would many sea captains. There was no effective way to make all of these people play by the company's rules, however. The only power that the company had over them was its control over the appointment of senior officers. But here again, the company had to avoid harsh penalties and too much control because the same people who broke trading rules protected the company's assets when these were threatened by the Dutch.

The formation of the three settlements brought this schism out into the open. The decision to spend money on the forts and cities annoyed the directors. The financial commitments, therefore, were often met from the private resources of the East India Company's senior employees, who were, in turn, indicted for private trading. In this way, George Oxenden and Gerald Aungier, who oversaw Bombay's formative period, faced disgrace. Such was the fate also of Francis Day, who had founded Madras. Job Charnock, an old India hand and the main figure behind Calcutta, was both chastised and praised by the directors. Yet in the presence of immediate threats to the branch offices, the rebel local officers appeared to the towns' populations to be more farsighted than the London directors.

Where did the threats to these settlements come from? The story of Madras began against the backdrop of the Mughal invasion of the Deccan. Similarly, Bombay emerged twenty years later in the wake of threatened attacks on the town by the Maratha warlord Shivaji's army. In the 1680s, the Mughal provincial army in Bengal attacked the English in southern Bengal. The Mughal emperor Aurangzeb left the English alone, however, in the belief that they were too weak to require more than a warning. But the Mughal threats made the European populations in the towns look to the local administrations for protection. The shadow of English politics, especially the conflict between those who supported the monarch (royalists) and those who espoused a republic (radicals), further complicated for the East India Company directors the task of administering the towns. The contest in English politics between the royalists and radicals induced the local administration to claim that they were acting as representatives of the Crown in defying their employers. In 1665, when a local officer, Edward Winter, refused to hand Madras over to the designated representative of the company, and in 1679, when Richard Keigwin, a sea captain, seized power in Bombay, the mutineers posed as royalists. In the end, the company had to come to terms with the autonomy of the towns by giving their governors a wide range of powers, including the power to make laws.

Although the division of power between the Crown and the East India Company was always a messy issue, hindsight suggests that the English company played the game of territorial control more effectively than did the French and the Dutch companies in the days before an empire was even a possibility. However, because the visible success of the English port cities overshadowed the experience of the other Western European settlements, less research has been done on the colonial strategies of the other powers. One exception, a study of Dutch Cochin, suggests that the Dutch, like the English, sought to turn Cochin into a self-financed territory by using local and land taxes when the income from its main local merchandise, pepper, became uncertain in the second half of the eighteenth century. To that effect, the small community of Dutch settlers forged new social ties with local and mixed-race families.[24] These moves, however, came to an abrupt end with the suspension of the Dutch company.

Despite their occasional political engagement, until 1740, Bombay, Calcutta, and Madras were little more than trading settlements conducting the routine business of the English East India Company. Although they had grown in naval power and population, there were no structural changes in the character of these towns, and clearly they had not been set up to fight wars with the Indians. But the political situation changed with two developments, the collapse of the Mughal Empire and the rivalry between England and France.

State formation, 1707–1765

In 1707, Aurangzeb, the last of the great Mughal emperors, died. Almost immediately afterward, the empire that had ruled over northern India for 180 years began to collapse and to split into independent states. In this way, Awadh, Hyderabad, and Bengal, formerly Mughal provinces, emerged as independent states, Marathas established dominion over Mughal provinces in central India, and warlords with more localized influence, including the Rajputs and the Nayakas of South India, consolidated their authority.

The Europeans stationed in Bombay, Madras, and Calcutta kept an eye on these upheavals. But the events did not threaten their survival, though they did require more negotiations with the new kings and warlords. Nor was there any indication that the London directors saw the negotiations to be of any strategic importance. If anything, they were as nervous as ever that the territories the company owned in India would be a drain on its profits. Although resenting the costs of fortification and harbor construction, the company head office came to accept the good sense of its having well-defended port cities in India.

And yet the propensity to join in politics was in some way inherent in the organization of the firm. In the middle of the century, local officers increasingly made friends with courtiers and kings and formed partnerships with

---

[24] Anjana Singh, *Fort Cochin in Kerala, 1750–1830: The Social Condition of a Dutch Community in an Indian Milieu*, Leiden and Boston: Brill, 2010.

the private traders. Territorial revenues in Calcutta, Madras, and Bombay were from the profits of the resident Indian merchants. In their turn, many of these merchants were refugees from decaying and anarchic states and were more than willing to pay the taxes against the custom of a wealthy port and wealthy business partners. These two lines, the empowerment of merchants and the weakening of states, merged in Bengal and the Carnatic in the 1740s.

In Bengal, repeated Maratha raids in the western districts saw Calcutta emerge as a safe haven for Bengali merchants. When Calcutta was established in 1690, the west bank of the river Hooghly was the more populous and urbanized. The English decision to locate their fort on the east bank of the river was unusual by the conventions of the time. The decision probably depended on the greater navigability of the river toward the east, as well as considerations of defense against the Dutch, the French, the Danish, and the Portuguese settlements, which were all on the west bank. Already by then, a small stream of migration of Bengali textile dealers to the town had begun, especially after the old river port Saptagram had suffered a decline in its fortunes due to silting of the port. This trickle now became a flood. In the 1740s, the population of the town doubled from less than a hundred thousand. To the same extent that Calcutta gained from the Maratha raids, the regional state grew weaker. Unable to militarily deal with the raids, the ruling nawab made peace and ceded a large territory to the Marathas.

Shortly before Bengal faced these raids, a succession dispute broke out in the Carnatic, a South Indian state. The disputing parties were individually weak and made alliances with the English and the French East India Companies. Between 1740 and 1760, the English and the French fought three wars in this region, the battles being triggered by a new succession issue and by two European wars (the War of the Austrian Succession [1740–48] and the Seven Years' War [1756–63]). The hostilities in Deccan effectively ended in 1760, when the English East India Company prevailed and succeeded in securing the friendship of this wealthy, strategically situated but militarily dependent, Indian state.

A showdown had already begun in Bengal. Calcutta and lower Bengal were emerging as a major field of enterprise for European private traders, who were friends of East India Company officers. The dispute in Bengal had much to do with the limits of the nawab's sovereign power to tax Europeans. Again, the French and the Dutch opposed the English, and the English won the key battles (1757–64). In deciding the outcomes of these battles, the English company's territorial acquisitions proved a great advantage. The company could move troops easily between Madras and Calcutta, and it received help from Indian merchants living under its protection. Some of these merchants became prominent negotiators.

In 1764, the English East India Company defeated a North Indian army and was formally recognized as the de facto ruler of Bengal. The significance of the conquest was not lost on the Indian powers. The main military force, the Marathas, had their base in Central and western India. Almost all the other major powers were willing to enter into alliances with the company to meet the Maratha threat. Some of these alliances led to dependencies and further territorial acquisitions in the late eighteenth century. The Marathas were subdued in the early nineteenth century, and by 1818, the company's empire in India had largely taken its final shape.[25]

Immediately after the East India Company assumed power in 1765, state revenues were used to purchase cloth. This phase of taxing the peasant to pay the artisan did not last long, because money needed to be diverted to warfare as well. Territorial acquisition, therefore, affected the company's own future as a trading firm. In Bengal and Coromandel, state power meant that the company enforced measures to take closer control of its purchases. The system of intermediaries was not abolished, but the intermediaries who remained were subordinated to paid officers of the state. These employees were usually outsiders to the world of the weaver, and they were ready to abuse their policing powers. The system, therefore, caused much conflict.[26]

---

[25] The relationship between the English East India Company and the local business and political environment during the period of transition is the subject of much scholarship. Representative works should include Lakshmi Subramanian, *Indigenous Capital and Imperial Expansion: Bombay, Surat and the West Coast*, Delhi: Manohar, 1996; Pamela Nightingale, *Trade and Empire in Western India, 1784–1806*, Cambridge: Cambridge University Press, 1970; Sushil Chaudhury, *From Prosperity to Decline: Eighteenth-Century Bengal*, Delhi: Manohar, 1995. P. J. Marshall discusses relations between the company and settlers in two colonies with divergent trajectories in *The Making and Unmaking of Empires: Britain, India, and America, c. 1750–1783*, Oxford: Oxford University Press, 2005.

[26] Om Prakash, "From Negotiation to Coercion: Textile Manufacturing in India in the Eighteenth Century," *Modern Asian Studies* 41(5), 2007, pp. 1331–68; S. Arasaratnam, "Weavers, Merchants and Company: The Handloom Industry in Southeastern India, 1750–1790," *Indian Economic and Social History Review* 17(3), 1980, pp. 257–81; P. Swarnalatha, "Revolt, Testimony, Petition: Artisanal Protests in Colonial Andhra," *International Review of Social History* 46(59), 2001, pp. 107–29; Prasannan Parthasarathi, *The Transition to a Colonial Economy: Weavers, Merchants and Kings in South India, 1720–1800*, Cambridge: Cambridge University Press, 2001; H. Hossain, "The Alienation

Access to land revenue raised the hope that dependence on silver imports could now end. For a few years that hope was fulfilled. But again, the diversion of revenues to other uses forced the company to import silver at times.[27] Its political power, however, had made the company highly creditworthy in the Indian money market, and business with the bankers was placed on a secure foundation. Although warfare drained the budget, it also increased the demand for imported iron goods, helping the company to better balance its trade. In the eighteenth century, Indian princes who had come in contact with British enterprise and society, the nawabs of Carnatic and Awadh, for example, purchased a great deal of prefabricated European iron goods; sometimes they had the goods made locally. Founding cannons with European help was a popular occupation for the regional princes at this time.

The assumption of political power was the beginning of the end for the English East India Company as a trading firm. Warfare made its finances precarious and forced the company to negotiate a large loan from Parliament in 1772. The Parliament approved the loan in exchange for closer regulation of Indian administration.[28] The volume of trade was generally depressed, except for a few years before the Napoleonic Wars (1799–1815). Furthermore, private traders continued to consolidate their commercial fortunes at the expense of the company. Although indirectly helped by the new empire, they also resented the company's monopoly charter. It was largely this new opposition that saw the end of the royal charter that had granted monopoly of Indian Ocean trade to the East India Company in 1813.

The company as a state now faced the vexing problem of regulating private trade, the same issue that had brought down the nawab. The first parliamentary enquiry on justice in Bengal noted that soon after 1765, Europeans, "with or without Consent of the Presidency, dispersed themselves over the Country, and engaged in its interior Commerce, which often led them to interfere with the Judicature and Government of the Country." Institutions of justice affiliated with the local courts were already crumbling, with the result that "the Banyas of English Gentlemen, wherever they reside, entirely Govern the Courts of Judicature, and that

---

of Weavers: Impact of the Conflict between the Revenue and Commercial Interests of the East India Company," *Indian Economic and Social History Review* 16(3), 1979, pp. 323–45.

[27] H. V. Bowen, "Bullion for Trade, War, and Debt-Relief: British Movements of Silver to, around, and from Asia, 1760–1833," *Modern Asian Studies* 44(3), 2010, pp. 445–75.

[28] On the place of the company in British politics after the empire began, see H. V. Bowen, *The Business of Empire: The East India Company and Imperial Britain, 1756–1833*, Cambridge: Cambridge University Press, 2006.

they even frequently sit as Judges in these Courts."[29] Such decentralized justice, formally endorsed in the case of disputes that broke out in the countryside, was convenient but contentious.

Until 1765, the English court in Calcutta was itself, in principle, merely a court conducted by an Indian landlord (zamindar). The company was no more than a Mughal zamindar after all. At the time, zamindari privileges included the right to "the Criminal, Civil, and Religious Jurisdiction of the District."[30] The English zamindari court in Calcutta began to supersede all other zamindari courts starting in April 1771, when, in a dispute between an English landlord of Calcutta and some of his defaulting agents, who had absconded to Rajshahi, the jurisdiction of the Calcutta courts was extended to all parts of Bengal.[31] The compass of the court was still extremely limited, and it covered commercial matters unevenly. Only in the nineteenth century did the court's scope become more general, as we will see in Chapter 7.

Transactions in knowledge

The collapse of the Mughal Empire and the efflorescence of merchant enterprise on the Indian coasts led to transactions in commercially useful industrial technologies. Recent scholarship has emphasized the fact that technological exchanges were two way. For example, European cotton-cloth printers in the eighteenth century developed capability by trying to reproduce techniques evident in Indian goods.[32] A similar argument has been made about cotton-spinning technology in eighteenth-century Britain.[33] That said, we know more about the technologies that came to India in the course of Indo-European trade than about the technologies that went out.

During the seventeenth century, Indian practices were behind the European ones in navigation. Instruments such as the telescope and

---

[29] British Parliamentary Papers, *Seventh Report from The Committee Of Secrecy Appointed To Enquire Into The State Of The East India Company. Together with an Appendix referred to in the said Report*, 1773, pp. 325–26.

[30] Ibid., p. 330.

[31] Ibid., p. 331.

[32] Giorgio Riello, "Asian Knowledge and the Development of Calico Printing in Europe in the Seventeenth and Eighteenth Centuries," *Journal of Global History* 5(1), 2010, pp. 1–28.

[33] Prasannan Parthasarathi, *Why Europe Grew Rich and Asia Did Not: Global Economic Divergence, 1600–1850*, Cambridge: Cambridge University Press, 2011.

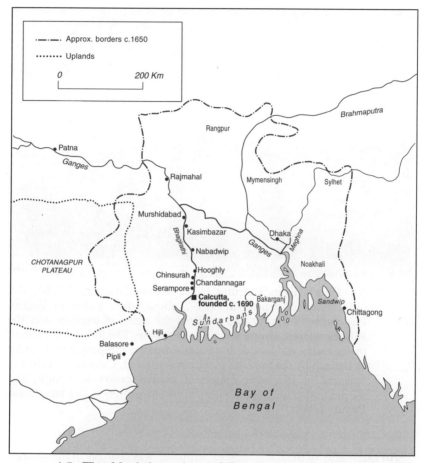

4.5. The Mughal province of Bengal showing towns and trade settlements, c. 1650.

compass were unknown in India. The heaviest Indian ships were constructed with little iron, which made them unsuitable for long voyages. European naval technology stimulated significant adaptation, learning, and improvement in India, one result of which was shipbuilding complexes such as Narsapur Peta on Coromandel.[34]

---

[34] Ahsan Jan Qaisar, *The Indian Response to European Technology and Culture (A.D. 1498–1707)*, Delhi: Oxford University Press, 1982, pp. 10–13; Zaheer Baber, *The Science of*

4.6. Fort William, Calcutta, by an unknown painter, c. 1750. The old fort was constructed in 1701–2, about a decade after the English East India Company had acquired the rights of tenancy over the villages where Calcutta town was to appear. The fort was the site of major events and battles that transformed the company into the ruler of Bengal. By the time the picture was painted, Calcutta had already emerged as the most important trading center in Bengal, but its political transition was still a distant prospect. © Mary Evans Picture Library.

An externality of the navigation experiments was changes in metallurgy. One description of Indian shipbuilding on the western coast in the eighteenth century remarked that "their anchors are mostly European, our iron being much better, and better worked."[35] There is considerable evidence that even though iron casting was not a well-developed indigenous industry, many ship anchors were manufactured in ports using indigenous iron and ironsmiths who worked under European direction. In the seventeenth century, the Dutch East India Company set up ironworks near Palakole,

Empire: Scientific Knowledge, Civilization, and Colonial Rule in India, Albany: State University of New York Press, 1996; Sanjay Subrahmanyam, "A Note on Narsapur Peta: A 'Syncretic' Shipbuilding Center in South India, 1570–1700," *Journal of the Economic and Social History of the Orient* 31(3), 1988, pp. 305–11.

[35] John Henry Grose, *A Voyage to the East Indies*, London: S. Hooper, 1757, vol. 1, p. 109.

4.7. Ruins of an eighteenth-century lighthouse located on the mouth of the Hooghly. *Source*: Rangan Datta

on the southwestern coast.[36] These works possibly contained a foundry, employed Indian blacksmiths, and represented a different technological paradigm in shipping, one that employed much more iron than did the Indian ships. Thomas Bowrey, an English merchant who lived in Bengal in the 1670s, observed that the works employed "Several black Smiths, make-inge all Sorts of iron worke, (necessarie for Ships) whereby they doe Supply most of theire fleets with Such Necessaries." The "necessaries" included "speeks," bolts, and anchors. Apart from iron parts, the cluster also pro-duced rope and twine for ship riggings; and it employed master shipbuilders "who have most of their dependencies Upon the English, and indeed learnt their art and trade from some of them, by diligently Observinge the ingen-uitie of Some that build Ships and Sloops here for the English East India Company and theire Agents."[37] Bowrey complained of their "falsehearted-ness" at having learned from the English but working for the Dutch. Read in a more positive light, the description hinted at an active labor market for skilled workers. A slightly later source that mentioned the casting of anchors for ships stated that the anchors were "not so good as those made in Europe."[38]

These ironworks belonging to the European companies were located near Balasore, where the English and the Dutch had trading stations before moving up north. One authority on iron suggests that the presence of larger-scale iron-smelting workshops in Kathiawad and near Masulipatnam were also legacies of European enterprise connected to shipbuilding.[39] The scope of such technological exchanges expanded with the growth of the Indo-European partnership in the private sector that the conquest made possible.

Private trade and new enterprise, 1765–1800

Profits in the India trade were ordinarily so high, and so well-protected by a coterie of shareholders, that every London merchant of sufficient means

---

[36] Subrahmanyam, "Note on Narsapur Peta."
[37] Thomas Bowrey, *A Geographical Account of Countries round the Bay of Bengal, 1669 to 1679*, Cambridge, 1895, pp. 102–5.
[38] Alexander Hamilton, *A New Account of the East Indies being the Observations and Remarks of Capt. Alexander Hamilton from the year 1688–1723*, Delhi, 1995, vol. 1, p. 392.
[39] A. K. Biswas, "Iron and Steel in Pre-modern India – A Critical Review," *Indian Journal of the History of Science* 19(4), 1994, pp. 579–610.

was tempted to sponsor trips to India. Many took this road. Not all of them were officially interlopers, as it was legal to conduct trade in those goods in which the English East India Company did not have a serious interest. A number of such goods moved between one Indian port and another. Grain and sugar bound for a port town; timber to be used for shipbuilding; and dates, wine, and horses from West Asia were legitimate fields of business for the short-haul private merchant in India. Many Europeans joined this coastal and short-haul trade.

The Europeans who took part in such segments of intraregional trade occasionally made forays into piracy as well. But the more ambitious among them were not satisfied with the small profits of coastal trade or the riskier earnings from piracy. The officers of the East India Company almost always sought out private merchants as partners in their personal trading schemes. The temptation to poach on the company's monopoly was too great. So was the temptation to make use of the company's extensive infrastructure for their own purposes. Such practices were a long-standing bone of contention between London and the overseas branches, but London could do little to stop them.

When the English East India Company began its rule of Bengal, private merchants there conducted their business in open defiance of the company's monopoly. In fact, the officers of the company's overseas branches were often more or less in league with the private traders. The political transition offered the private traders a new area of opportunity in the exploration of commodities that could be found only in the interior. European merchants and opportunists moved "up-country" in search of lucrative and formerly unknown business enterprises. The numbers were perhaps not large, but the range of enterprises started and abandoned was quite varied. The principal businesses that established roots at this time were the export of cotton and opium to China, the manufacture of indigo for export in plantations in Bihar and lower Bengal, and the supplying of grain, sugar, timber, and other goods for port-to-port trade.

The private traders' main strengths were their ability to forge partnerships with Indian merchants and their access to the business infrastructures of Bombay, Calcutta, and Madras. These three cities in 1800 were not just ports on the Indian coastline. They were cities with a different business culture than the older Indian commercial centers. Commercial profits, rather than land taxes, sustained these cities. Merchant migration created a more cosmopolitan settlement than in the interior. Unlike in the interior, which had no homogeneity in commercial law, in the company cities, English Common Law prevailed in order to protect expatriate interests. The three cities, in other words, offered an environment in which unorthodox forms of entrepreneurial activities could flourish. The biggest gainers were the private traders. As we will see in the next chapter, India-China trade was soon to become a major field of private investment.

A segment of these new enterprises was engaged in artisanal industry connected with country trade. The principal industry was ship building. Calcutta became the capital of Bengal in 1772, and, as the largest settlement of Europeans in India, needed artisans to produce consumer goods in demand in European households. As yet, the market was small; the settlement was no more than a few hundred families strong, and most of the goods they required were still imported. But there were a few items that it was sensible to produce locally. Ships and iron goods were the main examples.

In 1770, a colony of Armenian merchants who owned a dock resided on the west bank of the river Hooghly, from where the road going toward northern India started. In the 1780s, attempts to build oceangoing ships at this location began (significantly, an engineering industry developed here almost a century later). Colonel Henry Watson, an engineer with the East India Company, sought permission in 1781 to build a shipyard in Calcutta. Watson invested a large amount of his own money, and possibly lost much of it, but he launched a business that survived. Watson also erected a windmill in this location, which a court ordered closed because it overlooked the women's quarters of an Indian gentleman. In the last decade of the century, James Kyd's Calcutta docks produced small ships and boats. Kyd was the illegitimate son of Robert Kyd (1746–1793), who had been an army engineer and was the founder of the botanic gardens in Calcutta. Kidderpore, named after James, was the location of a government-owned Calcutta port that was built in 1795 using some of the old dock construction. In the 1770s, Kyd's docks on the Hooghly produced boats that became familiar on the southeastern coast in the early nineteenth century. And further south, a point of anchorage called Gloucester, later Gloster, possessed a ship-building yard that was later converted into a cotton factory and a distillery.[40]

At this time, cannons were an item of import into India. Attempts to substitute imports were sponsored by the importers themselves. In a mud fort on the opposite shore from Kyd's shipyard, a cannon foundry was in

[40] J. Holman, *Travels in Madras, Ceylon, Mauritius, etc.*, London: G. Routledge, 1840, pp. 448, 452.

existence by the mid-eighteenth century.[41] In 1768, a short time after they saw a similar enterprise run by the nawab of Awadh, company officers proposed that a cannon foundry be erected inside Fort William. Ten years later, a complete blast furnace was contracted, but not delivered, for the use of the Fort William foundry.[42]

European wars and the end of the companies

The Napoleonic Wars largely ended the careers of the Western European merchant companies. The French and the Dutch companies were closed, and the English company ceased to be a trader. Within a few years of the turn of the nineteenth century, the American reexport trade in Asian goods had increased to become as large as that of all the Europeans combined; it was accompanied by rapid American strides in shipping, ship building, and commercial finance.

American trading missions to India had begun in earnest in the 1780s amid patriotic fervor. Proposals to form chartered corporations in the European style were considered and rejected, and the trade remained in the hands of private individuals, mainly consortia of Philadelphia merchants. Ideological resistance apart, the coastline would have presented impossible challenges to any regulatory law. The trade, however, was small in scale, and the traders had difficulty finding goods for export. The demand for ginseng and furs in Asia eased that problem, but access to silver was still necessary. Trading missions, therefore, needed to maintain links with sources of supply for these goods, with entrepôts such as the Cape of Good Hope, and with the South American ports. Both the Pacific and the Atlantic routes to Asia were used, which gave American shipping considerable flexibility.

The decisive break in this pattern of expansion came in the 1790s, when the Americans found themselves in possession of the only neutral fleet in the world's oceans. War in Europe had spilled over into the colonial territories, as it had done on many previous occasions. On this occasion, however, the Dutch were drawn into the conflict. The Dutch East India Company was suspended during the years of the Batavian Republic (1795–1806, a client state of the French republic), the English company

---

[41] H. Yule, ed., *The Diary of William Hedges*, London: Hakluyt Society, 1887, vol. 1, p. ccxv.
[42] *Fort William–India House Correspondence*, New Delhi: National Archives, vol. 5, p. 156; vol. 7, pp. 43, 297.

was a shadow of its former self, and the French company was disbanded in 1793, leaving much of Europe either directly or indirectly dependent on American shipping for supplies of consumer goods such as tea, coffee, sugar, and cloth.[43] Their opportunistic moves in the Indian Ocean allowed the Americans to feed Asian goods to the American consumer market as well. It also allowed the traders to resource some goods already part of the American consumer basket, such as coffee and sugar, from Asia. The trade created a chain of "correspondence partners" in Europe, who arranged to deposit the sale proceeds into the London bank accounts of the merchant firms.

It is fitting to end the story of old-style Indo-European trade with a consideration of two larger questions that have driven much of the research in this field. Why did the European mariners and merchants succeed in improving their position in Asian trade progressively from 1500? And, how did the European factor influence and reshape the structure of Asian trade?

The meaning of Indo-European trade

The once popular phrase "European world economy" answered the first question by referring to the superior economic power and commercial skills that European merchants had and the backing of mercantilist states that they received.[44] The problems of applying this idea to seventeenth-century India, however, are many. The notion of European hegemonic control in the Indian Ocean does not live well with the presence of the empires that ruled Asia. The Asian exchange that the Europeans joined in about 1500 had been in existence for a long time and was organized on sufficiently capitalistic principles. The Europeans joined it from a position of commercial weakness rather than strength. The Europeans succeeded thanks to their entrenched position in the emerging global monetary exchange after the Spanish conquest of the Americas.[45] Until the beginning

---

[43] James Fichter, *So Great a Proffit: How the East Indies Trade Transformed Anglo-American Capitalism*, Cambridge, MA, and London: Harvard University Press, 2010. See also essays in John J. McCusker and Kenneth Morgan, eds., *The Early Modern Atlantic Economy*, Cambridge: Cambridge University Press, 2000.

[44] Immanuel Wallerstein, *Mercantilism and the Consolidation of the European World-economy, 1600–1750*, New York: Academic Press, 1980.

[45] Frank, *ReOrient*.

of industrialization in Britain, the Europeans found it difficult to sell European manufactures in India. Vasco da Gama's gifts to the king of Calicut in 1498 drew derisive comments from the courtiers. The English East India Company did not fare much better in using English goods to balance its trade. Indian Ocean trade was made possible by the steady flow of American gold and silver into the European money markets and beyond to the overseas traders. But this thesis begs the question of why Asians, with their superior commercial and artisanal skills and plenty of goods to sell, did not break into European exchanges first.

Should we then believe, after Frederic C. Lane, that an exercise of raw violence, here as elsewhere, was the distinctive feature of European capitalism?[46] It would be necessary to explain why firepower was so essential to trading enterprise in this case. In fact, it was needed in the Asian waters for different reasons. The Portuguese wanted to remove the Asians from the spice trade. The Dutch and the English wanted to deter each other. But such violence should weaken, not strengthen, the collective might of the Europeans. Indeed, thanks to such bickering, the military situation in the region was managed quite well by the land-based empires; the balance of power began to turn only in the eighteenth century because of the collapse of the Mughal Empire. The European-violence thesis is sometimes framed within an argument of Asian nonviolence, or of the peaceful coexistence of trading groups in Asian waters in the pre-European era. Kenneth Hall writes that the "Indian Ocean networks [before 1500] were based in economic and cultural dialogue rather than in dominance," the implication being that European entry changed the rules of the game in a world that had so far functioned on the basis of tolerance and mutual respect.[47] However, the Asian-nonviolence thesis is challenged by scholarship on the western Indian Ocean in late antiquity.[48] The Europeans did not introduce bullying in the Indian Ocean; the Asians were already familiar with the idea.

---

[46] Frederic C. Lane, *Profits from Power: Readings in Protection Rent and Violence-Controlling Enterprises*, Albany: State University of New York Press, 1979; Niels Steensgaard, "Violence and the Rise of Capitalism: Frederic C. Lane's Theory of Protection and Tribute," *Review (Fernand Braudel Center)* 5(2), 1981, pp. 247–73.

[47] Kenneth Hall, "Local and International Trade and Traders in the Straits of Melaka Region: 600–1500," *Journal of the Economic and Social History of the Orient* 47(2), 2004, pp. 213–60 (quote on p. 214).

[48] Roxani Eleni Margariti, "Mercantile Networks, Port Cities, and 'Pirate' States: Conflict and Competition in the Indian Ocean World of Trade before the Sixteenth Century," *Journal of the Economic and Social History of the Orient* 51(4), 2008, pp. 543–77.

If commercial acumen, American silver, and militarism are rejected, perhaps the distinctive new element could be found in knowledge and institutions? The Europeans brought into India maritime skills that embodied superior knowledge of long-distance navigation. The fields of knowledge were vastly different; the Europeans' included a knowledge of charts, ocean currents, instruments, routes, and building sturdier and larger ships,as well as a more numerous cluster of trading posts and victualing stops. It is not easy to establish whether the "conservative nature of Indic maritime traditions" was an effect of "the lack of a naval warlike impetus which would have made technological nautical change imperative," as one historian suggests, or its cause.[49] But that the two fields of navigational knowledge were unequal when a meeting occurred between them cannot be gainsaid.

Even more important were the organizational characteristics of European enterprise. As Neils Steensgaard reminds us, the English and the Dutch overseas trading enterprises were differently structured not only from Indian firms but also from the Portuguese Crown monopoly.[50] They functioned on the basis of joint-stock, which allowed them to pool large amounts of capital, spread and share risks, and build an elaborate infrastructure consisting of forts, factories, harbors, and ships. The monopoly charter that the English received from their Crown also reduced competition and allowed a larger scale of operations and, in turn, enabled greater investment in military capability and trading infrastructure. Ashin Dasgupta, in his assessment of the Indian merchant enterprise, suggests that the Indians by contrast were organized around informal associations of communities and families, which would have made them risk averse and even cause divisiveness.[51]

We should not overdraw the differences. The simplistic contrast between the informal community and the formal company can be misleading. It makes us overlook the strengths of the community (easier dispute resolution, for example) and the weaknesses of the company form. It also makes us overlook the fact that the English East India Company was not only the most powerful corporate entity in the City of London in the seventeenth and eighteenth centuries, it was also one of the

---

[49] Archibald Lewis, "Maritime Skills in the Indian Ocean, 1368–1500," *Journal of the Economic and Social History of the Orient* 16(2/3), 1973, pp. 238–64 (quote on p. 249).

[50] Steensgaard, *The Asian Trade Revolution of the Seventeenth Century*.

[51] Ashin Dasgupta, *The World of the Indian Ocean Merchant, 1500–1800*, Delhi: Oxford University Press, 2001.

most vilified and criticized. Its royal charter was far from an absolute right in the face of constant poaching by its own employees and agents. The company was a leaky vessel, but it was still a different kind of vessel than any Indian firm of the time.

Two further differences should be noted to explain the effects of Indo-European trade on business in India. The English East India Company was a highly specialized firm in the nature of its main businesses. It dealt in a few goods, which it bought on large scale. It specialized more than Indian traders did. Being specialized, the company contracted with a specific set of suppliers year after year and paid them sums of money as advances. These sums were distributed over an entire year. Contractual sale of goods was not unknown in India before, but contractual sale on such a scale by a single firm had no historical antecedents. These factors increased the chances of disputes occurring and the costs of dispute resolution in Indo-European trade. The institutional impact of European trade, even its political effects, cannot be understood without reference to these problems of contract enforcement.

Another sphere in which the Europeans made a significant change, urbanization, again invites us to the institutional and knowledge outcomes of the contact. Trade historians see in the emergence and meteoric rise of Bombay, Madras, and Calcutta merely a diversion of trade from the established centers such as Surat, Masulipatnam, or Hooghly. In fact, these three cities represented a different business culture in coastal India. For one thing, Madras and Bombay broke the geographically conditioned dependence of port cities on internal navigation and Mughal roads. Even more than Surat, these were ocean-bound ports. For another, Surat and Masulipatnam were cities that did not belong to merchants; in those cities the merchants did not make laws, in Bombay they did. The three cities were, institutionally speaking, worlds apart from the Indian littoral spaces.

It was in their status as sovereign legislating spaces that the prospect of using them as staging posts in a conquest lay embedded. But conquest also was owed to the very character of the East India Company. Although technically a joint-stock firm, the company did not represent a unitary command-and-control structure. Its overseas trading enterprise was possible because of the peculiar nature of the principal-agent relations that it entailed, combining modern joint-stock operation with a premodern form of partnership between risk-taking peripatetic sailors and soldiers and risk-averse sedentary town merchants. These two classes of people did share a common interest in the profits of Asian trade, but they were not friends otherwise. A decisive change of balance in the partnership could see the sailors-cum-soldiers try to establish a sphere of political authority thereby defying the wishes of their principals, the capitalists. Colonization was an outcome of the unstable partnership that formed the basis of these enterprises.

Conclusion

Looking at these 300 years of Indian Ocean trade, one result stands out. The littoral emerged from the upheaval with a new political and economic strength. The axis of politics had shifted to the maritime merchants. Bombay, Calcutta, and Madras were not just colonial ports. They were ports that dominated the interior. Such a relationship did not exist in Indian history before. They were cities where merchants could function without having to negotiate their status with the territorial powers. They had not invented rule of law in India. But they did represent a different rule of law, one that embodied a commitment to commercial law. Such a regime had no precedent in Indian history.

The phenomenal growth of Bombay, Calcutta, and Madras came out of this attraction, which drew Indian capital to them. Reflecting their freedom of enterprise and their autonomy from the state, merchants and entrepreneurs, whether Indian or European, whether a part of the East India Company or private actors, revealed a preference for empire. The strong form of implicit legitimacy that the empire commanded among Indian business contrasted with the weak and opportunistic support it received from the land-owning warlord elites. The cleavage came out into the open during the Indian mutiny of 1857, when both the warlords and the landed elites tried to shake off their dependence, and the merchants and bankers in the ports solidly supported the company's efforts to defeat them.

The British Empire was beginning to open many doors by 1800. Three of these were especially important: trade with China, export of agricultural goods, and new artisan enterprise. These new avenues required an innovative entrepreneurial spirit, and presented many problems as well, as we will see in the next chapter.

5   Trade, Migration, and Investment, 1800–1850

At the start of the nineteenth century, the English East India Company tried to encourage a few businesses in India to compensate for the declining role of cotton textiles in Indian exports. These were opium, indigo, and raw cotton. Opium was useful as a means of payment for Chinese tea, the company's main import. Indigo and raw cotton contributed to Britain's own expanding cotton-textile industry. These businesses retained some of the characteristics of the old Indo-European trade in that they were concentrated in the port towns and had been initiated by the company. But they were also exceptional in some ways. All three provided a larger scope for private enterprise and involved dealing with peasants rather than with artisans. Property rights over land were now a matter of interest to the conduct of foreign-export businesses.

A simple measure of trade volume based on incoming shipping tonnage (Figure 5.1) shows that trade to and from India grew quickly from 1850. By comparison with this explosive growth, in the first half of the century growth was more modest, but the acceleration started before 1850. The first half of the nineteenth century saw the consolidation of what I earlier called the imperial umbrella, a loose network of territories ruled by regimes that shared a commitment to market integration and a single official language and that had compatible laws. The umbrella created the opportunity for capital and labor to circulate within the network, with an additional impetus from Britain's own industrialization and the Asian country trade. Recent research has demonstrated how the removal of barriers to private trade imposed earlier by the chartered companies and the Chinese state aided the growth of intra-Asian trade, creating new axes of commerce that were to play a large role in the business history of Asia later in the century.[1] This chapter deals with the broad patterns of

[1] Kaoru Sugihara, "The Resurgence of Intra-Asian Trade, 1800–1850," paper read at the Global Economic History Conference, Pune, India, 2005. A shorter version can be found in Giorgio Riello and Tirthankar Roy, eds., *How India Clothed the World: The World of South Asian Textiles, 1500–1850*, Leiden: Brill, 2009.

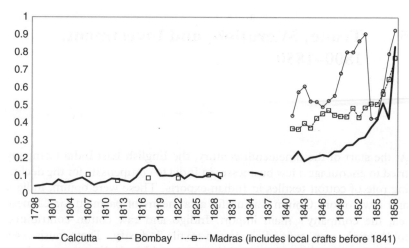

———— Calcutta   —o— Bombay   ---□--- Madras (includes local crafts before 1841)

5.1. Shipping tonnage (million) entering major Indian ports, 1795–1858. *Source*: *Statistical Abstract relating to British India*, various years.

commodity trade, capital formation, and labor migration in this phase and under these stimuli.

Alongside the emergence of freer trade, the first half of the century also witnessed the consolidation of the East India Company's empire in India. An older tradition of business history read the impact of this empire on Indian business through models of dependent or comprador capitalism. Critics of the view, although not disputing that the nineteenth century was indeed "the age of European domination," suggest that the Indians adapted to the new opportunities while making use also of their distinctively indigenous modes of doing business.[2] This is a valid argument, and so is the attendant point that Asian actors used the knowledge and skills that they accumulated in the next phase of Indian Ocean trade. That said, the division of the business world into Asian and European segments risks overlooking the differences within both Asian and European capital. And emphasizing the "sophistication" of Asian business institutions risks underestimating the persistent difficulties in forging collaborations between Asians and Europeans.

A better way, perhaps, of defining the time span that forms the subject of the present chapter is to suggest that this was a period of experimentation. We see innovation in the character of industrial enterprise, in the way

[2] Rajat Kanta Ray, "Asian Capital in the Age of European Domination: The Rise of the Bazaar, 1800–1914," *Modern Asian Studies* 29(3), 1995, pp. 449–554.

private traders established a link between India and China, and in the steps taken to establish labor migration. In trade, agricultural commodities were beginning to be procured in bulk, but such trades required the creation of stable contractual relationships among the peasants, local merchants, export firms, and the state. This requirement was addressed in quite different ways in opium, indigo, and cotton. In opium, the state bypassed the contractual issue by monopolizing production and processing in one region; in indigo, European capitalists set up plantations but were not too successful with contract enforcement; and in cotton, plantations were tried and given up because of ecological constraints, giving way to a system in which local trading networks played a prominent mediating role.

Opium and China

Between 1780 and 1833 the English East India Company and private traders invested on average more than a million pounds sterling each year in buying tea in Canton for export. The London-Canton trade was a monopoly of the company, but a monopoly that was becoming increasingly difficult to protect. The Canton-India trade was private from the beginning and conducted by "country" traders. India's Chinese imports consisted principally of tea, with a significant quantity of silk textiles, chinaware, and nankeen added on.[3] The company had difficulty exporting to China. Metals and woolens formed the main commodities sent. But the woolens sold at a loss and were often left unsold. To meet the balance of trade, the company relied on silver and, increasingly, on Indian goods.

At the turn of the nineteenth century, cotton from western India and opium from Bihar were used to balance the trade. The company did not directly import the opium in its ships, but depended on the silver that the country traders could obtain for the opium that they brought in and exchanged for bills on London. Besides, opium was grown under government license in Bengal, so that the company government there obtained a profit from domestic trade. In central India, in contrast, opium was legally grown in the territories of the princely states, and the government collected a transit tax on the goods.

The trading system in Canton was quite different from the systems in India and though lucrative, restricted the East India Company's options

---

[3] Nankeen was a cotton cloth from Nanjing that received its distinctive color and texture from the variety of cotton used.

5.2. Opium from Patna bound for China during the Opium Wars, by
the Indian School (19th century). *Source*: The Bridgeman Art Library

in a number of ways. In the South China Sea, the company was beleaguered by the Portuguese in Macao and by private traders everywhere, and
was required to do business through mediating Hong merchants. The
Chinese state and the principal officers of the Chinese court regarded the
company's trade with only marginal interest. Even diplomatic missions
failed to produce much in the way of stable rules for the trade. According to one assessment of the situation, the indifference was a matter of
deliberate policy, because elite members of the Hong guild also served as
agents of the state. But there was a cost attached to the policy; the state
appeared to be out of touch with maritime trade when the European
chartered companies demanded negotiations with the Chinese.[4]

---

[4] Weng Eang Cheong, *Hong Merchants of Canton: Chinese Merchants in Sino-Western Trade,
1684–1798*, Richmond: Curzon Press, 1997, pp. 11–20.

The ships conducting the Bengal-China trade were owned mainly by British merchants in Calcutta and by Parsis in Bombay and Calcutta. Marwari merchants were involved in the inland trade in Malwa opium. In this way, the commercial fortunes of Bombay, Calcutta, Canton, and Hong Kong became interconnected and rested on their shared dependence on opium.[5] Opium revenues were in this period the most important source of government income in India after land taxes and, via the exchequer, flowed back into the construction of canals and railways in India. In addition, the specie inflow into India in the 1830s ended the recession induced by a shortage of silver and by high taxes in southern and western India.[6]

Between 1772 and 1786, opium production was made into a government monopoly in Bihar and Benares. Licensed contractors drew up agreements between the state and the peasants regarding the extent of the land area to be sown with poppy and the price and quantity of opium to be delivered. Although forced cultivation was not to be the norm, it was understood that the contractors would possess some degree of informal and coercive power over the peasants. Peasants seemed unhappy with the arrangements, nevertheless, and tried to shortchange buyers by a variety of means. The offer of a fixed price made them careless cultivators, and in the 1790s many administrative attempts were made to secure the contracts on a sound basis by adding an element of incentive and reducing the opportunity for exploitation by the middlemen. It cannot be said that the problems were completely resolved, but the government increasingly acquired control over the process. The key step was taken in 1799 through regulations that tried to reduce the role of the contractors in the purchase process.[7]

---

[5] Michael Greenberg, *British Trade and the Opening of China, 1800–1842*, Cambridge: Cambridge University Press, 1969; Tan Chung, "The Britain-China-India Trade Triangle (1771–1840)," *Indian Economic and Social History Review* 11(4), 1974, pp. 411–31; R. K. Newman, "Opium Smoking in Late Imperial China: A Reconsideration," *Modern Asian Studies* 29(4), 1995, pp. 765–94. On the end of the trade, see Thomas D. Reins, "Reform, Nationalism and Internationalism: The Opium Suppression Movement in China and the Anglo-American Influence, 1900–1908," *Modern Asian Studies* 25(1), 1991, pp. 101–42.

[6] P. J. Thomas and B. Natarajan, "Economic Depression in the Madras Presidency (1825–54)," *Economic History Review* 7(1), 1936, pp. 67–75.

[7] British Parliamentary Papers (hereafter cited as B.P.P.), 1895 (C.7723) (C.7723-1), *Royal Commission on Opium*, vol. 6, *Final Report of the Royal Commission on Opium, Part 1, The Report, with annexures*, London, p. 123.

Indigo and Bengal

Similar problems to those discussed for opium arose with indigo, but these involved the private planter class. Indigo was needed in Britain as a textile dye. Although India had been a producer and user of indigo, the availability of alternative sources in the United States and the Caribbean had made India a less important supplier until 1800. In addition, competition for the indigo that sold in the market was already quite keen. In the early years of the seventeenth century, a rivalry reportedly developed between Portuguese traders and the Dutch East India Company in the procurement of North Indian indigo (*Indigofera tinctoria*) for export to Europe. The trade was nearly killed, however, by regulations prohibiting the use of indigo, instituted under pressure from woad (*Isatis tinctoria*) traders and manufacturers. When the prohibition was finally lifted in the 1660s, the English East India Company joined the business. But not until the close of the eighteenth century, when American sources of supply of the dye became unreliable because of stronger planter interest in coffee and sugar, did the English company start buying Indian indigo on a large scale. In the 1790s, total British import of indigo increased from 1,000 to 2,000 tons, Bengal's share rising from less than one-third to about three-fourths. The quantity at the peak of the trade (1820–50) reached 5,000–6,000 tons on average, when private traders had replaced the company completely.[8]

Indigo was purchased from northern India and Bengal. In northern India, the agents of exporting firms preferred to buy crude indigo from the peasants and retail merchants. In Bengal, European planters produced indigo in factories located near agricultural land. Much of the indigo procured, and nearly all of the Bengal output, was made on lands owned or leased by European capitalists. Although called planters, they were in reality owners of the factory that processed the indigo leaves and extracted the dye.

It is believed that the first planters in Bengal were a group of Frenchmen who started factories in 1770. The English company's directors followed their experience closely and persuaded some West Indian planters to relocate to Bengal. Between 1786 and 1804, the company purchased nearly a million pounds sterling worth of the dye from these planters. In this early and somewhat obscure phase, planters often went bankrupt. But there were also entrepreneurs who made fortunes in the business.

---

[8] Tirthankar Roy, "Indigo and Law in Colonial India," *Economic History Review* 64(S1), 2011, pp. 60–75.

A Mr. Williams of the Bengal administration spent a great deal to buy and fit a ship, loaded it with indigo, sent it to England, and earned a large return on his investment. John Prinsep, a private trader and the father of two nineteenth-century Indian administrators and orientalists, built his family's wealth on indigo. Legends like these men did more for Bengal export than the company's campaign. By the 1820s, Bengal plantations were the most important field of investment for foreign capital in India.

A petition submitted to the government by the leading indigo agents in 1829 stated that the land engaged in indigo amounted to 1.2–2 million acres; the gross output value of the crop was £2.5–4 million, about a quarter of which was remitted to Britain as profit. The extent of cultivation was large for a minor commercial crop. The total acreage in cultivation in lower Bengal, where indigo plantation was concentrated, could not have exceeded 10 million acres. Indigo, then, would have engaged 10–20 percent of the net crop area. Considering that a third of the plantations could be found in a few districts (Jessore, Pabna, and Rajshahi), the importance of the crop for these districts can be easily guessed. Planters were foremost among the rural notables in these districts, sharing the honors uneasily with the landlords. They lived like country squires on large estates, "rode to hounds, kept racing studs, revelled in pig-sticking, and entertained their friends on a princely scale."[9]

An important factor behind the rise of Bengal indigo was the established position of Calcutta as a financial hub, a port, a point of information exchange, and a political center. Until 1833, private merchants formed partnerships with servants of the East India Company, thus securing a degree of political and policing power in the countryside. The company's servants deposited their savings for remittance in these firms. After 1833, new enterprises in the business were started, often by individuals unconnected with the government. Political tensions generated by the indigo business arose in the countryside starting in the 1830s. In order to see the origin of these tensions, it is necessary to look at the property right in land.

In 1766 the East India Company prohibited its employees from holding land in India. The regulation implicitly applied to all British-born subjects. In practice, however, land could be held by proxy and leased through agents. Although indigo planters complained about these restrictions, the land law did not stop them from entering the business. Land ownership in the first half of the nineteenth century was vested with the zamindars, or landlords, of large estates who were in possession of secure

---

[9] Asiaticus, "The Rise and Fall of the Indigo Industry in India," *Economic Journal* 22(86), 1912, pp. 237–47 (quote on p. 237).

ownership rights. The manufacturers could either buy zamindari estates or lease land from a zamindar or from a superior tenant. In either instance, they could decide to grow the indigo themselves or to contract with peasants to grow the crop on land to which they had tenant rights. Before 1829, almost all land held by a planter was on leasehold but was usually not in the name of the planter. Direct leasehold was made possible by a new law in 1829, though restrictions on Europeans' owning or leasing land continued. In 1837, Crown subjects were made equivalent in the right to acquire or hold land in perpetuity. Thereafter, a few planters bought estates, but the average planter, whose interest was exclusively confined to indigo, was reluctant to own land on a large scale. In 1860, the proportion of cultivation on the planters' own land was still small, not exceeding a quarter of the estates.

Those who owned farms had to deal with the difficulty of procuring large numbers of wage laborers and borrowing money from the local moneylenders to meet seasonal shortfalls. Buying an estate was expensive in the densely populated districts of lower Bengal. While owning farms often gave planters access to the best lands for growing indigo, namely, sandbanks formed out of alluvial deposits in the rivers of the delta, few planters wanted to become full-fledged farmers. On the other hand, contracting kept the contracted prices of goods within established convention but required close monitoring. Boundary disputes were frequent between the lessor and the lessee. The zamindars, who also had a share in the profits of the competing rice trade, were wary of planter power and exerted both overt and covert influence on the peasants' crop choices.

The planters adopted two strategies to enforce contracts. One was the old device of a six-month contract signed on payment of an advance. The contracts specified not the quantity of the crop to be delivered, but the extent of land to be sown with it, as well as the amount of the advance payment. At the prevailing prices in the 1820s, 1830s, and 1840s, the advance generally settled the accounts, and the peasants took these contracts willingly. Although the contract was referred to as a legal paper, there was in fact no contract law covering it, and the document was, therefore, not much more than a legal gesture. Enforcement of such a contract was not easy. There were cases of the peasants' sowing a smaller area than agreed, underreporting yield, and even disappearing when the fields had to be sown. Thus some of the planters located in the remote areas adopted a second enforcement method. They maintained armies of *lathials*, literally, "bludgeonmen," to protect the estate and make the peasants fulfill the terms of the contract. Their usual method of enforcement was to descend on the land of a contract-bound peasant who had sown rice instead of indigo, and either burn the crop or imprison the farmer until the advance was returned or a promise to sow indigo was extracted.

The indigo business in the interior, therefore, had a reputation for violence. The Bengali press and literary works of the time, as well as much historical scholarship, suggest that such violence derived from collusion between state officials and European capitalists.[10] This is overdrawn. In a large measure, the element of violence reflected the weakness of the contract to protect planter interests, the ambiguous legal status of the paper, and the widely held belief among the planters that in applying force they were merely following an established Indian custom already used by zamindars and wealthy creditors. "The native merchants," a report in 1829 found, routinely "had recourse to the illegal restraint of his debtor."[11] Until 1859, actual cases of violence were few, were confined to only a few districts, and were often directed against the landlords and superior tenants. These cases, nevertheless, received publicity, and some of them were brought to the magistrate courts. Although the magistrates underscored the need "to subject the indigo planters and their servants to the control of law," the planters and agency houses countered that the violence was the frustrated response of the creditors to the absence of a "more effectual execution of contracts relating to the cultivation and delivery of the indigo plant."[12]

A serious breakdown of law materialized in the 1859–60 indigo season. For some time past, rice prices had been going up, inducing contracted peasants to change their minds about planting indigo after taking an advance. The planters approached the courts and magistrates with the legal papers that they called agreements; however, the authorities usually rejected these documents as the basis for forcing performance of the contract. Some of the planters and their Indian officers tried to enforce performance of the contracts by violent means, and the peasants in turn resisted them. There disturbances drew a sharp reaction from the Christian missionaries who had taken up the peasants' cause.

This outbreak of violence, which became known as the Blue Mutiny, drew attention to the long-neglected question of law, especially when the

---

[10] B. B. Kling, *The Blue Mutiny. The Indigo Disturbances in Bengal, 1859–1862*, Philadelphia: University of Pennsylvania Press, 1966, p. 148.

[11] B.P.P., 1831–32 (734) (735-I) (735-II) (735-III) (735-IV) (735-V) (735-VI), *Report from the Select Committee on the Affairs of the East India Company; with minutes of evidence in six parts, and an appendix and index to each*, London, p. 300.

[12] Ibid., pp. 290–92.

parties involved were European merchant firms and Indian peasants and artisans. Political connections and indigenous customs could no longer compensate for the absence of law. Fifty, or even thirty, years before, the company's directors had taken a soft line on the planters, even though the planters had long ceased to be their business partners in any direct sense. In 1835, an aggrieved planter could still hope to find a "reasonable member of the Calcutta Board of Revenue, who condescended to listen to my oft repeated prayers."[13] But by 1860, professional civilians wanted to distance themselves from old-style Indo-European business. The Indigo Commission that reported on the incident, therefore, also cleared the way for legislation on contracts.[14]

Already by 1860, Adolf von Bayer had successfully tested synthetic indigo. Indian exports did not begin to diminish until the last decade of the nineteenth century; but the little that was exported thereafter (800–900 tons about 1900) came from the planter-landlords of Bihar rather than Bengal.

Cotton and western India

Cotton was an indigenous crop in India, and grown in several regional clusters, of which the most important ones before the nineteenth century were coastal Gujarat, eastern Bengal, Khandesh, the Narmada Valley, Malwa, eastern Rajasthan, Rayalaseema, and the Coimbatore region. The growth of cotton cultivation in many of these clusters resulted from the growth of local demands for textiles. For example, the Bengal cultivation expanded because of the need for long-staple varieties in the Dhaka muslin industry. The Narmada Valley supplied the demand in the Deccan states, especially Bahamani and Vijayanagar states. Malwa, Rajasthan, and Narmada cotton also went to Sironj, which was a center for dyeing cotton yarn in northern India. The rise of North Indian Indo-Islamic empires facilitated east-west transactions in knowledge, and one of the visible effects of that process was that cotton cultivation traveled from eastern Bengal to eastern Rajasthan.

Descriptions of the Arabian Sea trade before European entry sometimes recorded a trade in Indian cotton. Little is known as to how large or how systematic the trade was. It is safe to assume that cotton formed part

---

[13] G. Lamb, "The Experiences of a Landholder and Indigo Planter in Eastern Bengal" (pamphlet), London: Edward Stanford, 1859, p. 5.
[14] Roy, "Indigo and Law in Colonial India."

of a diversified basket of goods carried by general merchants and did not yet involve a specialized trading system. This was to change in the early modern times, under the impetus of first, Indo-European trade in cotton textiles, and second, the Indo-European trade in cotton itself. The expansion of textile production for export in Gujarat, Coromandel, and Bengal imparted an expansionary effect on cotton production and marketing in certain regions.[15] Descriptions of Banjara bullock caravans in the eighteenth century report cotton as one of the principal items transported, along with grain and salt. By caravans and by boats, Narmada Valley supplied cotton to coastal Gujarat, and Deccan to the Coromandel. Bengal drew cotton along a west-to-east trade axis from Gujarat, and from Berar via markets in Mirzapur.

Before 1750, only a small quantity of cotton was imported by Britain, where it was used as candlewick. Clothing manufacture using cotton yarn, rather than a mixture of cotton and linen, developed in the eighteenth century, mainly in response to the importation of Indian cotton yarn. Once the trade began, the growth in demand was rapid. In 1697, the annual import of cotton into Britain was less than 1,000 tons. In 1775, imports were 3,600 tons; in 1800, 27,000 tons; in 1840, 220,000 tons; and in 1860, 680,000 tons. The initial impetus came from patents taken out by James Hargreaves for the spinning jenny (1770) and Richard Arkwright for the spinning frame (1769), as well as from the wide adoption of the steam engine in factories. Thereafter, rapid cotton mill building took over. In addition, Samuel Crompton's spinning mule (1779) made it possible to spin yarn as fine as that used in the Bengal muslins.

Until the middle of the 1790s, the main supply sources of cotton for Britain were the Caribbean, South America, and Turkey. Thereafter, the source switched to North America, where Eli Whitney's saw gin (1793) helped the United States keep pace with Britain's increased demand for cotton. Still, such an order of growth in demand could not be met by only one source. In the early 1780s, a small quantity of Indian cotton reached Britain via Flanders and Denmark, and, in 1788, the English East India Company placed an order for 250 tons of Indian cotton. The proposal threw the company's Indian branches into confusion because they did not know how to carry out the order. After some research and procurement

---

[15] Joseph Brennig, "Textile Producers and Production in Late Seventeenth-Century Coromandel," *Indian Economic and Social History Review* 23(4), 1986, pp. 333–55; Amalendu Guha, "Raw Cotton of Western India: 1750–1850," *Indian Economic and Social History Review* 9(1), 1972, pp. 1–41; Pamela Nightingale, *Trade and Empire in Western India, 1784–1806*, Cambridge: Cambridge University Press, 1970.

efforts, a few tons of Gujarat cotton were sent from Bombay. In 1800, the quantity was much larger, but was still dwarfed by the scale of the Anglo-American trade. The government in Bombay, in charge of encouraging procurement, found it difficult to divert the trade toward the company ports. Moveover, because of high internal transport costs, Indian cotton was expensive. A large part of Gujarat cotton still went to Bengal overland, and the prices offered did not succeed in diverting this flow into the export trade.

The East India Company sustained its efforts to get more cotton from India. The most promising policy, it seemed then, was to encourage European- and American-owned cotton farms in the style of indigo plantations. A Dr. Anderson was appointed to import and popularize Bourbon (Mauritius) cotton, and a private merchant named Hughes used these seeds on his Tirunelvely farm. The small supplies of "Hughes' cotton" were recognized in the Liverpool market as having distinctive quality and commanded a slightly higher price than American cotton. In 1797, a spice farm owned by one M. Brown in the uplands of Malabar also tried these seeds and managed to sell some of the cotton. In 1799, the naturalist William Roxburgh (see also Chapter 7), succeeded in culturing cotton in Calcutta, but its commercial significance cannot be established.

The Napoleonic Wars changed the situation. Trade with the United States became uncertain, and in the same proportion, trade with Asian sources became more attractive than before, regardless of the price. It was clear to everyone that the demand was growing too fast for a government-managed scheme of cultivation to cope with. Enquiries, therefore, were made also of the domestic trade and production, and two Scottish firms, Forbes and Company and Bruce, Fawcett and Company, were hired to procure cotton for the East India Company. In 1809, when more than 13,000 tons were exported, the price of cotton in Bombay was pushed to an unprecedented high. Bombay's shippers, who had by then started selling a few thousand tons of Gujarat cotton to China, faced losses. The new system seemed to favor the foreign trading firm, and the government's entry into trade revived unsavory memories of the days when the company had been tapping Indian revenues to carry on trade. These circumstances, however, made the export market profitable for the peasants. Although the government soon stepped away from direct trade, the viability of Indian cotton as an export item to Europe was demonstrated.

Securing a future for the trade demanded attention to two obstacles – the quality of the ginning and the poor yield of indigenous cotton varieties. There was no one method of ginning and cleaning cotton practiced in India. Descriptions from the mid-nineteenth century suggest the prevalence of highly labor-intensive methods in the southern Maratha countryside. In one of these, workers, usually peasant women, rolled the cotton with their feet on an iron roller until the seeds were separated from the fiber. Only slightly less labor intensive was the use of the wooden charkha: two rollers were turned by a handle, and the cotton passed between the rollers. Seeding was achieved, by both these methods, but not cleaning. Bits of dirt and leaves continued to be mixed with the fibers unless someone hand-picked them out. When the women of a peasant spinner family ginned the cotton, they also handpicked the dirt out. However, this task received little attention when cotton was exported. The Whitney saw gin addressed both problems at once, by the dual mechanism of a series of circular saws that deseeded the cotton and a cylinder surrounded with brushes that cleaned it. The saw gin also did something that the charkha did not; that is, it kept the cotton fibers together rather than have them fly around the room. The first saw gin in India arrived as early as 1794 but was not adopted outside of the European farms, possibly because of the heavy expense associated with them. The gin worked better if a thresher loosened the fibers beforehand.

Trade volumes in cotton were far too large for either the single- or the double-roller systems to cope with efficiently. It was too expensive to hire the laborers to clean cotton by means of the ordinary methods employed by the peasants. In 1795, professional cleaning by the hand method in Surat added 20 percent to the cost of cotton.[16] The cotton that came to the ports for loading, therefore, was generally of poor quality.

But there was more than the cost of cleaning involved in the quality problem. The administration thought that there was also deliberate adulteration by the local merchants. The cotton dealer firms of Bombay made advances to undercontractors, who in turn made advances to and contracted with the peasants or local merchants. When the crops were delivered, the local dealers "treat the purchaser with an insolence which reduces him to the dilemma of either taking a bad article on their terms, or running the hazard of losing the advance he had made."[17] Following this logic, when the market was depressed, the quality improved, and when the market was brisk, the quality went down. The dealers did not spend any money on cleaning the cotton properly; they also mixed different varieties, stored the cotton in damp godowns, and added moisture to increase the weight. The agents of the exporting firms colluded with the local merchants

---

[16] Guha, "Raw Cotton," p. 16.

[17] B.P.P., 1812–13 (306), *Papers relating to Revenues of India, and on Growth of Hemp and Cotton*, p. 19.

to take a cut of the latter's profits, and kept quiet about the quality of the cotton that they brought to Bombay. The company's agents shrewdly recognized that the "dishonesty" of the merchants in some fashion offset the distortions that resulted from government procurement of the cotton.[18]

A further difficulty with Indian cotton was the low volumes usually traded, an effect of poor yield. About 1850, there were four main cotton varieties cultivated in India, three of which were not indigenous: Bourbon was introduced in India from Mauritius in the 1790s; New Orleans was the main variety the East India Company tried to popularize in India; and Egyptian was adopted to a limited extent in Madras. The fourth and principal variety was the indigenous plant, a short bush that produced about half or even less on average than the American varieties.

The government's preferred solution to the supply problems was to encourage the European plantations and to enlist the support of amateur botanists. These measures, it was thought, would solve two issues at once, the low yield of Indian cotton and the poor quality of its processing. As early as 1788, the East India Company funded an experiment in Bengal to develop cotton cultivation in Dhaka, on the assumption that the famous Dhaka muslin derived its fineness from the quality of the cotton. The experiment did not lead to useful results, and scientists like Roxburgh believed that the quality of the muslins had more to do with their spinning than with the cotton.[19] In the 1820s, an organization called the Agricultural Society of India sought government funding for a farm in Bengal to try commercial culture of American cotton, and after a series of setbacks to the enterprise, received a go-ahead in 1830. The project was declared a failure in 1833 and ended.

In the early-1840s, the most important government experimental farm was started in Coimbatore under Robert Wight (1796–1872). Wight was trained and employed as a surgeon when he enlisted in the company's service in 1819.[20] Stationed in Madras, he turned his attention to botany and was appointed as a naturalist in 1826, after a collection of plants that he sent to England established the potential value of his amateur research. While on furlough in 1831–33, he published a series of accounts of Indian flora. Some of his projects were never completed, but Wight returned to India in 1834 as the head of the Agri-Horticultural Society gardens of

[18] Ibid., p. 20.
[19] Ibid., pp. 245–46.
[20] R. K. Basak, "Robert Wight and His Botanical Studies in India," *Taxon* 30(4), 1981, pp. 784–93.

Madras. In 1841, he was asked to lead the farm in Coimbatore set up to popularize American cotton and the saw gin. This project too was ultimately deemed a failure and ended, but not before twelve years of operation and possibly some demonstration effect, as we will see.

The other arm of government policy was the encouragement of private plantations. Between 1835 and 1850, several attempts to grow American cotton on Indian soil received the company's blessings. About a dozen "practical men from America" expected to "be put in communication with scientific men in India" and to explore the possibilities of cotton plantations in various parts of India.[21] Other collaborating parties in the project included indigo planters in Bengal and North India, a few zamindars, and some merchant firms that exported Indian cotton to Britain. These experiments happened in a somewhat unsystematic fashion. There was, in the end, no serious laboratory or "scientific" input that went into the work of the commercial groups.

The histories of these odd plantations are now obscure. We know of one Mr. Huffnagle, who had a farm near Calcutta; a Mr. Terry, who first started a farm in Bundelkhand and then shifted to Rangpur in Bengal; and a Blount, a Bell, a Duncan, a Vincent, a Jackson, and a Price. None of their enterprises survived beyond a decade at the most. The model that many of them wanted to emulate was that of the indigo plantations of Bengal, wherein the planter contracted with peasants who had secure rights to land and persuaded them to use different seeds and to change their methods. The cotton planters faced the same kinds of difficulty as did the indigo planters. The peasants took advances and proved indifferent about following instructions. After the Blue Mutiny of 1859–60, this model was, politically speaking, obsolete.

But contract failure was not the only reason why these experiments did not succeed commercially. The main problem was that the American seeds were not as well adapted to the Indian environment as the indigenous varieties were. Most experimenters chose Bengal, possibly because of its proximity to the administration and the indigo business. A May sowing made the young plants vulnerable to a late arrival of the monsoon, or if the monsoon was too heavy and too persistent, vulnerable to too much moisture. The soil on which a rice paddy was grown was often found unsuitable for cotton. In addition, the sandy soil of the riverbanks, which was good for the plant, was exposed to inundation. If such was the experience in Bengal, plants were also at high risk in drier conditions.

[21] J. Forbes Royle, *On the Culture and Commerce of Cotton in India*, London: Smith, Elder, 1851, p. 244.

The indigenous cotton plant was a short one, rarely rising more than two feet. The New Orleans plant was taller, but its roots did not go deep, so that it was more susceptible to droughts. In the western Doab and in Bundelkhand, the months leading up to the monsoon proved to be too dry for the young plants.

The biggest problem was pests. Bengal, again, turned out to be the wrong choice. The vegetation and moisture of Bengal made it a haven for pests. Indigenous cotton, "being harder and more hairy," was less attacked by insects. The Sea Island or Bourbon, on the other hand, was defenseless against the army of red, green, and gray caterpillars that feasted on the fruit and the boll. The peasants had no remedy against them. The only way forward was to study "the natural history of the several insects," a job for the scientists, which was never properly pursued for want of coordination.[22]

We should not, however, dismiss these experiments as inconsequential too quickly. Although the individual firms failed to make a profit, the knowledge of the seeds diffused among the peasants and they were moderately successful with the New Orleans variety. There were also significant positive spillover benefits, as we see from the fact that the average cotton yield did creep up from its low base in the 1840s (less than 75 lb. of clean cotton per acre) to a more respectable level in about 1920 (above 100 lb.). The failure of innovative businesses in this period points to the many obstacles that foreign capitalists needed to overcome to set up viable businesses in the Indian countryside. Trade costs were large and arose from contracts, transportation, and communication. In the end, cotton trade settled into a more sustainable trade model – reliance on the local merchant. It was a less than perfect solution from the quality point of view, but a better utilization of the respective advantages of foreign and local traders. Furthermore, such choices meant that the foreign and global firms would remain mainly engaged in trade.

Global merchants

Historians who have studied the relationship between British capitalists and the British Empire emphasize the role of the financial interests in the City in pushing for overseas expansion.[23] Other scholars, however,

---

[22] B.P.P., 1812–13, *Papers*, pp. 248–49.
[23] P. J. Cain and A. G. Hopkins, "Gentlemanly Capitalism and British Expansion Overseas I: The Old Colonial System, 1688–1850," *Economic History Review* 39(4), 1986, pp. 501–25.

suggest that the capitalists who had a possible stake in the empire in fact formed quite a diverse group, especially prior to 1850.[24] There is supporting evidence for the former view, in that some of the pre-1850 firms were connected with the City. But by and large, the firms with an Indian interest were too small and too diverse to be easily characterized as a class or to have exerted much political influence. Nevertheless, politically influential figures sometimes did arise from the London financial world.

Unlike modern multinational corporations, foreign firms that established their major fields of operation in India and China did not have a head or a parent located somewhere outside these areas. Called "investment groups" by S. D. Chapman, and "free-standing companies" by Mira Wilkins, they arose from "small-to-middling business" origins, remained family concerns, and registered themselves as partnerships and private concerns.[25]

The diverse origins of the agency houses, their loose links with the City, and their closer links with the provincial manufacturers who led the Industrial Revolution seem to confirm the second view. Although started under license from the English East India Company, or as agency houses, as they grew larger, they challenged the remaining privileges of the company and successfully campaigned to end the monopoly. As we will see, these firms also supported the empire, for their own survival depended on the political ties that connected Hong Kong and Singapore with Calcutta and Bombay.

The period of the emergence into prominence of the India firms started soon after 1813, with the end of the company's Indian monopoly. In China, Sino-European partnerships flourished after 1833, when the company's trading monopoly ended. Good business prospects in Bengal indigo and opium in the 1820s attracted deposits to these firms, and away from the company and its debts, which allowed the firms to expand and to extend their banking and insurance businesses. If these facts suggest that

---

[24] Anthony Webster, "The Strategies and Limits of Gentlemanly Capitalism: The London East India Agency Houses, Provincial Commercial Interests, and the Evolution of British Economic Policy in South and South East Asia, 1800–50," *Economic History Review* 59(4), 2006, pp. 743–64.

[25] S. D. Chapman, "British-Based Investment Groups before 1914," *Economic History Review* 38(2), 1985, pp. 230–51; Mira Wilkins, "The Free-Standing Company, 1870–1914: An Important Type of British Foreign Direct Investment," *Economic History Review* 41(2), 1988, pp. 259–82; S. D. Chapman, "British Free Standing Companies and Investment Groups in India and the Far East," in Mira Wilkins and Harm Schroter, eds., *The Free Standing Company in the World Economy, 1830–1996*, Oxford: Oxford University Press, 1998, pp. 202–17.

they were mainly picking up businesses abandoned by the company, the impression has been disputed.[26] The individuals who established these firms often had to take great risks, not the least political risks, in both India and China. Their survival through the major business recessions of the mid-nineteenth century was due to their diversification away from old trades and into newer fields like steam navigation and railways.

The typical agency businesses were exposed to high price risks. The prices of indigo and opium were volatile. Speculation in these goods could easily make fortunes, or destroy them. Before the intercontinental telegraph lines, these firms had few means to collect information on demand and supply. A long run of high prices made them careless about such information. When, therefore, indigo prices crashed in 1830–33 and again in 1846, they responded to the low prices by raising the volume of production, on the expectation that the depression could not last. That expectation soon turned out to be wrong. But it was too late for the deeply indebted firms to adjust their strategy. The banks and the insurance firms that supported these traders lacked a diversified portfolio and followed their clients into bankruptcy. This was far from the end of the story, however, for a number of firms survived beyond these crashes, and on the foundation laid by the pioneers, new firms entered in the 1840s, as we will see in the next chapter.

Among the most famous pioneers, the Calcutta firm of Paxton, Cockerell, Trail, later renamed Palmer and Company, had its main interests in Bengal and lent money to firms in other Asian ports. Palmer and Company was established in 1810 by a son of William Palmer (1740–1816), an East India Company officer and a contemporary of Warren Hastings, the first governor-general (1732–1818). Palmer was a partnership between the brothers George Palmer (1772–1853) and John Horsley Palmer (1767–1836).[27] The Scottish firm of James Finlay (1727–1790) began in 1765 as cotton mill owner and textile trader in Scotland and continental Europe. James's son Kirkman (1773–1842) was based in Glasgow but developed an export market for his goods in Africa, Europe, the Levant, and eventually America. As the geographical extent of his commercial operations expanded, he turned into a

---

[26] A representative of the old view is Greenberg, *British Trade*. For a critique, see W. E. Cheong, *Mandarins and Merchants: Jardine Matheson and Co., A China Agency of the Early Nineteenth Century*, Atlantic Highlands, NJ: Humanities Press, 1980.

[27] Anthony Webster, "An Early Global Business in a Colonial Context: The Strategies, Management, and Failure of John Palmer and Company, 1780–1830," *Enterprise and Society*, 6(1), 2005, pp. 98–133.

campaigner for the end of the English East India Company's monopoly in East India trade. As soon as the company's charter ended, Kirkman Finlay had a branch of his firm established in Bombay. The branch specialized in selling cotton yarn. In the 1830s, it started buying cotton from India. In the 1870s, the firm of Finlay opened jute mills in Calcutta and, in the next decade, started selling Indian tea in Europe. By 1900, the firm owned the major part of the area under tea in the Anaimalai and the Nilgiri Mountains, which was consolidated under four companies listed in London. Their other ventures included a cotton mill in Bombay and a sugar refinery in Uttar Pradesh. In the 1830s, ownership of the firm had passed to a former partner, John Muir; the firm stayed family controlled until 1924. Its core business by then was selling tea worldwide, a business in which the London companies played an important role.[28]

A member of a later generation, James Matheson (1796–1878), took up employment in a Calcutta merchant firm in 1815, and after a difficult start, established himself in country trade between Canton and Calcutta. His partnership with William Jardine (1784–1843), a surgeon-turned-merchant, launched in 1832 what was to become a pioneering British firm, Jardine, Matheson. Their country trade interests continued, and selling opium for tea and silk was the main business of the firm for as long as Jardine remained in China. But after James Matheson died, the main field of operation for the firm was China. Already by then, the firm had established itself in Hong Kong.[29] From a beginning in opium, the firm diversified so successfully into shipping, insurance, warehousing, and trade that in more recent times it has emerged as business historians' favorite example of the adaptive firm.[30]

In recruiting managers, all these firms relied on personal ties. The important role that tacit knowledge of commodities and regions played in their business success left room for such informal ties to develop. Owing to this flexibility, they were entrepreneurial in integrating related businesses. In the Finlay case, the move from tea trading to plantations was an example of such integration. The histories of such firms also point to the connections

---

[28] C. Brogan, *James Finlay and Company Limited*, Glasgow: Jackson, 1951; Roger Jeffery, "Merchant Capital and the End of Empire: James Finlay, Merchant Adventurers," *Economic and Political Weekly* 17(7), 1982, pp. 241–48.

[29] M. Keswick, ed., *The Thistle and the Jade: A Collaboration of 150 Years of Jardine, Matheson and Co.*, London: Octopus Books, 1982; Cheong, *Mandarins and Merchants*.

[30] C. M. Connell, "Jardine, Matheson & Company: The Role of External Organization in a Nineteenth-Century Trading Firm," *Enterprise and Society* 4(1), 2003, pp. 99–138.

that they maintained with London, Liverpool, Manchester, Glasgow, and Dundee, and, further afield, with Scottish firms in Africa, Latin America, and Southeast Asia. These networks created scope for complementary businesses and facilitated the exchange of tacit knowledge. Through such networks, skilled foremen came from Lancashire to work in the mills of Calcutta and Bombay.[31]

In the case of mobile capital, the British Empire was present as a facilitator, but only indirectly. With mobile labor, the imperial agency was a more direct one, as will be seen in the next section.

Labor migration

The extreme seasonality of Indian agricultural work posed risks to lives and livelihoods. The same syndrome also ensured a plentiful supply of labor for nonagricultural work. On average, the male member of a peasant or rural labor family worked full-time for half the year. The intensity of farm work increased slightly in the paddy areas and fell away sharply in the Deccan plateau and Rajasthan. A large peasant family could manage the necessary supervision of cultivation with even fewer days per person. The availability of a labor surplus, therefore, was ingrained in agricultural operations. Within the village, there were few lucrative avenues of non-farm work. The generally small land yield depressed demand for industry and services in the village itself. But it was a different matter with urban construction, manufacturing, mines, and plantations, which could tap the same labor pool at wages that were among the lowest in the contemporary world. This market turned global in the 1830s.

It is possible that Indian sailors had served on board the East Indiamen before 1800, but we know little about who they were, where they ended up, and the conditions of their service. The earliest overseas migration of Indian workers on which definite reports exist involved Tamils found in the Straits Settlements, and a motley group of eastern Indians in Tenasserim. Both territories came under British control about 1826, but migration itself was essentially still outside state regulation, so that the numbers again remain uncertain. The Indians performed domestic labor and agricultural labor, and worked as sailors. Although unconfirmed reports

[31] Geoffrey Jones and Judith Wale, "Merchants as Business Groups: British Trading Companies in Asia before 1945," *Business History Review* 72(3), 1998, pp. 367–408.

of the migration of laborers to Mauritius and Réunion date such movements back to 1819, the first recorded enterprise occurred in 1830, when a French merchant, Joseph Argand, sent 130 artisans from Calcutta to Mauritius. It appears that the laborers had signed an indenture committing them to a five-year term and entitling them to an extraordinary 8 rupees/month wage. In 1832, two members of Argand's group complained to the police in Calcutta that their wages had not been paid. The complaint was rejected, but the British government had for the first time become involved in overseeing a labor contract.

As a result of such complaints, emigrants to the Indian Ocean islands were required to appear before a magistrate and declare their willingness to go. When slavery was officially abolished in the British Empire in 1834, Mauritius, then a British colony with a French sugar planter settlement, was driven to exploring the indenture route more actively. Between 1834 and 1837, several thousand Indians left Calcutta port. For the first time, reports reveal the rather striking fact that nearly all of the emigrants came from the Oraon and Munda population groups who lived in the Chota Nagpur uplands. Almost all of them were men.

The year 1837 saw the first of many legislative moves to regulate the flow of emigrants. The question of regulation had been ambiguous until then. By the implicit contract that the British maintained with respect to Mauritius, the laws of the colony would not be interfered with. But Mauritian labor ordinances could be quite harsh, whether because of the legacy of slavery or the fear that the indenture was not a secure enough deed. On the other side, the indenture was entered into in Calcutta or Madras, which required Indian law to take notice of it. A trickier problem to address involved workers who were being taken to a non-British colony: how deeply should the British government be involved in protecting their welfare and interests? In 1837, the Law Commission hoped to settle these problems by ruling that no legislation was mandatory. Nevertheless, a law (Act XXXII) was passed that required police and magisterial checks at the ports of embarkation. The magistrates were instructed to look at the contract and speak to the contractee. The police were responsible for issuing permits to the ships that were transporting workers and for checking that the vessels carried the proper quantity of water and food for the workers. Seamen contracts were exempt from these regulations.

Whether or not the police and the magistrates performed these roles diligently, from this time onward we begin to have reliable numbers for those migrating overseas. The first group of roughly seven thousand workers who left Calcutta under the new legal provisions again hailed predominantly from Chota Nagpur. But a substantial number came from middle Bengal. A small but noticeable number of the emigrants were artisans, such as the silk winders who were being sent to Batavia "to teach their art."[32] Possibly nine out of ten migrants went to Mauritius, with the remaining one headed for the West Indies. In 1838, there occurred the first and last direct embarkation for Australia.

These transactions stopped for the next four years because of a prohibition engineered by an antislavery group led by Lord Chancellor Henry Brougham. Private reports processed in Calcutta detailed the abuses that the workers suffered. Some workers had been intimidated into signing the contracts. Others had been denied six months of wages, which were instead divided between the recruiting agents and the ship captains. Some workers complained of bad treatment at their destinations. The situation in Bourbon was more or less unknown, but it was easily assumed to be much worse than in Mauritius. The prospective emigrants were housed in merchant homes in Calcutta while they waited for their ships. Visitors to these "depots" were horrified by the sight of a disorderly and filthy human mass living in opium-induced stupor, while the gates were guarded by armed North Indian soldiers. In other words, the Calcutta underworld and the brutal planter seemed to be playing an unduly large role in deciding the welfare of the workers. In this interregnum, much data were collected on recruitment systems, wages, and welfare provisions, and constant pressure was mounted on the government to ease the restrictions. A few workers did board the ships from Ceylon in this interregnum, but the numbers were small. By 1842 the economic pressure had become too strong, and emigration was allowed to resume. A new law (Act XV of 1842) provided for a salaried agent employed by the government to be in charge of reporting on the business. Many of the other provisions and checks continued as before.

An unrealistically low estimate of labor requirements may have played a role in the relaxation of the prohibition. It was believed in 1842 that an annual flow of between fifteen hundred and two thousand Indian workers should be more than enough to meet the needs of the planters.[33] It was soon apparent, however, that the very supply of Indian workers created a new demand for them by inducing the planters to expand cultivation. Many more hands were needed, and many workers embarked on the ships headed to Mauritius. For their part, the planters complained of the wages being too high and the workers deserting before their indenture ended. It had been estimated that the total stock of Indian workers needed in all

---

[32] B.P.P., 1874 (314), *Mr. Geogheghan's Report on Coolie Emigration from India*, London, p. 5.
[33] Ibid., p. 13.

parts of the empire was twenty thousand, which one agent could provide well enough. But between 1842 and 1870, the total number that left India for all overseas destinations was slightly more than half a million, or about twenty thousand per year. Fewer than one in five who went abroad returned to India during this time span. Bombay and Madras joined the traffic in the 1850s, and emigration to Africa and the Atlantic colonies began.

The system, if it can be called a system, of recruitment of indentured workers was the following. There were licensed emigration agents at the major ports of embarkation. There were also depots where the workers waited for their ships. The agent was responsible for overseeing the required medical and police checks and for making sure the ships complied with regulations regarding space and provisions. In towns in the interior such as Patna, Muzaffarpur, Gorakhpur, Kanpur, and Allahabad, there were depots managed by licensed private agents. These agents, in their turn, hired subcontractors who traveled to the bazaars of the smaller market towns, farther into the fairs and weekly markets in Chota Nagpur. These places were the first points of contact between the prospective migrants and the professional recruiters.

According to the emigrants' testimony, in an unusually large number of cases, a young man would leave home on an indefinite search for a job in the city, or after quarreling with the parents or community elders, or simply because there was not enough food to eat at home. Wandering into the village fair or market, he would meet the subcontractor. In some cases, the subcontractors' spies made the first move. When a few of these young men had been gathered, they would be taken to the private depots and then on to Calcutta. That the worker's migration was rarely a family decision was evident from the fact that families usually learned of the decision years later when a letter arrived from overseas.

This pattern was no doubt broken many times. For example, during famines whole families would wander from their homes and villages, often meeting a recruiter, and not wholly by chance. Another significant exception occurred when a returnee went back to his village seeking fresh migrants. Sometimes, married women and children joined the men. But in the default case, where wandering individuals were spotted by an agent, women were rare, if conspicuous for that reason. Almost all of the single women migrants that we know about had left home after a failed affair or had gone away with their boyfriend. Of course, the single female migrant faced great danger. It is almost certain that there were more cases of single women trying to enlist and ending up in the brothels of Calcutta than we know about.

The standard contract in the mid-nineteenth century was for a five-year indenture, renewable for five more years with the same employer or with another employer. Such renewals left the worker in an almost identical status for a long time. In the last quarter of the nineteenth century, legislation and a general tendency of maturation of the labor market saw a progressive contraction in the scope of the long indenture.

Indo-European industry

As a way to deal with interlopers, the East India Company had long discouraged licensed migration of Britons to India. Its anxiety spilled over into the various restrictions imposed on British subjects in India regarding land ownership (see the earlier discussion of the indigo trade). "Among British residents in India," an 1813 petition written by the company stated, "there is a strong disposition to assert what they conceive to be their constitutional and indefeasible rights, a general leaning towards each other, and a common jealousy of the authority of Government."[34] Interestingly, the petition picked on a propensity of the private traders to form communities. In the indigo business, mutual help clubs among the company's own servants, private merchants, and local administrators sometimes embarrassed the state. These alarmist discussions ended in 1813.

Every year between 1814 and 1831, fifty to one hundred British citizens took out licenses to go to India.[35] Possibly the largest single group consisted of partners and assistants in private commercial establishments. But there was also a noticeable number of artisans, advocates, planters, and, of course, Christian missionaries. Among the indigo planters and agency houses, a certain number were French. The missionaries included a few Germans. These numbers were not large by any standard. But the effects of this migration cannot be measured by numbers, since almost all of these migrants brought to India either capital or special skills. Outside this society, a much larger body of European soldiers was already settled and formed part of an Indo-European society that could not have been smaller than one hundred thousand in 1800.

During this time, the movement of skilled artisans into the cities fostered innovative businesses. An example was shipbuilding. As a recent

[34] B. P. P., *Report from the Select Committee of the House of Commons on the Affairs of the East India Company*, London, 1832, p. 352.
[35] B.P.P., 1831–32, *Report from the Select Committee*, pp. 268–70.

work on the shipbuilding industry of Bombay has shown, in the first half of the nineteenth century, Indian shipbuilding maintained a close link with country trade.[36] Indian ships were only rarely made for the Atlantic trip; the Napoleonic Wars created the only exceptions to this rule. It is still not clear whether the specialization was enforced by the company's policy, by indigenous knowledge, or by the sponsors of the industry who were themselves engaged in country trade.

The transition to steamships changed the engineering skills required for running shipyards. A certain number of Indian shipwrights made the transition successfully. The most important examples came from among those Parsi individuals who had been apprentices in machine maintenance in Bombay and England. In 1838 the great shipwright of Surat, Nowrojee Jamsetji, sent his son and his nephew to England to learn the craft of building steamships. Their journey is memorable for an unrelated reason. The cousins recorded their impressions of female education and gender equality in the English society of the time, urging their own community to take up a program of female education in view of "the host of amusements and recreations that by education are afforded to females."[37] These writings must have resonated well among the Parsis, who by about 1900 had a proportion of female literacy far exceeding the Indian average.

More is known about Ardaseer Cursetjee, the head of the dockyard in Bombay in 1852. Cursetjee was the "chief engineer and inspector of machinery," that is, he was in charge of the repair and maintenance of ships in the government marine under the East India Company.[38] He was born c. 1808 and at the age of fourteen was apprenticed to the master builder of the Bombay dockyard. Conversion to steam began in earnest by the time he was a senior assistant. On the recommendation of the master, he took training in England in constructing and maintaining steam engines; he was appointed to head the Bombay dockyard in 1848. Shortly thereafter, his son traveled to England to receive training as shipwright.

At the time Cursetjee took over, the dockyard produced boilers, built small engines on the principle of marine engines, and "cut and lengthened" iron ships, but it did not build complete iron ships. Cursetjee employed the European engineers of ships docked in the port as foremen of the different dockyard departments. His core workforce consisted of

---

[36] Anne Bulley, *The Bombay Country Ships, 1790–1833*, Richmond, VA: Curzon Press, 2000.
[37] Anon., "Journal of a Residence in Great Britain, by Jehungeer Nowrajee and Hirjeebhoy Merwanjee, of Bombay, Naval Architects. London. 1841," *Calcutta Review* 4, 1845, Miscellaneous Notices, pp. i–xii.
[38] B.P.P., *Select Committee*, First Report (2), pp. 87–90.

5.3. Parsi schoolgirl, from a postcard printed in 1897. Close business partnerships with Europeans sometimes contributed to reformist social movements among Indian business communities, one area of collective action being the education of girls. © Images of Asia

several hundred Indian workers. Like himself, the senior assistants from the Indian pool were as skilled as the European ones, but the difference in salary was large. A European boilermaker could not be hired for less than Rs. 200 a month, whereas an Indian of comparable skill but less experience received Rs. 16. Cursetjee described a system of apprenticeship that was quite different from the Indian models and adapted elements of the English system. That is, the employer offered wages tied to experience on the job, distinguishing workers into three classes. There was no mention of the employment of Indian intermediaries in making decisions about seniority and wages. The workers came from diverse backgrounds and did not necessarily hail from any specific caste or community. A significant number were considered "Christian half-caste."

There were at this time also dockyards constructing sailing ships in Surat and Cochin. Much of the wood used in Bombay was teak from Malabar. The business of procuring teak for the shipyard was an old one in the Malabar foothills; it merely changed direction toward Bombay as the demand increased there. The advantage that men like Cursetjee possessed in Bombay and that a British shipwright would not have was their knowledge of the old timber trade and their experience in dealing with local suppliers.

Although Calcutta was a much smaller center of shipbuilding than Bombay, the business flourished there in the first half of the nineteenth century because of the expansion in shipping in Calcutta after the East India Company's monopoly of India trade ended. In the 1840s, apart from the government docks, there were several European-owned private shipyards in the region of Howrah. These enterprises built mainly vessels for coastal or river transport. They also repaired and maintained ships that called on these ports and in the process strengthened indigenous skills in ship repair. Further south of Calcutta, Fort Gloster also possessed a shipbuilding yard. Here between 1811 and 1828, twenty-seven ships were built, averaging 350 tons each. We know of yet another experiment in Titagarh, where a massive sailing ship was constructed early in the nineteenth century, but the site had to be abandoned because the river changed course.[39]

By far the most important set of experiments in manufacturing was related to iron making. In the nineteenth century, artisan-entrepreneurs having some connection with the company tried to erect viable iron shops after the English model. They were driven by a quite realistic conception

[39] "Calcutta in the Olden Times. Its Localities," *Calcutta Review* 18, 1852, pp. 275–321.

of comparative advantage. In this view, "they have labor cheap, and they have abundance of ore cheap, but they want skill and capital."[40] What they did not factor in, though, was transaction cost. In any event, these entrepreneurs expected that with a change in scale they could bring down the average costs of iron making substantially. Despite the mention of "capital" in this quotation, these individuals were far from capitalists. They were artisans brought up in the British tradition. In this respect, they fitted the flow of migrant artisans and laborers from Britain to India better than the foreign investment that went into tea, jute, and indigo.

Some of these adventurers, including Andrew Duncan and Josiah Marshall Heath, had been established iron masters. Duncan had worked for more than fifteen years in Scotland and Russia before arriving in Bengal in 1810.[41] He was engaged by the East India Company to carry out a survey of and prepare a report on the prospects of finding iron in Midnapore and Balasore and to construct a smelting shop and a foundry, on the promise of a sales contract with the government. Duncan's surveys eventually took him to the Birbhum district in western Bengal.

In this region, mining in the forested uplands and small-scale artisanal smelting were already established. Between 1770 and 1870, licenses to mine or to produce iron in large furnaces or both were procured by a broker of the East India Company (Indranarayan Sharma); by Messrs. Mott and Farquhar; by several small zamindars; and by the Birbhum Iron Works Company, which had been founded by Messrs. Mackay and Company of Calcutta. The first of these ventures never began; the second fought exhausting battles with the principal zamindari in Birbhum over rent and with local smelters over access to material; the third's zamindari enterprises fought with each other; and the fourth faced prohibitive costs to transport wood for fuel as forests receded rapidly starting in the second quarter of the nineteenth century. Unlike these enterprises, Duncan, who arrived in the district in 1812, was already experienced in smelting. He set up an experimental smelting shop in Birbhum. When the landlords discovered that Duncan was not a government employee, they bribed and

[40] B.P.P., 1859 Session 1 (198), *Select Committee to Inquire into Progress and Prospects for Promotion of European Colonization and Settlement in India Report, Proceedings, Minutes of Evidence, Appendix, Index*, pp. 245–50 (quote on p. 250).

[41] I draw on Tirthankar Roy, "Did Globalization Aid Industrial Development in Colonial India? A Study of Knowledge Transfer in the Iron Industry," *Indian Economic and Social History Review* 46(4), 2009, pp. 579–613, where the original source citations appear.

chased his workers away and destroyed his buildings. Despite these troubles, he still managed to produce some iron over the next seven months.

The Birbhum experiment taught Duncan that the main obstacle to setting up a large-scale workshop was people. Duncan found it impossible to secure workers willing to learn how to operate the machines that he had brought with him. The problem inclined him toward finding a location where European foremen would be more easily available, though he still contemplated employing and training a mainly Indian workforce. The new site would be at a confluence of two rivers, with relatively easy access to Calcutta. He received financial support from the East India Company, which thought the enterprise would be useful to it. In 1814, when the building was completed, the government officers dealing with this enterprise had second thoughts and appointed a committee of engineers to assess the project. The committee reported that Duncan was a good ironmaster but a bad accountant who had underestimated the costs of getting material and machinery from abroad. The subsequent history of the enterprise is not clear. The factory possibly manufactured a few cannon shells, but there is no mention of a body of workers being employed there.

The best documented modern venture in smelting was the Porto Novo factory.[42] Porto Novo (Parangipettai), a small town located on the north bank of the Vellar River where the river meets the Bay of Bengal, was a one-time port used by European ships. Here, in 1825, Josiah Marshall Heath, an East India Company servant, sought permission to set up an iron-making factory "embracing the process of smelting, puddling, and beating out into bars."[43] Heath requested an exclusive lease covering ores occurring in the region for the legally maximum time for such lease, twenty-one years. The grant of an exclusive license drew a threatening response from George Jessop, who had, with his brother, successfully established a foundry in Calcutta (which lives on today as a state enterprise). On the other hand, Heath received the backing of Thomas Munro and along with him a powerful section of Madras's administration.

[42] Earlier descriptions of these enterprises appear in Morris D. Morris, "Growth of Largescale Industry to 1947," in Dharma Kumar, ed., *The Cambridge Economic History of India*, Cambridge: Cambridge University Press, 1983, vol. 2, pp. 553–676; R. S. Rungta, *The Rise of Business Corporations in India, 1851–1900*, Cambridge: Cambridge University Press, 1970. None offers an adequate explanation of the failure of the enterprise.

[43] B.P.P., 1852–53 (634), *Despatches, Minutes and Reports from Madras Government on Origin and Transactions of Porto Novo Iron Company*, p. 3.

The factory would produce four thousand tons of bar iron, at a cost of £12 per ton. The price of English pig iron was £8.3 per ton at this time. In Heath's license application, the price of bar iron was set at £34–40 per ton in England and £18–24 in India; both figures were possibly exaggerated. In both markets, Heath managed to convince the concerned company officers that his enterprise would make profit. The enterprise was troubled from the start. Heath soon found himself in debt to the Calcutta agency house, Alexander and Company, to the extent of Rs. 100,000 for the property purchased in Porto Novo and needed a large loan from the company to proceed. The Porto Novo Iron Works also raised capital in Madras by persuading company surgeons and the advocate-general in charge of drawing up the contract to become shareholders. It does not appear that the ironworks managed to pay either a dividend or interest at any time. By 1840, Heath's company was hopelessly in debt.

As late as 1849, a memorandum from the accountant-general stated that "the causes of the total failure of the undertaking are at present inexplicable."[44] While the iron was high priced, a lack of demand was not the reason for the works' failure. In 1859 Sheffield imported a small quantity of Indian pig iron. In an estimated annual consumption of 35,000–40,000 tons, Indian production, almost all of it from Porto Novo, supplied slightly less than 1,000 tons, a small proportion but large enough to draw attention. In this market, Porto Novo iron was known for superior quality. After he returned to England in 1837, Heath complained about the lack of cooperation in Sheffield, about the fact that his goods did not find a market in India, and about the government's refusal to respond to his call for a marketing contract.[45] In Sheffield, however, a different perception prevailed. Heath's problem was not demand, not quality, and not the price; it was the impossibility of increasing the supply. Sheffield, in fact, wanted more of Heath's iron, which was considered unequaled for steel tools, but Heath "indignantly rejected" the offer of a contract to supply a larger and steady volume. "The fact was, he knew he could not do it."[46] The problem was on the supply side.

In current scholarship, the explanation of why Porto Novo failed remains conjectural, and therefore, not always persuasive. One work suggests that the enterprise suffered from capital shortage.[47] This interpretation would

[44] Ibid., p. 467.

[45] Ibid., pp. 32–35, 259.

[46] J. Ochterlony, Engineer on J. M. Heath's enterprise, cited in ibid., p. 17.

[47] Prasannan Parthasarathi, "Iron-smelting in the Indian Subcontinent, c. 1800," paper presented at the S. R. Epstein memorial conference, London, London School of Economics and Political Science, 2008.

be convincing but for the fact that the company managed to continue on for twenty years with borrowed money. An earlier study surveyed a few other examples of failed European adaptation of indigenous smelting processes and attributed the failures to incompatibility between an indigenous work organization and the scale of the new enterprise.[48] It is true that the two knowledge orders were too far apart and too incompatible to develop working partnerships. However, it is not clearly stated how this factor was relevant to the failure of Porto Novo. I would argue that the main supply problems in this case were posed by the costs of labor and materials.

The report of a study conducted in 1833 stressed the importance of "steady intelligent workmen" and a steady supply of charcoal to make the enterprise a success.[49] Another report in 1837 was more candid: "The persons in immediate charge of the machinery at Porto Novo appear to have been not educated men, but merely working artificers," which contributed to the delayed commissioning of the works. The machines ordered from England were incomplete, using cattle power to operate bellows did not work, the European workmen arrived a year after the machinery did, and "adequate arrangement had not been made for the provision of fuel."[50] There is no evidence that Porto Novo ever employed Indian workers above the most unskilled tasks. Given the character of indigenous smelting in the interior regions, it would have been difficult to contemplate making use of smelters usually engaged in operating small furnaces.

The transportation of wood fuel was a huge problem in this region, which still had neither railways nor good roads. The ores had to be transported from the iron-rich areas around Salem town by rivers and canals that were navigable only for about six months of the year. One small canal used by the factory to transport charcoal dried up.[51] In a further blow to the prospects of the works, the workshop did not have, and despite tortuous negotiations for over a decade, never could establish, undisputed property rights over resources. The Board of Revenue asserted the rights of the people to the common forest lands in the region, including the right to collect wood and ore.[52] The collector of Salem, from where the

---

[48] S. Bhattacharya, "Cultural and Social Constraints on Technological Innovation and Economic Development: Some Case Studies," *Indian Economic and Social History Review* 3(3), 1966, pp. 240–67.

[49] B.P.P., 1852–53 (634), *Despatches, Minutes and Reports*, p. 161.

[50] Ibid., pp. 266–67.

[51] Ibid., p. 434.

[52] Ibid., p. 325.

company tried to procure iron and charcoal, stated that "the hundreds of native furnaces at work" in his jurisdiction were already able to provide "any quantity of iron required by the people," that "very many make their livelihood by burning charcoal and bringing it for sale to the iron smiths," and that it was his duty to protect these livelihoods.[53] After all, India was not a New World colony where the settlers could write their own laws. Natural resources such as wood, water, and iron were entangled in complicated legal and customary rights, which some officers of the government felt it their duty to protect.

Another contemporary venture on which some information is available is the Kumaon Iron Works, which was formally launched in 1856. It had been officially known for at least thirty years before that date that Kumaon had indigenous smelting and ore, and plenty of wood fuel. In 1856, the government considered producing charcoal iron in Kumaon with the help of private capital. It appears that two small smelting workshops under government supervision had already been working in this area. Two private agents, Davis and Company and one Drummond, took over these workshops. These two firms merged in 1862 to form North of India Kumaon Iron Works Company. The enterprise had its eye on potential demand for iron from the railways. But it faced an insurmountable obstacle in accessing and transporting wood.

These examples show that European enterprise in India did not succeed because of its persistent underestimation of transaction costs and the costs of complementary inputs. It faced high energy cost, for wood fuel was costly to transport in regions that did not have many navigable rivers. The European workforce often proved unreliable and inexperienced. Property rights and rights to the commons were not distributed to the advantage of a factory. And given that these works failed to make convincing attempts to address these problems, the government was only a half-hearted partner in these ventures. Finally, there was the misperception of demand. These enterprises understood the colonial market that consisted of the army, public construction, and the railways and believed that a promise to supply these markets would enable them to get concessionary licenses on ore, wood, and market. The colonial market was an unreliable partner, however. Porto Novo made an attempt to sell an iron plow to peasants but did so too late and too hesitantly to make any difference to its profitability.

---

[53] Ibid., p. 339.

The shaky nature of Indo-European industry, indeed, the experience of the deeply indebted Porto Novo ironworks itself, revealed a major obstacle that innovative businesses in the early nineteenth century faced, which was the raising of finance. Capital was costly in India; even the best interest rates in transactions that did not involve known and related partners exceeded 12 percent per year. The East India Company restrained capital market integration and foreign exchange banking in order to ensure stability in meeting its own obligations. Repatriation of merchant profits was done by means of bills drawn largely on a half dozen firms in Calcutta – Palmer, Fergusson, Alexander, Colvin, Macintosh, and Cruttenden – until 1833. But these firms had a divided interest between trade and banking. When they failed in 1833 (Fergusson was refloated, to fail again in 1842) because of a trade recession, the effect on banking and remittance was immediate and deep. Thereafter, exchange banking was left in a limbo for some time, to be carried out by smaller agency houses. In the early nineteenth century, therefore, the difference between the money markets in India and in England, where "sixteen million people have nearly a thousand Banks and Branch Banks," was large and growing.[54] In the middle decades of the nineteenth century, a number of proposals for banks licensed in India to conduct foreign-exchange business were floated. The movement would reach maturity in the second half of the century (see Chapter 6).

Overland trade

In the early nineteenth century, caravan trade in the western Himalayas needed to reinvent itself. The horse trade was as good as over. However, the empire, in desperate need to fix its borders with its potentially hostile northern neighbors, took great interest in the trans-Himalayan trade routes. A series of explorations in the early nineteenth century yielded a great deal of systematic knowledge of Himalayan commerce. The end of the horse trade had reduced the political significance of overland trade, and yet trade in textile articles such as cotton, silk, and wool was to grow in importance in the early nineteenth century. Silk came from Central Asia and China, and wool came from Tibet. Encouraged by the extension of the imperial domain, Sindhi merchants and bankers of Shikarpur joined the business of financing trade. Notwithstanding the presence of bankers who could source cheap money from parent firms in Sind, the trade entailed huge risks

---

[54] Cited text from Anon., *East India Bank* (pamphlet), 1840.

and high transportation costs, and though not insignificant to the local economies, it was almost certainly dwarfed by the scale of maritime trade.

In the northwestern Himalayas, caravans would leave the plains of Punjab and cross the mountains to reach markets in Tibet, China, and Central Asia in one of two directions: westward via the Khyber Pass to Kabul and onward to Khokand, Yarkand, Khotan, and Bokhara; or northward toward Leh and into Central Asia via the Karakoram Pass. The former route was easier for traffic, and was good even for carts for part of the way, but it was reputed to be unsafe because of the possibility of predatory attacks. The latter route could not accommodate anything other than small caravans of ponies, sheep, and camels, but the journey was punishing on the animals. The road, an 1866 report stated, "is so exceedingly dangerous and difficult that the traders are obliged to take three spare horses for every one laden, and the calculation is that 25 per cent of the animals die on the road."[55] Not surprisingly, therefore, the cost of transport by this means was extremely high – the hire of a horse load for the journey cost Rs. 42–50.

It seems that the Indo-Tibetan trade revived in the late nineteenth century, after a long lull starting in the seventeenth century. However, the earliest detailed descriptions available pertain to the turn of the nineteenth century. The Bhotiya traders of the Kumaon-Garhwal region traversed the passes with sheep and goats, for no other animal could survive the journey and the elevation, to connect Tibet with the pilgrim towns in the plains, mainly Hardwar. They also sold their wares at major fairs in the foothills, such as Bageshwar, and in the Tibetan plateau, such as Gyanema and Gartok. The exports from the plains consisted of cloth, dyes, guns, and sugar, among other goods, and the imports included horses, Tibetan mastiffs, and borax. Borax was a material used in refining gold. The Kumaon-Garhwal region probably did not have gold mines as was believed by the Mughal chronicles, but there was a small-scale industry in gold washing along some of the rivers. The "antiquity of many of these items may be traced to a much earlier period [than 1800]," one study suggests.[56] Nevertheless, the export items that figure in the preceding list were partly supplied by British goods imported into Calcutta.

[55] H. C. Rawlinson, "On Trade Routes between Turkestan and India," *Proceedings of the Royal Geographical Society of London* 13(1), 1868–69, pp. 10–25 (quote on p. 13). See also, Janet Rizvi, "The Trans-Karakoram Trade in the Nineteenth and Twentieth Centuries," *Indian Economic and Social History Review* 31(1), 1994, pp. 27–64.

[56] Maheshwar P. Joshi and C. W. Brown, "Some Dynamics of Indo-Tibetan Trade through Uttarākhanda (Kumaon-Garhwal), India," *Journal of the Economic and Social History of the Orient* 30(3), 1987, pp. 303–17.

Compared to these two routes, commerce in the eastern Himalayas was much less integrated with trade in the plains, confining itself to supplying local needs for subsistence. The Indo-Burma-China frontier, nevertheless, was growing in significance for a different reason, prospecting for tea, as we will see in Chapter 6.

Conclusion

It is possible to boil down the myriad forms of enterprise tried out in the first half of the nineteenth century into two key words, "experiments" and "consolidation." There were experiments with institutions, with law, and with knowledge and ideas. And there was consolidation of occupational groups, of foreign capital, of Indian merchants, and of Indo-European entrepreneurship in manufacturing. There were many failures and much unfinished business, too.

A new factory producing iron and steel in 1840 would need to build railways and canals, enter protracted negotiations on mining or land acquisition at a time when property rights had been redefined and allocated, wait indefinitely for machines to arrive and then have them faultily assembled, and face rising costs of purchasing charcoal if a charcoal-using factory or of transporting coal if a coal-using one. In the presence of the high costs of so many complementary inputs, it is little wonder that so many businesses failed. The role of the state in the early nineteenth century was minimal, among other reasons because many actors within the state understood the barriers that private capitalists needed to overcome. By contrast, in the second half of the nineteenth century, the prospect of effective state intervention brightened as the costs of accessing machines, material, and labor declined. Increasingly, the only remaining barrier to the success of large-scale enterprise was the cost of capital.

Business risks were still high in the second half of the century. But some things had changed. Unlike in earlier periods, with a new regime in place that was in principle more interventionist than the East India Company from 1858, the resolution of disputes invited legislative and administrative action or, at any rate, discussion about the appropriate policy (see also Chapter 7). Furthermore, with the construction of the railways, trade costs were brought down dramatically. The land-based foreign trade that had been trying to establish itself entered an era of lower costs and smaller risks. It is this era of globalization that is considered in Chapter 6.

6   Trade, Migration, and Investment, 1850–1920

Although dependent on the taxation of landed wealth like any other regime in the past had been, the British Empire was especially interested in overseas trade. India was beginning to play a major role in Britain's own engagement with the world economy, as a market for its manufactures, chiefly textiles, machinery, and metals; as a source of food, unskilled labor, and industrial raw materials; and as a destination for capital going into the railways, tea, jute, and banking. Britain, likewise, was crucial to a vast range of new capitalistic enterprises run by the Indians, and for sustaining the consumption of cheap cotton cloth.

A new land and sea frontier for Britain had opened up in Burma after the conclusion of the Anglo-Burma wars (1823–26). The conquest yielded the British control of the Tenasserim isthmus and the Arakan state, and allowed the British to become entrenched in Rangoon and Pegu. The direct value of these territories for private commerce was not great, but the conquest made the prospect of overland transactions between India and China brighter than before. In the 1820s, the attempt to grow tea in India led enterprising Europeans to take an interest in the Burmese trade with Yunnan. The immediate economic possibility, however, was located in Burma itself. Lower Burma was beginning to become a commercial hub, not least because of the diversion of Burma's cotton exports from the overland China route to overseas trade. The protection of these newly developed commercial interests fueled further rounds of colonization in Burma, continuing up to 1885.[1]

In the second half of the nineteenth century, there was a large increase in the volume of long-distance trade from India. The distinctive aspect of this change was not only a rise in the scale of foreign trade, but a conjoint rise in domestic and foreign trade. Railway construction integrated the land and the sea by making possible a large decrease in the carriage costs of low-valued high-bulk commodities. Steamships connected coastal trade

[1] Eric Tagliacozzo, "Ambiguous Commodities, Unstable Frontiers: The Case of Burma, Siam, and Imperial Britain, 1800–1900," *Comparative Studies in Society and History* 46(2), 2004, pp. 354–77.

with international trade in a manner that would have been hard to conceive in the days of the East India Company. As this chapter will show, the region continued to be a base for both global capital and global labor; but capital turned toward export-oriented plantations within India, and mobile labor looked for jobs in the niches opening up within the region, in Assam, Burma, and Ceylon, among other destinations.

Bridging the land with the sea

Between 1850 and 1900, the world's fifth largest railway network developed in India. The discussions and the policies leading up to the beginning of railway construction is a well-researched subject and can be omitted here.[2] It bears repeating, though, that one of the main motivations behind the project was interest of the cotton trade, and that the expectation was largely fulfilled, as we will see.

Some numbers illustrate the extent of the change. The Gangetic plains had some of the principal highways for carrying goods of the prerailway era. An estimate for 1844 placed the quantity of goods carried by boats on the river on the Calcutta-Delhi route at 3 million tons, whereas in 1900, the East Indian Railway conveyed 10 million tons of goods along the same route.[3] Of the total tonnage carried by railways in 1900, 43 million, the greater part came from regions that had no serviceable all-weather roads, nor, in 1844, any worthwhile bulk trade. In the Deccan plateau, the cargo carried in domestic trade increased from a few thousand tons in 1790 to at least 8 million tons in 1900. These numbers for domestic trade parallel an equally impressive rise in shipping tonnage. The total tonnage capacity of ships entering the three major ports (Bombay, Calcutta, and Madras) was below 100,000 in 1800, totaled 1.2 million in 1844, and reached 4.2 million in 1900.

Considerable scholarship exists on the effects of the railways on trade and business enterprise in India.[4] It is well known from existing studies

---

[2] See, for example, Daniel Thorner, *Investment in Empire: British Railway and Steam Shipping Enterprise in India*, Philadelphia: University of Pennsylvania Press, 1950.

[3] Anon., *Indian Railways and Their Probable Results*, London: E. Newby, 1848, p. xviii.

[4] M. B. McAlpin, "Railroads, Prices, and Peasant Rationality," *Journal of Economic History* 34(3), 1974, pp. 662–84; I. D. Derbyshire, "Economic Change and the Railways in North India, 1860–1914," *Modern Asian Studies* 21(3), 1987, pp. 521–45; John Hurd II, "Railways and the Expansion of Markets in India, 1861–1921," *Explorations in Economic History* 12(4), 1975, pp. 263–88; Mukul Mukherjee, "Railways and Their Impact on Bengal's Economy, 1870–1920," *Indian Economic and Social History Review* 17(2), 1980, pp. 191–208; Tahir Andrabi and Michael Kuehlwein, "Railways and Price Convergence in British India," *Journal of Economic History* 70(4), 2010, pp. 351–77.

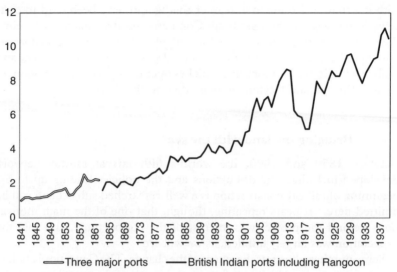

6.1. Shipping tonnage (million) entering Indian ports, 1841–1939.
Source: *Statistical Abstract Relating to British India*, various years.

that the railways cheapened the cost of cargo in domestic trade by a large factor. But how large was the savings? And who gained?

Data for one region, the western Gangetic plains, suggest that the cost savings depended on the mode of transportation available as an alternative to the railways.[5] In general, boats could be hired more cheaply for the carriage of bulk goods than could carts, but carts were cheaper than pack bullock caravans. But the prospect of internal navigation was more or less limited to the Gangetic plains, especially its eastern parts. Before the railways, therefore, the east-west traffic followed the Ganges up to Mirzapur and then switched to carts or caravans to go further west, south, or north. Along this riparian highway, which connected major commercial centers like Calcutta, Patna, Benares, and Mirzapur, cost of carriage was low enough to effectively compete with the railways long after the railways came into existence. It was only after the rail network had acquired sufficient scale, and was partially nationalized, that the rail tariffs would come down to competitive levels. This stage was not reached until 1900. Not only was the eastern Gangetic plains fortunate to have all-weather waterways, it also had some of the best roads for wheeled traffic (see Table 6.1). Even in relation to the cost of hiring carts, the railways made a relatively small difference.

[5] Derbyshire, "Economic Change."

Table 6.1. *Transport cost of cargo (Rs. per ton per mile).*

	1804[a]	1828[b]	1845–49	c. 1860	1854–60 (rail)	1920 (rail)
Bengal and Bihar, goods by bullock caravan	0.270				0.047[h]	0.010[i]
Bengal and Bihar, riverboats	0.017	0.010	0.042[c]	0.058[g]		
Bengal and Bihar, rice by bullock cart	0.052			0.140[g]		
Mirzapur–Calcutta by bullock cart			0.084[d]			
Bombay-Deccan, transporting cotton by bullock caravans			0.250–0.470[e]		0.052[i]	0.014[j]
Berar, transporting cotton by bullock caravan			0.630–0.840[e]			
Narmada Valley, to Bombay by cart			0.185[f]			
Assam, hauling coal by river to Bengal seaport				0.017[h]	0.047[i]	0.010[j]
Assam, long-distance carriage				0.053[h]		
Madras, carriage of government store			0.229[c]		0.052[i]	0.014[j]

[a] H. T. Colebrooke, *Remarks on the Husbandry and Internal Commerce of Eastern India,* Calcutta, 1804, p. 164. Rice from the interior of Bihar and Bengal to the port.

[b] Montgomery Martin, *The History, Topography, and Statistics of Eastern India,* London: W. H. Allen, vol. 1 of 2, p. 385. Carriage of grain from Patna to Calcutta.

[c] Standard rate of boat hire (converted into per ton/mile) on Ganges and Hooghly, c. 1844. Anon., *Indian Railways and Their Probable Results,* London: E. Newby, 1848, p. xliii; Appendix, p. xxii.

[d] J. Forbes Royle, *On the Culture and Commerce of Cotton in India,* London: Smith Elder, 1851, p. 269.

[e] The bullock-cart transportation cost for cotton from Khamgaon to Bombay in 1847 was, according to sources cited by Amalendu Guha, between 0.6 to 1.01 d. per lb., or Rs. 0.25–0.47 per ton per mile. "Raw Cotton of Western India: 1750–1850," *Indian Economic and Social History Review* 9(1), 1972, pp. 1–41.

[f] British Parliamentary Papers, 1863 (372) "Doctor McClelland's Report on Coal-Fields of India," 1868, p. 65.

[g] Mukul Mukherjee, "Railways and Their Impact on Bengal's Economy, 1870–1920," *Indian Economic and Social History Review* 17(2), 1980, pp. 191–208.

[h] R. N. C. Hamilton, "Note on the Transport of Coal from the Pits at Sonadeh to Bombay, by the Nerbudda," *Journal of the Asiatic Society of Bengal,* 1849, pp. 594–600.

[i] R. D. Tiwari, *Railways in Modern India,* Bombay: New Book, 1941, p. 133.

[j] S. C. Ghosh, *A Monograph on Indian Railway Rates,* Calcutta: Government Press, 1918, pp. 40–41; the rates are quoted per maund per mile, but these were scaled by distance, "class" (most bulk goods were placed in the lowest-fare class), and weight carried; different railway systems applied different minimum rates. In the reconstructed figures, only for the lowest-tariff class, a standard weight of 500 maunds is the tariff per mile taken; figures reflect differences in the railway system.

The river-rail story was quite different in regions that depended mainly on carts and caravans, the Deccan peninsula, for example. This region had few navigable rivers and depended on carts and caravans to transport goods. Bullock carts provided economies of scale and were cheaper, on average. But caravans were used far more extensively in carrying grain and cotton because of the scarcity of roads fit for wheeled traffic in the uplands. Because of these differences, before the railways, the cost of carriage varied widely between regions. In the 1840s, thanks to a heavy dependence on bullock caravans, the cost of carrying cotton from central or southern India to the ports could be from five to twenty times greater than the cost of carrying grain in northern India. The railways had, relatively speaking, a deeper impact in these regions. It was here that the cost of carriage dropped the most and the earliest. This vast region contained some of the best cotton tracts.

The Deccan peninsula was the main field of operation of the Banjara caravan runners. An East India Company document placed the scale of the Banjara caravans that carried grain, cotton, and salt between North and South India and across the Deccan plateau at 170,000 bullocks (c. 1790).[6] According to H. T. Colebrooke, the average load carried by a medium-sized bullock was 75 kg (the maximum load being 140 kg, but only for short journeys and exceptionally large animals).[7] The carrying capacity of the overland system, possibly at the very peak of its career, was a little over 10,000 tons. In 1901, goods carried by the two main South Indian railway companies (Madras and Southern Mahratta, and South Indian) totaled over 5 million tons. If we add the Great Indian Peninsular railway, which connected Bombay with the western part of the Deccan plateau, the number would rise to 8 million tons. This was an increase of 800 times. Surely these comparisons would be misleading when the caravans carried valuable goods, for example, horses across the trans-Himalayan routes. But with items like grain, salt, cotton, and sugar, a rise in volume is a fair measure of a rise in the value of trade. Colebrooke's conclusion, that "except in cities, the bulk of the people is every where subsisted from the produce of their own immediate neighbourhood," held true for regions far away from navigable rivers.[8]

---

[6] Cited by John Briggs (Persian interpreter in the Hyderabad court), "Account of the Origin, History, and Manners of the Race of Men called Bunjaras," *Transactions of the Literary Society of Bombay*, London: John Murray, 1819, vol. 1, pp. 170–97.

[7] H. T. Colebrooke, *Remarks on the Husbandry and Internal Commerce of Bengal*, Calcutta, 1804, p. 163.

[8] Colebrooke, *Remarks*, p. 161.

Trade cost depended not just on the cost of freight but also on the amount of time saved. Here again, the extent of the change was on average more impressive in the Deccan. Cotton from the Narmada Valley to Bombay, for example, took 8–12 weeks to traverse the distance of 700 miles, whereas the railway train took 24 hours to cover it. Costs also depended on the depth of the rental market. Colebrooke mentions that the costs of carriage varied according to whether the means of transport were owned by the transporters or hired by them.[9] In the Banjara case, traders by and large did not own the means of transport, but the specialized transport operators did. Although river transport was cheap, the risk of damage from exposure to rain, damp, and piracy was so great that merchants often treated 20 percent of the value of the cargo as a possible waste. Not surprising, then, "the insurance from Calcutta to Rajmahal (distance 200 miles) is as high as from London to Calcutta" in 1844. To avoid the insurance, many merchants would send goods by roads despite the high costs.[10]

A similar saving in time and money was evident for passenger traffic. A rich merchant traveling from Calcutta to Benares in 1844 had the choice between taking a steamboat on the Ganges, which would cost Rs. 400 to hire and one month's journey, or finding a seat on the East India Company's horsedrawn mail carriage along the Grand Trunk road, which would cost Rs. 500 and eight days. The train ticket in 1860 cost Rs. 50 for a middling class, and the journey was completed in twenty-six hours.[11] In 1844, an estimate placed the number of passengers traveling by road or river between Calcutta and Delhi at about one million. In 1900, the two major railways that served this route carried more than 29 million passengers.[12]

Economists writing on the aggregate effects of the railways on the Indian economy have paid particular attention to market integration. The definition of integration is a fall in the cost of moving goods as well as the cost of information and transaction between markets located physically far apart. A measure of integration is convergence of prices of the same good between markets. Although prices in regional markets did converge in the late nineteenth century, the role of the railways was probably not large in making it happen.[13] That it was not large should not surprise us. Measurements of the extent of price and wage convergence tended to overlook the fact that the effects were different in

---

[9] Ibid., p. 163.
[10] Anon., *Indian Railways*, p. xliii.
[11] Ibid., p. 42.
[12] Ibid., p. xxi, and *Statistical Abstracts for British India*.
[13] Andrabi and Kuehlwein, "Railways and Price Convergence."

6.2. Opening of the Madras railway, 1856. Possibly the artist's impression based on an eyewitness account, the picture suggests that the opening of a major railway station in the nineteenth century was both a social event and a political spectacle. From the author's collection

scale between northern India and southern India. The drop in direct costs was far larger in the south. That being said, market integration also owed something to nonrailway factors. The telegraph, for example, enabled low-cost and speedier information exchange. The large merchant firms that entered agricultural export trade in the nineteenth century had agents stationed in the interior. More information passed between the branch offices and the head office of these firms. In addition, political consolidation and growth in the insurance business reduced the high insurance costs of the mid-nineteenth century. The main result of the railways, however, was the growth of peasant exports.

From opium to cotton

Opium continued to be a successful export for India until the third quarter of the nineteenth century. But increasingly it was becoming embroiled in a debate over the desirability of the trade. On the one side, a growing international lobby urged the claim of "morality" over the revenue interest

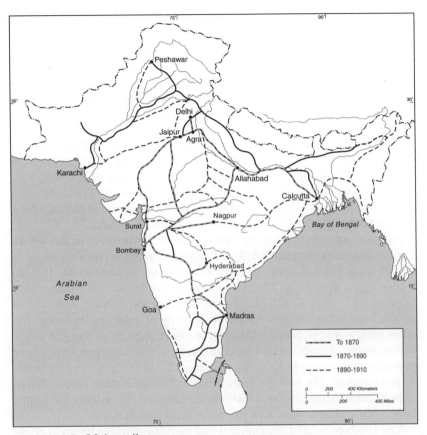

6.3. Major railways.

of the government. On the other side, having made an expensive expenditure commitment, "our Indian administrators are now able to urge the plausible excuse that the abandonment of the traffic would entirely derange the revenues of India, and create a deficit large enough to put an end to all expenditure for public works."[14] The battle continued on into the 1870s, when the volume of Indian exports to China began to fall. It is not obvious that the campaign against consumption and trade was the immediate cause of the decline. Alternative sources of supply from within China and from Persia also contributed to the fall. Only when the

---

[14] Anon. (on behalf of the Aborigines' Protection Society), *The Opium Trade between India and China in Some of Its Present Aspects* (pamphlet), London, 1870, p. 6.

Republican government in China imposed stronger restrictions did the opium trade and revenue finally dwindle.

By contrast, India's cotton trade entered the second half of the century unchanged. It was a large but stagnant trade. And efforts to find a solution to quality and yield continued as before, if with diminishing hope. A second cluster of sponsored experiments took shape in the 1860s in the Bombay Deccan. The aim again was to encourage cultivation of American cotton. Like the earlier experiments, the ones in the1860s also failed. But in this instance, European plantations were no longer actively encouraged. Instead, district administrators tried to induce peasants to switch to different seeds and practices, but the peasants proved reluctant to take what they considered would be undue risks. The mere appearance of a government scientific representative could not break the preference for a known system that produced known, even if small, returns.[15]

Although specific enterprises failed, a slow transformation did set in. Export of cotton between 1825 and 1840 remained on average close to 30,000 tons, still a fraction of American supplies to Lancashire. But the Indian figure was rising. The price of raw cotton fell almost continuously between 1815 and 1840. This fact should suggest to us a diversion of cotton from other markets to exports because of a decline in demand in those other markets. Some expansion in cotton cultivation was also likely. Broadcasting of seeds and mixtures of cotton with other crops, which were practices common in India in the early nineteenth century, became steadily less popular. The saw gin or its variations became more visible. When railway construction in the 1850s again increased the market for Indian cotton, the peasants were well placed to meet that demand.

The 1860s presented the peasants and merchants with a boom in prices of an unprecedented order. The American Civil War (1861–65) created sudden shortages in cotton, Lancashire mills were forced to find ways of using more Indian cotton, and the cotton price in Bombay soared. Before peasants had time to adapt to the new level of demand, local merchants made a killing. And the old problem of adulteration returned with a vengeance. In 1861, the Cotton Supply Association of Manchester, in a memorandum to the government of Bombay, urged the administration to play a role in preventing the adulteration of cotton. On top of the long-term problem of poor cleaning technology, speculation now encouraged the deliberate mixing of dirt and moisture with the cotton in response to the rise in prices. The rumor that Lancashire was willing to pay good

[15] Peter Harnetty, "The Cotton Improvement Program in India, 1865–1875," *Agricultural History* 44(4), 1970, pp. 379–92.

money for any quality product encouraged adulteration. The trade was powerless to control the actors at points of production and was paying high prices for poorer quality.[16]

Eventually, the Bombay Cotton Frauds Act passed in 1863 and made the adulteration of cotton a criminal offense punishable by imprisonment. Because it was a toothless piece of legislation, it produced few convictions. The cheats remained at large, and the act was repealed in 1878. In the end, it was the trade itself that punished the wrongdoers by dropping prices to a fraction of what they were when American supplies resumed. After this ruinous depression, trade slowly regained ground. The adulteration problem, however, persisted until the Bombay and Ahmedabad mills began controlling the trade. At the same time, the export merchants found that the form of their contract at the Liverpool end had changed to their detriment. Unable to predict the cotton's quality after the forward contracts had been entered into, the Liverpool merchants classified all cotton and wheat from India as "fair," that is, inferior grade. The contract acted as a disincentive for those Indian suppliers who were spending money and effort to secure better quality.[17]

Wheat

An almost identical problem to that of the cotton trade, leading to identical solutions, occurred with grain exports. The quantity of grain sent overseas from Calcutta was negligible in the early nineteenth century, not exceeding a few thousand tons in the 1820s, and much of it was carried as ballast.[18] The situation did not change in the remaining years of the East India Company's regime. Steam made some difference to the average volumes in the middle of the century, but a serious increase in rice and wheat exports began only after railway connections opened up between the ports and the interior. Indeed, it was this breakthrough that doomed the Bengal indigo industry by drawing peasants away from that crop.

Unlike in cotton, in the grain trade, British interest in Indian supplies was of a political, as well as commercial, nature. As an officer of the India Office explained, "In case of war, all sources of European wheats might be stopped, and it would be desirable that wheats should be shipped from

---

[16] F. A. Logan, "India's Loss of the British Cotton Market after 1865," *Journal of Southern History* 31(1), 1965, pp. 40–50.

[17] HMSO, *Reports and Papers on Impurities in Indian Wheats*, London, 1888–89, p. 11.

[18] H. H. Wilson, *A Review of the External Commerce of Bengal, 1813–14 to 1827–28*, Calcutta: Baptist Mission Press, 1830, p. 73.

our Colonies."[19] On the commercial plane, imported wheat increased the scope of mixing the flour of different varieties, a strength of European milling and baking businesses compared with American ones. Homegrown wheat was often stored in damp conditions. Imports arrived dry. Mixing the grains was an effective solution to dampness. Above all, imports from the colonies were cheaper than American, Canadian, and Argentinian wheat.

Indian wheat, nevertheless, was available in small quantities for foreign markets before 1873. In 1873, an ad valorem export duty was repealed, with the result that exports, which had not exceeded 17,000 tons until then, increased sharply. The trade would have reached supply constraints thereafter but for continuous expansion in canal irrigation. Although technically classified as rain fed, little of the India crop could be grown on rain-fed land. Wheat was a canal-irrigated crop in Punjab and western Uttar Pradesh. In Sind, wheat was grown on double-cropped lands that received moisture from inundation canals in summer. Between 1881 and 1911, the major expansion of irrigation in Punjab was completed. Overall, the area irrigated by government canals increased from 11 million to 22 million acres.

The surprising feature of the trade was how quickly it seemed to reach a ceiling. In 1880, India had 14 percent of the world's wheat lands (26 million of 192 million acres), and accounted for 11 percent of the world's wheat production (259 million of 2,258 million bushels).[20] The average annual export volume at the turn of the twentieth century was less than a million tons, though in some years, exports were several times that quantity. Ordinarily, not more than 5 percent of the estimated output was exported. The export volume generally fluctuated from one year to the next; these fluctuations were seemingly unrelated to price fluctuations. Why was the trade volume so unstable?

The wheat exported from India contained a level of dirt that put milling machinery at risk. The dirt problem was of a serious order in Calcutta, and only slightly less so in Bombay. Like cotton, wheat was routinely adulterated on its way from the farm to the ports. There were four main agents involved in the process of export. The peasant and the export houses were at the two ends of the chain, and between them were the shipper's agent, who bought grain from the local grain merchants, who, in turn, bought grain from the peasants either directly

---

[19] HMSO, *Reports and Papers*, p. 24.
[20] J. F. Unstead, "Statistical Study of Wheat Cultivation and Trade, 1881–1910," *Geographical Journal* 42(3), 1913, pp. 254–73.

or through the mediation of another set of dealers. The export houses lost money because of the adulteration and were absolved of responsibility on the matter. The peasant sold the wheat in small lots in which adulteration would easily be spotted.[21] The agent of the export house had too much to lose by manipulating the quality of the grain. That left only one actor, the traders who lived in the small market towns and who were ordinarily too remote from the shippers to attract any penalty. They were not only the agents responsible, but they proved impossible to be brought to book, or worse, to be dispensed with.

Being unable to deal with the matter, the trade imposed a 5 percent "refraction" tax on the price of Indian grain. Once the charge was in place, it made economic sense for everyone to mix loose earth into consignments of wheat. The traders did this now with a clear conscience. Because the system refused to discriminate between cleaner and dirtier wheat, suppliers of cleaner wheat either stopped selling their wheat or even growing it altogether or started mixing dirt into their consignments. Adulteration was a specialist field of knowledge; some forms of impurities were relatively easy to clean by steam-threshing machines, and some were not. Straw, chaff, and earth were one thing; grains commonly used as cattle feed were another. The machines were not able to clean fine grain mixed with coarse grain. The manager of Dumraon estate in Bihar, one of the suppliers to the Ralli Brothers in Patna, explained how he had to discover from the market what articles should be mixed to make the wheat impure exactly to the order expected by the trade.[22]

Crashes in the indigo business and the decline of opium trade in the second half of the century had bankrupted many of the country traders. But some of the firms survived these episodes and diversified from trade into mining, plantation agriculture, and manufacturing.

Capital: Global firms

By the end of the nineteenth century, almost all of the surviving agency houses had reinvented themselves as manufacturers, financiers, and transporters of cargo. They were no longer an offshoot of the world economy tied to the business of the chartered East India companies;

[21] HMSO, *Reports and Papers*, p. 9.
[22] Ibid., p. 10.

rather, they were actors in a world economy founded on coal, cloth, colonies, and private enterprise.

Recent scholarship suggests that the pattern of entry in the early nineteenth century and the pattern in the second half of the nineteenth century were somewhat different. In both periods, Asian markets and materials attracted merchants based in Britain. In both times, a substantial number of firms maintained a simultaneous presence in the imperial port towns and treaty ports, such as Bombay, Calcutta, Singapore, Manila, Canton, Hong Kong, and Shanghai. In the earlier period, entry tended to follow the fortunes of the East India Company in Asian trade and to move into the businesses the company vacated because of the end of its charter. Indigo, opium, tea, silk, and Manchester piece goods were the main articles of trade. In the later period, businesses diversified into manufacturing of various kinds, and the scale of local assets and investments increased greatly. The global firms that entered Asia later in the century knew their trades better and handled risk by specialization and vertical integration. They were less diversified than the earlier generation of agency houses. Their relationship with the empire was not mediated any more by the vexed question of the company.

Managerial style also changed in the late nineteenth century. As Anthony Webster has shown in a study of John Palmer and Company, the personalized style of functioning inside the early nineteenth-century agency houses involved frequent disputes among partners and between European owners and their Indian agents.[23] On average much larger, the global firms of later vintage had a distinct and prominent role for professional managers in relation to the partners and their family members.

One of the leading firms in the second phase was Mackinnon, Mackenzie. It had its beginnings in Glasgow, where William Mackinnon (1823–1893) had begun his career as an employee in an East India trading firm. In 1847, Mackinnon and his friend Robert Mackenzie (d. 1853) went to Bombay and started a company to import cotton goods into India. A major diversification occurred about ten years later, when the firm set up a steam-navigation company to share the growing traffic between Calcutta and Rangoon. Thus began what was to become one of the largest shipping companies in the nineteenth-century world, the British India Steam Navigation Company. Their commercial success was secured

---

[23] Anthony Webster, "An Early Global Business in a Colonial Context: The Strategies, Management, and Failure of John Palmer and Company, 1780–1830," *Enterprise and Society* 6(1), 2005, pp. 98–133.

further on their receiving a mail contract from the government. William Mackinnon's own interests shifted westward, first to the Persian Gulf and later to British East Africa. Within India, Mackinnon, Mackenzie invested in tea estates and jute manufacturing, and was one of the leading managing agencies in Calcutta between 1860 and 1900.[24]

Another Calcutta firm that developed extensive interest in Burma shipping and timber was Gillanders, Arbuthnot. Started in 1833 in indigo and textile trades, it moved into jute and acquired interests in Burma at the end of the nineteenth century. Harrisons and Crosfield started as a Liverpool tea-trading firm in 1844, venturing into tea estates in Ceylon and South India only in about 1900. By then, the firm's distribution network was spread over a large area in Asia and the Pacific, and the company was beginning to produce rubber in Malaya. It abandoned the partnership form quite late, only in 1908. Gillanders, Arbuthnot was an associate of a Liverpool-based merchant firm, Ogilvy, Gillanders, with interest in India. The association ended in 1842, when Thomas Ogilvy left the partnership. Gillanders, Arbuthnot, thereafter, grew firmer roots in Calcutta.

One of the more interesting groups was that of David Sassoon (1792–1864), a member of the loosely constituted eastern Mediterranean Jewish diaspora, who established a base in Bombay and joined the opium trade in 1830. His son Elias David (1820–1880) sailed for Canton and Hong Kong a year after the Opium Wars ended. The firm that the son set up, E. D. Sassoon, was the leading agent of the opium trade during the middle decades of the nineteenth century. The Sassoon family were social leaders in the small community known as Baghdadi Jews; nearly all members of this group were connected in some fashion with E. D. Sassoon. The Sassoons cultivated their oriental image even as they supplied unconditional political support to Britain and the empire. In their ambiguous position as an ethnic cartel, the Sassoons in Bombay and Shanghai somewhat resembled the Parsis. Although beginning in the opium trade, the Sassoons started textile mills in Bombay when opium's future became uncertain.

Not accidentally, the Asian identity of the global firms grew in the late nineteenth century, in effect through the conscious political and social positioning of a new generation of partners. Mackinnon, Mackenzie, and

---

[24] J. Forbes Munro, "From Regional Trade to Global Shipping: Mackinnon, Mackenzie & Co. within the Mackinnon Enterprise Network," in Geoffrey Jones, ed., *The Multinational Traders*, London: Routledge, 1998, pp. 48–65; Munro, *Maritime Enterprise and Empire: Sir William Mackinnon and His Business Network, 1823–1893*, Woodbridge: Boydell Press, 2003.

Jardine, Matheson are cases in point. The Baghdadi Jews again produced colorful orientalist characters. From the Sassoon umbrella emerged the Shanghai millowner Silas Aaron Hardoon (1851–1931), for some time a partner in E. D. Sassoon and in later life a symbol of interfaith relations thanks to his marriage to a Chinese Buddhist. Another community member, I. R. Belilios, was a Hong Kong industrialist who had been born in Calcutta and maintained links with both cities. Such a hybrid characterization was perhaps possible only in the port cities from which the colonial global firms operated. Cultural practices, furthermore, were useful as mechanisms to hold "transregional networks" of business together.[25]

Although fierce critics of the East India Company as long as the company lasted, these firms provided a bulwark of support for the British Empire in Asia, for their own survival depended on the political ties that connected Hong Kong, Singapore, and Calcutta. In the late nineteenth century, leading figures in Asian firms like Mackinnon, Mackenzie or Jardine, Matheson played prominent roles in British politics and shaped opinions on colonial expansion. In doing this, the individuals often used a reconstructed oriental identity. They were British in political sympathy, sometimes British in origin, but self-consciously Asian in business and managerial practices and experience. It was their knowledge of and rootedness in Asia and Africa that made them influential in the political mainstream.

Global banking

International trade gave an impetus to international banking. Banks in India were prohibited from transacting in foreign exchange, which was at first monopolized by the East India Company and later allowed under license. A pioneering "exchange bank" was the Bank of Western India, established in Bombay in 1841. The bank soon had branches in Colombo, Calcutta, Hong Kong, and Singapore. The bank later acquired a royal charter and was renamed the Oriental Bank. The charter empowered the bank to operate in India without the company's authorization of its status. When in 1853 the Chartered Bank of India, Australia, and China was incorporated, the Company raised obstacles to the grant of a royal charter. Another bank, the Mercantile Bank of Bombay, had started in 1853 and

[25] C. Plüss, "Baghdadi Jews in Hong Kong: Converting Cultural, Social and Economic Capital among Three Transregional Networks," *Global Networks* 11(1), 2011, pp. 82–96.

6.4. "Coast cruiser" off Coromandel, early-1900s postcard. The picture represents one of the standard sailboats that engaged in coastal trade in southeastern India. © Images of Asia

received a charter in 1857. With the end of the East India Company's rule in India (1858), the discord over royal charters ceased. With the opening up of Japan to Western trade (1853), the business of international banking expanded in the Asia-Pacific region. By 1900, these banks formed a network of branches that interlinked every maritime city of the British Empire in Asia.[26]

These banks were established by merchants engaged in foreign trade, usually with the tacit support of individual administrators. Their custom consolidated the reputation of other trading firms. Bills drawn on Indian importers of foreign goods would usually come for collection to the Indian branches of exchange banks. The acceptance of a trade bill by a major bank conferred on the purchasing firm a standing in the market. The main business of the exchange banks, however, was in financing exports. The India Office sold Council Bills in London, which the banks purchased,

[26] Geoffrey Jones, *British Multinational Banking, 1830–1990*, Oxford: Clarendon Press, 1993. See also Tirthankar Roy, *The Economic History of India, 1857–1947*, 3rd ed., New Delhi: Oxford University Press, 2011, on the operation of the exchange system in colonial India.

6.5. Boat in Madras going out to a ship, 1876. Compared with the building of the railways, harbor construction started late and hesitantly. Even as late as the nineteenth century, the major ports in India did not have all-weather harbors. In Madras, a pier was not rebuilt until the 1880s (an earlier and weaker construction had been blown away by a storm). Until then, *masula* boats were used to transport cargo and passengers between the shore and the ships. From the author's collection.

sent to India, redeemed at the Treasury, and used to finance trade demands for money. The receipts in London were used to meet the government of India's obligatory payments to Britain on account of pensions and interest on debt. Alternatively, the banks could also buy gold and silver in London, ship it to India, and use these as a means of payment in foreign trade transactions (that is, to redeem the bills of exporting firms). However, the bullion business of the banks was less connected with monetary transactions and rather more with nonmonetary demand for gold and silver in India. Yet a third method for remitting money was to buy sovereigns and ship them to India to be exchanged in the Treasury for the rupees necessary to purchase the exporters' bills.

Labor

Like capital, in the late nineteenth century, the channels of labor supply turned toward homegrown businesses. The bridge between these new employments and the overseas ones was again European firms.

The cost of journeying by railway and ship fell drastically between 1850 and 1900, encouraging more migration and more seasonal migration. In overseas markets, a government-appointed emigration agent oversaw the traffic by hiring undercontractors. But increasingly, private recruitment overtook the operations of the public office. As long as the contracts went through a registration process, the private agents were allowed freedom not only to recruit but also to change the terms of the contract. The 1860s brought in new laws, for the business of supplying labor had grown to be almost uncontrollable. A series of disasters seems to illustrate this point.

In 1861, a cholera epidemic caused havoc on board a ship carrying several hundred passengers. There were also constant complaints that some of the professional recruiting agents located "upcountry" had kidnapped youth from wealthy families and released them on payment of a ransom. In 1871, a particularly nasty case of kidnapping came to light and reopened the debate about recruitment and voluntary agency. On August 21, 1865, the ship *Eagle Speed* left Port Canning and was traveling along the river Matlah when the steam tug that was pulling it ran aground and the 262 people on board all perished. Investigators found that the ship's officers and crew were all down with sickness and the tug not fit for the job, and that Port Canning was a dangerous point of embarkation. At about the same time, a fire on board the *Shah Jehan* took 300 lives. In 1864–65, a typhoid epidemic on board several ships bound for the West Indies killed almost a third of the passengers. In 1869, a "fever" outbreak on board the *Shand* killed almost half the people on board. Subsequent investigations revealed that many among those who died had already been ill or weak when they embarked. The first indication that emigration had become an escape route for the famine stricken was in evidence.

But the news was not all bad. Nor was it the case that emigration was the result of "push factors" alone. The first systematic surveys of returnees from the West Indies brought to light "what can be earned by a frugal, industrious immigrant."[27] From British Guiana, four thousand returnees interviewed in 1869–70 had brought with them, in cash, bills, and gold,

---

[27] Report of the Emigration Board, cited by British Parliamentary Papers 1874 (314), *Mr. Geogheghan's Report on Coolie Emigration from India*, London, p. 66.

Rs. 300 each, which was the equivalent of eight to ten years of wages in agriculture at the time. From Trinidad, thirty-five hundred emigrants returned with Rs. 166 each. Individual ships surveyed in 1869 revealed even higher figures per head. The Mauritius numbers were unavailable, but were believed to be considerably smaller. Whereas individual accidents on ships could result in high mortality, partly because the ships had grown bigger, average mortality on board in the 1860s was relatively low at 1–3 percent. The net emigration continued to be high, suggesting that a large majority of those who completed their indenture stayed on in the colony. Surveys done in Mauritius showed that about two-thirds of the people in that class reengaged with a new employer or with the old one. However, the decision to reengage was not always a voluntary one. The requirement that those who had completed their indenture should carry photo passes and those with an employer carry their contracts, or face conviction, created a perverse incentive to get back into indenture. But the positive incentive to stay on in the colony was growing too.

In the last quarter of the nineteenth century, several new destinations began to receive greater numbers of Indian immigrants, including Ceylon, Malaya, Fiji, Burma, and South Africa (Natal). Mauritius, Trinidad, and British Guiana, which had dominated the first thirty years of migration, received comparatively smaller numbers. The shift had much to do with the changing fortunes of sugar as an article of international trade. Sugar export in Mauritius reached its peak of 68,000 tons in 1860 and began to fall thereafter. In the first decade of the twentieth century, the average sugar export was about 30,000 tons. This story was repeated in Guiana and Trinidad. Only Fiji, where migration of indentured Indian workers began in 1882, continued to expand in sugar. Some of the new destinations produced and exported new consumer and industrial goods such as coffee, tea, rubber, minerals, and grain. Burma exported rice, Malaya tin and rubber, and Ceylon and Assam tea. The term-expired Indians in the older sugar colonies were growing rice, by contrast, in their own private plots.

In some of these new and later destinations, capital chased labor, in a pattern resembling European migration to the New World. In Burma, Ceylon, East Africa, and Malaya, the migrants included relatively few workers under contract, and more workers recruited by headmen, as well as bankers, traders, and financiers. In these colonies, European employers did not recruit Indian laborers through agents. Rather recruitment became an Indian private enterprise, a form of service exported along with many other services. Burma was a particularly appropriate example. In lower Burma, rice acreage increased from half a million hectares in 1860 to three and a half million in 1920, a growth that far outstripped the addition to the local labor force, and needed workers, financiers, and providers of semiskilled services. These streams of services originated mainly in Bengal and South India. Unlike in the other tropical colonies, the flow reversed swiftly after 1930 in the wake of the end of Burma's export boom and a backlash against immigrants.

The societies in the old sugar lands had diversified in livelihood and were pronouncedly South Asian by the end of the nineteenth century. Indians formed not more than 10 percent of the population of Mauritius in 1840; by 1870, the Indians were 60 percent of the population. About a quarter of the Indian population in 1870 had been born in Mauritius. In 1840, 5 percent of the immigrant population had been women. In 1870, 50 percent were women, thanks to the rising number of Mauritius-born Indians. Social conditions, or what contemporary sources called "moral conditions," approached benchmarks of normality in Guiana or Trinidad more slowly than in Mauritius. In the West Indies, the numbers were smaller, and the proportion of women was low. The scarcity of women created a demographic problem. Local births were relatively low per 1,000 among the immigrant population, whereas death rates were initially high.[28] This imbalance called for a constant injection of migrants into the pool to keep the workforce growth steady. In the second half of the nineteenth century, the imbalance was beginning to shrink.

By 1880, the indenture contract was past its peak. There was the beginning of a drift away from the contract toward recruitment by worker-intermediaries. Indian capitalists had taken over the job of sending out people. Legislation in Mauritius in the 1870s removed the restraints on term-expired workers, whereas these restraints had never been strong in the other colonies. As a result, the standard practice of reindenturing the term-expired worker on another standard five-year contract began to fade away. New laws hastened this process by obliging employers to offer one-year contracts to term-expired workers. The more important factor behind the beginning of the end of indenture was the increasing prefer-ence of employers for recruitment through senior workers rather than professional agents. For the employers, such a practice solved several problems – supervision, training, and recruitment – at once, while also making it more likely that whole families rather than single males would join the pool of migrants.

[28] For data on convergence in birth rates in Ceylon, see Great Britain, *Report of the Committee on Emigration from India to the Crown Colonies and Protectorates*, London: HMSO, 1910, p. 30.

The exception in overseas migration in the nineteenth century was Ceylon. Ceylon had a much older history of labor transactions with mainland India than did any of the other colonies to which the Indians migrated. A part of Ceylon's transactions was seasonal and agricultural. Between 1870 and 1900, the scope of permanent migration increased with the establishment of plantations. The number of settled Tamils in Ceylon increased from half a million to a million. In this case, almost all recruitment of the permanent plantation workforce was done outside indenture by headmen, known as kanganies.

Inside India, the Assam plantations were beginning to emerge as a major competing field of recruitment. Here again, the employers were divided in their preference between the indenture and the headman system, and most planters pursued a mixture of the two in the late nineteenth century. That is, the headman recruited relations and friends, but an indenture contract secured the individual worker's legal obligations to serve the plantation. This hybrid system continued until legislation made recruitment by the garden sardar, or team leader, the only legal method of recruitment. In the other emerging recruitment grounds, Burma and Calcutta, there was no indenture to begin with.

The scale of net migration varied considerably between colonies. Clearly, distance was a factor. Few among the Caribbean cohort returned to India. The proportion of returnees was higher for the Mauritius migrants. And the number of those who returned from Malaya constituted 50–80 percent of those who went out. This was the situation also in Burma. Ceylon continued to have both a circulating and a settler component among the migrants. Few attempts were made officially to track the returnees, who quickly disappeared from the field of vision of monitoring agencies. Surveys done in about 1870 with returnees at the Calcutta port showed that, whereas the Caribbean returnees did carry some wealth, the returnees from the Mauritius cohort usually came back with little savings. The colonies were legally obliged to send back those who were destitute or incapable of working and wished to return to India. Such people did not have good things to say about their experience.

By 1920, persons of Indian origin residing outside India numbered more than a million. They formed two-thirds of the population of Mauritius; a third to a half of the populations of Trinidad, British Guiana, Dutch Guiana, and Fiji; and nearly 10 percent of the population in Ceylon, East Africa, and South Africa. In the older settlements, the occupational profile of the immigrants had changed from mainly plantation workers to peasants and retail traders. In the newer settlements, many immigrants came in as merchants. This was especially the case in British Kenya and German

Tanganyika, where Gujarati merchants established retail businesses in the colonial cities. These communities remained sandwiched between the African native population and the European settlers. They lacked both the force of numbers of the one and the privileged status of the other, but made up for it, if imperfectly, with their entrepreneurial spirit. In the older destinations, the indenture contract was a thing of the past. It had never been used in Ceylon and Africa. Where it once was used, individual migration and migration induced by friends or through family channels had taken over. In short, a labor market dominated by local and Indian factors rather than by expatriate capital had emerged.

Postwar research on the history of Indian migration considered whether the societies formed out of the migration had distinct features when compared with the societies that the migrants had left behind. One of the differences observed was the tendency of caste hierarchy to disintegrate in the diaspora.[29] The implicit reference is to the situation of migrants within India who remained "segmented," socially speaking, even after migrating to modern work sites, and with whom this segmentation influenced mobility, on-the-job training, mobilization into unions, and relationships with employers.[30] It seems indisputable that these structures were either weak to begin with or dissipated faster when Indians went abroad to perform labor.

The transformation in social structure can be understood with reference to at least four factors. Three of these characterized the earliest emigrants: the relative equality in economic and earnings status that the early immigrants experienced; the scarcity of women in the nineteenth century, making it impossible to follow restrictive marriage rules; and the fact that the majority of the early migrants to Mauritius and the Caribbean came from the uplands of eastern India, where caste was a weak force to begin with. Adapa Satyanarayana has emphasized another factor particularly applicable to the later migrants – many of them came from the lower castes and adopted migration as a strategy to break out of hierarchical orders.[31] Such discontinuity between societies at origin and societies at

---

[29] For one study, see Elizabeth M. Grieco, "The Effects of Migration on the Establishment of Networks: Caste Disintegration and Reformation among the Indians of Fiji," *International Migration Review* 32(3), 1998, pp. 704–36.

[30] The literature is very large; the interested reader will find brief discussions in Roy, *Economic History of India*, ch. 7.

[31] Adapa Satyanarayana, "'Birds of Passage': Migration of South Indian Labourers to Southeast Asia," *Critical Asian Studies* 34(1), 2002, pp. 89–115.

points of settlement, however, was not necessarily so sharp in the case of the merchant migration and migration to locations (such as East Africa or Ceylon) that allowed frequent circulation between origin and destination of members of the same trading firm.

Conclusion

The differences between the late nineteenth century and the early nineteenth century were striking indeed. Let me illustrate the point with reference to entrepreneurship. The early nineteenth century saw the rise of private merchants from the ashes of the East India Company's interests. These firms mainly did business in traditional goods for intra-Asian markets. In the second half of the nineteenth century, a new breed of global merchant firms came into being who moved further afield, especially into Africa and Southeast Asia. Some of them owned shipping, as the Mackinnon, Mackenzie group did. The late nineteenth century was also quite distinctive owing to the rise of organized banking, stock markets, and corporate law. Unlike the private trade era, when merchants and producers formed distinct classes, in the mill era, the merchant firms were closely integrated with the mill system. The two groups were almost identical and shifted capital from trade to manufacturing and manufacturing to trade all the time. Their own trade costs, therefore, were smaller and more predictable than those of the private traders. This factor also gave stability to the growth of modern businesses in this phase. Market integration and a new breed of commercial actors, in other words, made industrialization more feasible than before.

These conclusions would be welcomed by the classical liberal economists, some of whom saw in India a vindication of their optimism about market integration, as well as by cautious modern-day liberals like the institutional economists. In the historiography of Indian development, however, market integration and nineteenth-century commercialism have been seen in a more or less uniformly negative light. The presence of a colonial state, it is said, distorted the positive potentials of these developments. How do we read the Indian evidence on development in the presence of such divergent views? The next chapter considers this question.

7   Colonialism and Development, 1860–1920

The British Empire represented a watershed in the relationship between India and the world economy, one with far-reaching effects on both enterprise and labor in the region. Yet, the processes by which the empire led to economic change often get obscured in ideological debates about development and underdevelopment. What were these processes? In this chapter, the question is explored. I suggest that market integration via institutional and technological change should be the starting point in this project. It is necessary, however, to begin with a developmental discourse on the empire.

Perspectives on empire

Early theories of economic imperialism, introduced by J. A. Hobson and V. I. Lenin in particular, held that the nineteenth-century European expansion into the tropics expressed a necessity for capitalism to reach out to the periphery in order to avert a falling return to capital in the core. Critics of the view countered that the attraction of the periphery was a more important driver behind capital export than was crisis at the core. Sporadically from the 1950s, and more systematically from the 1960s, Marxists helped place this debate at the heart of the discourse on comparative development. The European empires in Asia and Africa emerged during a period that also saw the onset of modern economic growth in Europe and a rise in economic inequality among regions of the world. Did empires cause inequality? The Hobson-Lenin process did not imply a rise in inequality; in fact, it could very well lead to the transmission of modern economic growth from Europe to the colonized world.[1] The Marxists

---

[1] Apart from being too British and too nineteenth century, the theory implies a hard-to-prove link between empire, crisis, and foreign investment. See D. K. Fieldhouse, "'Imperialism': An Historiographical Revision," *Economic History Review* 14(2), 1961, pp. 187–209.

agreed that there was a link between empires and inequality but disputed the nature of the link.

The scholarship exploring the relationship between imperialism, dependency, "backwardness," and underdevelopment from a Marxist perspective is large.[2] Formative writings by Paul Baran, Walter Rodney, and especially André Gunder Frank considered imperialism to be the main cause of underdevelopment. Interpretations of the mechanism emphasized either exchange relations (trade) or production relations (class) or a mix of both. For example, it was often argued that the power of metropolitan capital, buttressed by the colonial state and by local collaborators, could potentially lead to manipulation of the prices of tradable goods and services. Such a prospect does predict a rise in inequality. Much of this analysis had little in common with classical Marxism except a shared interest in surplus generation through production and surplus appropriation through the exchange process. The varieties of Marxists also shared among themselves a rejection of the modernization theory that attributed comparative development to the divergent internal characteristics of societies rather than to international relations.

It would not be wrong to say that the orthodoxy on India's tryst with the world economy during the raj is even today fundamentally a neo-Marxist story. Studies done within this framework consider that the empire impoverished India by causing deindustrialization, draining resources, and nurturing an exploitative class structure.[3] Economic policy in British India, it is recognized, was guided throughout by the desire to achieve market integration between Britain and India. This drive showed up in attempts to keep Indian commodity markets open to British goods, hold the exchange rate steady, and ensure sufficient export earnings to meet sterling obligations that arose from foreign borrowings and

---

[2] Useful references are R. I. Rhodes, *Imperialism and Underdevelopment: A Reader*, New York: Monthly Review Press, 1971; Jorge Larrain, *Theories of Development: Capitalism, Colonialism, and Dependency*, Oxford: Basil Blackwell, 1990; and Geoffrey Kay, *Development and Underdevelopment: A Marxist Analysis*, New York: St. Martin's Press, 1975. Within analytical economic history, another strand saw colonialism as a complicating factor in the already "semi-feudal" relations in agriculture; see essays reprinted in Amit Bhaduri, *On the Border of Economic Theory and History*, Delhi: Oxford University Press, 1999. The Marxists' enduring contribution was a rejection of "Eurocentrism" and a turning of development into a problem for global history.

[3] Discussions on Indian history in Amiya Kumar Bagchi, *The Political Economy of Underdevelopment*, Cambridge: Cambridge University Press, 1982; Irfan Habib, "Colonialization of the Indian Economy, 1757–1900," *Social Scientist* 1, 1975, pp. 20–53; and Aditya Mukherjee, "The Return of the Colonial in Indian Economic History: The Last Phase of Colonialism in India," *Social Scientist* 36(3/4), 2008, pp. 3–44.

administrative expenditures. As the empire integrated markets, the advanced manufacturing industries of Britain destroyed artisan enterprise in India and induced Indian peasants to produce crops for export.

According to the Marxists, the foreign trade was "forced" on the ordinarily risk-averse peasants by a class alliance of rural moneylenders, noncultivating landlords, and revenue officers. The gains from trade were dissipated in rent, interest, and taxes, impairing the peasants' capacity to invest in land improvement. In turn, the export receipts maintained a payment that India made to Britain on account of interest on debt and a variety of services. This payment was a "drain" of potential investment funds and by implication constrained public investment. It was the availability of sufficient exchange earnings from peasant exports that created the capacity to import the services that were paid for partly out of the government's budget.

The underlying presumption in some variants of Marxism is that the economic system outside Europe had been noncapitalist to begin with. Such a presumption stands largely discarded and would be difficult to fit with this book anyway. That production for foreign markets was "forced" is questioned in studies showing a positive response of peasants' crop choices to profitability.[4] Whether market integration was voluntary or involuntary is usually decided by the choice of theoretical perspective, for few peasants left a testimony suggesting that they had been forced to grow crops for export. The measurement of "drain" is a notoriously crude affair and a problem so much written about that we can leave it alone.

Furthermore, the notion that payments on account of factor services caused Indian underdevelopment suffers from an analytical flaw. The real puzzle about nineteenth-century India was that, within the colonized tropics, India forged ahead by some benchmarks of modernization. A large factory industry, one of the biggest railway and telegraphic systems, and some of the best banks, ports, universities, and hospitals developed in colonial India. Far from deindustrializing, India industrialized. Even the artisanal sector did not do as badly as was often claimed. This development was made possible because many kinds of scarce skills and capital could be purchased from Britain. Nineteenth-century Indian economic growth was reliant on the purchase of services from abroad with money earned by selling goods abroad. A part of these services was tied to the imperial administration, defense, and railway construction. But the major part was payment for services rendered to foreign trade, modern business, education, and health. The so-called drain was not a payment for empire;

[4] See the discussion in Tirthankar Roy, *The Economic History of India, 1757–2010*, 3rd ed., Delhi: Oxford University Press, 2011.

it was the price paid for the gains derived from market integration that the empire made possible. The railways represent a major example of a state-sponsored scheme to connect the ports with the interior. More silently, the empire facilitated private transactions in useful knowledge, in the end adding to the capability and skills of Indian capitalists and workers.

Historians of science and technology might respond with the argument that in the sphere of state-mediated technological transactions, many new ideas did come in by way of railway construction, civil engineering, and medical services; but there was an underlying bias for technologies that helped the colonists rule India.[5] Diffusion of technologies received sponsorship only if the knowledge systems concerned were "useful to the imperialists."[6] In short, the empire did facilitate transactions in knowledge, but the process empowered the expatriates. This pessimistic view on technology merges with a similarly pessimistic view on science. Scientific development in India, according to this position, was a political process. Western science had political authority behind it and manipulated knowledge to serve political ends. "Science, modernization and domination all marched together."[7]

The argument outlined is unduly restrictive. For one thing, it overlooks the public goods character of technologies. The railways may have been created for imperial defense, but once they were built, their use could not be restricted to just that one purpose to the exclusion of, say, profitable

[5] On distorted choice of technology, see Daniel Headrick, *The Tools of Empire: Technology and European Imperialism in the Nineteenth Century*, New York: Oxford University Press, 1981, p. 10. See also for interpretations in this vein, Zaheer Baber, *The Science of Empire: Scientific Knowledge, Civilization, and Colonial Rule in India*, Albany: State University of New York Press, 1996; Ian Inkster, "Colonial and Neo-Colonial Transfers of Technology: Perspectives on India before 1914," in Roy Macleod and Deepak Kumar, eds., *Technology and the Raj: Western Technology and Technical Transfers to India, 1700–1947*, Delhi: Sage Publications, 1995, pp. 25–50; and Inkster, "Science, Technology and Imperialism in India," in S. Irfan Habib and Dhruv Raina, eds., *Social History of Science in Colonial India*, Delhi: Oxford University Press, 2007, pp. 196–228. The "main purpose" of colonial education, Inkster writes, "was not ... transfer of Western ideas and artifacts, but ... transfer of loyalties" ("Colonial and Neo-colonial Transfers," p. 42).

[6] Headrick, *Tools of Empire*, p. 205. See also Roy MacLeod, "Nature and Empire: Science and the Colonial Enterprise," *Osiris* 15(1), 2000, pp. 1–13.

[7] Deepak Kumar, "Science and Society in Colonial India: Exploring an Agenda," *Social Scientist* 28(5/6), 2000, pp. 24–46 (quote on p. 26); Ashis Nandy, *Science, Hegemony and Violence*, Delhi: Oxford University Press, 1990. With science in context, the relationship between colonial rule and colonial modernity is explored in Gyan Prakash, *Another Reason: Science and the Imagination of Modern India*, Princeton, NJ: Princeton University Press, 1999. For a survey of the historiography of colonial science in relation to the modernization project, see David Arnold, *Science, Technology and Medicine in Colonial India*, Cambridge: Cambridge University Press, 2000.

7.1. India, 1920.

private enterprise by Indians. For another, the empire-centered approach to scientific and technological transactions ignores the arena of private choices. Much of the import of technology by the private sector was driven by the profit motive. Knowledge transactions aided market integration, and vice versa.

Empires, markets, and institutions

If empires were not such state-dominated economic systems as Marxists might think, what were they? It is necessary to recognize that what is at stake is a variety of highly indirect effects. The empire in India could hardly have a direct agency in development or underdevelopment, since the colonial state in India was one of the poorest states in the contemporary world. In the 1820s, the average tax per person in the three "presidencies" of India (major administrative units, Bengal, Bombay, and Madras) was less than one-tenth of that in England, and was half or less in relation to almost all the other British colonies, whether located in the temperate or the tropical regions. In terms of tax-per-person or tax–GDP ratio, the relative position of British India worsened in the early twentieth century when compared with the other emerging economies of the time, chiefly Japan and Russia. Geography and climate reduced the productivity of land to exceedingly low levels, and depressed tax collection in turn. The policy of limited interference in local political structures, a form of indirect rule, made it difficult to raise revenues by almost any means other than the land tax. However powerful the raj might pretend to be, its reach as a state was as severely constrained by these factors as that of any pre-European state in India.

The empire shaped economic change in many indirect ways. For one thing, it sponsored the construction of railways as a private enterprise operating under state guarantee. In the long run, however, its record on physical infrastructure was rather poor. Facing a resource constraint, British India perfected a technique of rule that relied on relatively inexpensive public goods. For example, it was a legislating state to a degree unknown in Indian history. The colonial state adapted to its own small size by taking a "night watchman" stance.[8] It saw itself as the means to create enabling conditions for private enterprise to flourish, by offering a single umbrella of property and contract law, security of property, one official language, one leading currency, and uniform channels of transaction in knowledge. By bringing different world regions within one institutional setup, the empire broadened the scope for market transaction. True, the passive stance and limited capacity also restricted the scale of any change that the state could directly shape, and this incapacity can be called a "failure." Still, British India represented a more modern kind of state insofar as it created the economic institutions necessary for global capitalism to function, which should be seen as a "success."

We should not imagine that market integration was a smooth process. It gave rise to unintended effects. It gave rise to discord, as we have seen in earlier chapters. An example of the unintended effect would come from the very first field in which institutional intervention occurred – property rights in land.

[8] Morris D. Morris, "Towards a Reinterpretation of Nineteenth-Century Indian Economic History," *Journal of Economic History* 23(4), 1963, pp. 606–18.

Agriculture: Markets and institutions

The challenge of raising money to finance ongoing warfare presented itself almost as soon as the East India Company assumed effective control over the revenues of eastern India (1765). Land supplied more than 80 percent of the revenues. Therefore, efforts to overhaul the taxation system focused on the structure of landed property. Although the peasants' right to their landed property was generally secure, the peasants shared the right with their tax-collecting landlords, called zamindars. This situation made the landlords too powerful an agent in the fiscal system. More than that political anxiety, there was also a growing realization that the entanglement of rights had made landed property unmarketable. In theory at least, market transactions could not play a role in correcting inefficiencies in the use of land.

In 1793, after a series of failed experiments, the British governor-general in India, Charles Cornwallis, converted private rights to land into a proprietary right defensible in a court of law. The move took the tax-collecting powers away from armed landlords and gave them to the state. In other words, it made the obligation to pay revenue a legal-contractual matter rather than a political one, made private property ownership the only legally recognized right on land, and tried to create incentives for private investment in land by this means. Ironically, circumstances forced the company to award the new property rights to the old tax-collector elite, a mix of warlords and merchants, turning the peasants into a body of rent-paying tenants of landlords. This arrangement, which came to be known as the zamindari system, or Permanent Settlement, was different from the land rights introduced in western, southern, and northern India. When these territories were acquired, property right reforms were done in a state of greater information and confidence. In these regions, therefore, the individual peasant or peasant kinship unit was made responsible for taxation and received the property right in exchange. The general principle came to be known as ryotwari.

Critics of colonial law argue that the decision to privilege ownership over user rights disproportionately empowered the landowner over users such as tenant farmers and pastoralists. When the owner was not a peasant, but an "absentee landlord" living off rent, the effect was the empowerment of a parasitical element. Even when the owner was a peasant, the effect was increased inequality, because all customary rights had become insecure in the new regime. Local notables could manipulate the settlement procedure to strengthen their hold over land.[9] The peasant-proprietor borrowed money recklessly using the new collateral, fell into a debt trap, and had to part with income to pay the moneylender. All of these effects pointed to one outcome, that the cultivator would have too little money to invest in land improvement.

These arguments need to be treated with caution. In zamindari areas, peasants were themselves differentiated by the quality of their user rights and were often organized in collectives that were politically strong and economically useful to the zamindar. In ryotwari areas, from where most exportable commodities came, there was evidence of investment and dynamism. Without recognizing these processes, we would not be able to understand the stories of indigo, opium, cotton, and wheat that the two previous chapters dealt with. Whereas the rate of investment in land improvement was undoubtedly low, there can be an alternative explanation of such a low rate, namely, the scarcity of a complementary input, water. The government constructed canals. But canals were feasible in regions, such as the plains of the Ganges or the Indus, where snowmelt rivers supplied large volumes of water throughout the year. They were more difficult to construct in the rivers of the Deccan plateau. Moreover, the high risks and high capital costs of digging irrigation wells in the arid lands restricted private investment in wells.

An obvious difficulty in applying these ideas, therefore, is that the regions had variable experiences, depending on their resource endowments and not only the property rights reforms. The fundamental distinction was that between irrigated and dryland agriculture, which is admittedly a stylized distinction but a useful one nonetheless.

Whether forced or unforced, agrarian commercialization happened on a limited scale. At its peak, only 10–15 percent of crop land was devoted to nonfood exports. Exportable goods came from just a few districts. The rest of the region participated little in the export boom. Exports did create gains for the peasant, however. Standards of living improved, but only in the presence of a rare conjunction of sufficient land, well-defined property rights, cheap water, and access to the railways. Outside the few districts that had this conjunction and that supplied the bulk of exportable wheat and cotton, the quality of land was generally poor, and agricultural production had to adapt to the extremely skewed seasonal distribution of rainfall by means of a concentration on low-valued but sturdy millets. Water scarcity and poor soil characterized much of the region outside the

[9] For an interesting study of this problem, see Neeraj Hatekar, "Information and Incentives: Pringle's Ricardian Experiment in the Nineteenth-Century Deccan Countryside," *Indian Economic and Social History Review* 33(4), 1996, pp. 437–57.

river deltas. Water scarcity in turn limited the possibilities of fertilizer application. The difference in yield between rain-fed and irrigated agriculture varied in the nineteenth century by as much as a factor of four. With less than 10 percent of the cultivated area under irrigation, the rain-fed scenario influenced average yield, making it one of the smallest in the contemporary world. Therefore, even when peasants sold in profitable markets, they sold too little.

Market integration, then, imparted an uneven effect on peasant well-being. As we will see, a similar argument can be made for industrialization.

Factory industrialization

Between 1860 and 1940, employment in factories increased from about one hundred thousand to two million, at an average annual rate of 4 percent. The most growth occurred between 1870 and 1921 (employment growth rate 5.3 percent per year), with the First World War providing a strong boost. The net income produced in factories rose at the rate of 4.3 percent per year between 1900 and 1947, and employment at 3.6 percent.[10] Impressive as the expansion was, factory construction was still concentrated in two sites, Bombay and Calcutta. Between 1860 and 1947, the share of the two cities in employment fell, but it remained high, at over half, even at the end of the span. Why did industrialization happen? Why was it so concentrated?

In common with other parts of the colonized tropics, India did not possess well-developed capital and labor markets in the nineteenth century, nor was its indigenous artisanal tradition poised to experience a technological revolution. It did have cheap labor, some cheap raw materials, and community-bound entrepreneurial resources, but interest rates were high, large-scale labor markets were nonexistent, transportation costs for raw materials were exceedingly high, and merchants did not understand machinery. India's colonial connection was instrumental in overcoming these obstacles. The railways brought down carriage costs, British capitalists and shareholders invested in India, and Bombay's merchants found it easy to hire foremen and buy machinery from the cities with which they already had trading links. The reduction of costs favored those industries, such as textiles, in which India had a relatively strong advantage. In cotton textiles, for example, in the early

---

[10] S. Sivasubramonian, *National Income of India in the Twentieth Century*, Delhi: Oxford University Press, 2000, pp. 201–3, 287–88, 293–94.

nineteenth century, the costs of cotton and labor were low, but the costs of technology and skilled foremen were high. These costs were reduced when the Indian port cities became more closely connected with the British economy after the Suez Canal opened in 1869. In other industries, such as iron and steel production, the required minimum scale of investment was considerably higher than what the limited easing of the capital constraints could sustain, and these industries were slow to develop.

The first industrialists in India had made their money in the Indian Ocean trade, were based in the company cities, and had a history of partnership formed with the private traders who led the Asian maritime trade after the decline of the company. The enterprise and capital engaged in the cotton textile mills of western India, for example, originated among Indian trading communities, members of which had made money in Indo-European trade. The Parsis, for instance, were traditionally not traders or financiers, but artisans, carpenters, and weavers. They turned brokers, merchants, and shipbuilders after European ascendance in Indian Ocean trade. Trading firms frequently performed banking services. There were also specialized banking houses that formed a prominent segment of the business community in Ahmedabad. In the eighteenth century, some of these had been money changers, had issued and discounted bills of exchange, had lent funds to governments, and, occasionally, had taken up revenue contracts, but, in the nineteenth century, they switched to the cotton or the opium trade. When mill construction began in earnest, many individuals who invested in the business had already been engaged in cotton and textile trading, and they traveled frequently between Bombay and Liverpool.

The first steam-powered factory producing cotton yarn appeared near Calcutta in 1817 or 1818 and was set up by a European. But a sustainable factory enterprise in textiles had to wait until a Parsi merchant of Bombay established a mill in 1854, overcoming great odds. It is not surprising that the first attempts began in the 1850s and that the move was undertaken by the cotton merchants of Bombay. Cotton export trade had grown in the previous decades. The railways promised to connect the cotton-growing regions with the port, cutting down transportation time from three months to one day. In the next decade, a spike in cotton prices created enormous gains for the Bombay merchants. Much of the money that they earned was invested in mills once the boom ended. In 1865, there were 10 cotton textile mills, the majority in Bombay. By 1914, the number of mills had risen to 271, and average daily employment was two hundred sixty thousand.

Between 1870 and 1914, the main buyers of Bombay yarn were the handloom weavers in China. The close trading contacts between India and China were in part owed to their proximate locations and compatible resources. The emergence of an India-China axis, however, cannot be fully understood without reference to the role that private traders played in connecting these zones, especially after the East India Company's monopoly trading rights ended. Yet the company continued to force its way into an open trade regime in East Asia. The trade regime consolidated in the second half of the century, and took on a new dimension with the industrialization of Japan.

A broad division of labor was maintained between Lancashire and Bombay in the Indian market for yarn, the former specializing in finer counts of yarn and middle-quality cloths, and the latter in coarser yarn counts and on spinning alone. An "Indianization" of the market began only at about the turn of the century, when Bombay lost the China market to Japan. Mills in Bombay started weaving their own yarn, and spinning and weaving finer counts of yarn. Both these moves brought the Indian mills into competition with the mills in Lancashire.

A growth of comparable magnitude took place in the Calcutta industry of jute processing. The manufacture of jute textiles was even more intimately connected with the globalization process than was cotton. Jute is a natural fiber grown mainly in southern Bengal. It was used as a raw material for sacking cloth. The demand for sacks increased in the nineteenth century in direct proportion to the volume of international trade. Until the 1870s, Bengal raw jute was processed into sacking mainly in Dundee and in Germany. Already, mechanized jute spinning and weaving had started near Calcutta. George Acland's mill in 1855 was the pioneer. In a short while, the Indian industry grew to become a virtual monopoly in the world. As with cotton mills, for the first fifteen years the jute industry faced unstable conditions and slow growth. After 1870, expansion was rapid. Between 1869 and 1913, the number of jute mills increased from five to sixty-four, and employment rose from between five thousand and ten thousand workers to two hundred fifteen thousand.

Whereas cotton mills were a mainly Indian enterprise and shifted toward Indian markets, jute was a firmly European enterprise catering to the world market for packaging. Historians of India have asked why Indian and European business communities specialized in distinct fields instead of working either in partnership or in direct competition. Although both groups shared an equal facility in buying technology, they drew capital from different markets. Europeans raised money from London; Indians raised money from personal resources. Furthermore,

Raw Jute entering Mill. Calcutta.

7.2. Raw jute being unloaded at a jute mill in Calcutta, c. 1900.
The jute mill at this time was owned by European capitalists. Its main
business associates on the production side were the Bengali peasant
and the Marwari jute merchant. The dealings among these disparate
agents were fraught with the kinds of contractual problems common
in Indo-European business for over two hundred years. © Images
of Asia

the Atlantic consumer market was more accessible to the European trading networks, whereas the Indians understood buyers in India and China
better. Europeans relied on indigenous agents for the procurement of raw
material. The Indian industrialists had been raw material traders themselves.[11] These differences were in the making for a long time; the origin,
strategies, and political positioning of the "global firms" discussed in
the two previous chapters set a pattern for European enterprise in late
nineteenth-century India that could not but be outwardly oriented.

Besides jute textiles, plantations provided an opportunity for foreign
capital. The East India Company was keen to sponsor tea growing in India
as an alternative source to Chinese tea and an area of promising employment for its own capital after the textile business ended. One obstacle to

[11] Morris D. Morris, "South Asian Entrepreneurship and the Rashomon Effect, 1800–1947,"
Explorations in Economic History 16(4), 1979, pp. 341–61.

the growth of tea estates in India was scientific and required a search for the right kind of natural habitat for the crop. When this problem was solved, the company ventured into tea production but failed to make any profits from the business. Given the remoteness of Assam, where the estates were thought to offer the greatest promise, there still remained the economic problem of creating a risk-free environment for capital. Estates eventually did start in upper Assam, Bengal, and Cachar, but only after appropriate institutions were set up, as we will see.

Reinvention of the artisan

The empire enhanced the capability of Indian artisans in quite a different way. In this story, Indian consumers played an especially important part. The legacy of the Indian craft workshop that had proven so successful in the eighteenth century is a controversial subject. Nationalist historians believed that the craftsmen of India disappeared because of the competition from cotton cloth and yarn imported from England in the mid-nineteenth century. This was an overstatement, for more than ten million artisans continued in business in 1900, which led to speculation that the market integration somehow strengthened the artisan sector.[12] Later research discovered evidence of a complex pattern of transformation. A number of artisans had changed jobs, lost jobs, or migrated away in the nineteenth century. But there was also considerable survival. Because of differentiated markets for textiles, not all expensive handmade goods competed with the cheap machine-made ones. Those artisans who did not have to compete gained from market integration by being able to access technological knowledge, cheaper raw materials, and export markets.[13]

[12] Morris, "Towards a Reinterpretation."

[13] The alternative view on the economic history of Indian crafts under colonialism, which recognizes that a large segment of the crafts may have gained rather than lost from wider and deeper contact with the world economy, is stated in Tirthankar Roy, *Traditional Industry in the Economy of Colonial India*, Cambridge: Cambridge University Press, 1999; "Acceptance of Innovations in Early Twentieth-Century Indian Weaving," *Economic History Review* 55(3), 2002, pp. 507–32; Roy, "Out of Tradition: Master Artisans and Economic Change in Colonial India," *Journal of Asian Studies* 66(4), 2007, pp. 963–91. See also Douglas Haynes, "Artisan Cloth-Producers and the Emergence of Powerloom Manufacture in Western India, 1920–1950," *Past and Present* 172, 2001, pp. 170–98, and Haynes, "The Labour Process in the Bombay Handloom Industry, 1880–1940," *Modern Asian Studies* 42(1), 2008, pp. 1–45; and Douglas Haynes and T. Roy, "Conceiving Mobility: Migration of Handloom Weavers in Precolonial and Colonial India," *Indian Economic and Social History Review* 36(1), 1999, pp. 35–68.

In the well-researched example of handloom weaving, a revival was aided by the access to knowledge embodied in new tools, machines, and processes. The more successful small tools adopted by the weavers, such as the fly-shuttle slay, the frame-mounted loom, the jacquard, the dobby, the drop-box, and synthetic dyes, had been invented in Europe, many of them in the eighteenth century. These adaptations reduced the costs of production, increased productivity, and enhanced the scope of product differentiation. Between 1900 and 1930, the volume of handloom-cloth production about doubled, even as the number of workers and looms did not change.

Artisanal iron production illustrates the same pattern of differentiated change as the textile industry.[14] Iron ore and charcoal were available along the fringes of the Deccan plateau and in some Himalayan regions. These sites were located far away from the cities and the ports, where the wealthy consumers were based in precolonial India. Iron smelters and blacksmiths lived mainly near the ores and served the agricultural demand for iron tools. These groups were at times miners, smelters, and smiths rolled into one. Because of the small scale and lack of specialization, production costs were high relative to the much larger smelting workshops in Western Europe, but the Indian industry was protected by high transport costs. However, when European iron began to come into India on a large scale in the early nineteenth century, the local industry fell obsolete quite quickly. Wood fuel began to become scarce, as forests were reserved, woods ran out, and alternative demands for wood in construction, shipbuilding, and railways grew.

Interestingly, imports seemed to encourage domestic production of iron goods. The consumption of iron increased from 0.9 kg per capita in 1788 to 3.2 kg in 1914. The proportion of imports in total consumption increased from 30 to 78 percent, but there was still an increase in domestic production to be accounted for. The key to the puzzle is that imports, while destroying the indigenous smelter, made the blacksmiths more competitive than before. The blacksmiths based in the towns served a wealthier clientele. The city, the ports, the barracks, and the public works allowed for greater knowledge exchange between European and Indian artisans. The skilled blacksmith experienced a steady increase in real wages, and village blacksmiths joined the urban foundries and forges when they could. By 1900, in towns located in prosperous agricultural tracts, urban blacksmiths

---

[14] I draw mainly on Tirthankar Roy, "Knowledge and Divergence from the Perspective of Early Modern India," *Journal of Global History* 3(3), 2008, pp. 361–87; and Roy, "Did Globalization Aid Industrial Development in Colonial India? A Study of Knowledge Transfer in the Iron Industry," *Indian Economic and Social History Review* 46(4), 2009, pp. 579–613.

belonged in "a substantial and prosperous class."[15] They procured their anvils from England. The larger of these tools, as well as the steel parts of the chisels and mallets, were "made of English steel, many by the carver himself."[16] Blacksmiths also preferred English plates, dies, and taps – tools they had seen at work in the ordnance factories.[17]

If in iron and textiles, imports replaced the production of inputs by hand methods, in tanning, the world market created a new demand for semi-processed inputs. The preparation of hides was a chemical rather than a mechanical process and remained labor intensive. The labor was relatively cheap in India because the castes and communities engaged in tanning were ordinarily poor and socially marginalized. Furthermore, the abundance of livestock in the region, and the limited domestic demand for leather as well as for meat, also made hides a cheap resource. From the 1860s, the European markets responded to these advantages, and hide export began to increase rapidly. Within a decade, however, concerns were raised about the quality of the chemical processing in the Indian artisanal production. As with cotton and grain exports, the infrastructure and the knowledge required to achieve standardization did not exist in India. The trade reacted to the excess demand by supplying poor quality goods and easily got away with doing so because the individual artisans and leather merchants were so far removed from the more organized segments of the export trade. Eventually, the trade adapted to these disputes by developing steady contractual deals with a newly emerging class of urban factories located in Bombay, Madras, Calcutta, Agra, and Kanpur. These yards became the sites for the limited experimentation in chemical processing and industrial organization that the tanning industry experienced in the late nineteenth and early twentieth centuries.

A distinctive feature of these adaptations in leather related to entrepreneurship. The factory owners in the tanning industry were rarely leather artisans by background, though there were some exceptions in Agra. In the main, they were leather merchants already based in the port cities or at major points on the railways, which was another reason for the concentration in the exporting side of the business. Seemingly, leather processing was considered a degrading industry and therefore was not the preferred mode of employment of capital for many Hindu business groups, leaving

[15] A contemporary report, cited in ibid., p. 58.
[16] J. A. G. Wales, *A Monograph on Wood Carving in the Bombay Presidency*, Bombay: Government Press, 1902, p. 8.
[17] E. R. Watson, *A Monograph on Iron and Steel Works in the Province of Bengal*, Calcutta: Government Press, 1907, p. 34.

entry into the business relatively open. Muslim merchants from northern India became prominent in leather production in the factories. Hakka Chinese immigrants also entered the business in large numbers during World War I, when the demand for Indian leather increased. A small Chinese artisan community had made Calcutta its home for at least a century before the war. An 1850 census of the town reported that the Chinese were engaged mainly in carpentry and found them to be "very industrious," even prosperous, "though not very abstemious," possibly in reference to their gambling.[18] The decisive break for them came with their entry into the leather industry. During the war, the Chinese became the most dominant group in the tannery business of Calcutta.

As in textiles and iron, the relatively skill-intensive finished goods side of the leather industry remained broadly a preserve of traditional artisans.

7.3. The brick building in the middle of the picture, which was closed because of a dispute in the 1980s, is iconic of Calcutta's Chinatown. It housed the Tong On Church on the upper floor and, on the lower floor, the Nanking Restaurant, said to be the first Chinese restaurant in the city. Source: Rangan Datta

[18] Cuthbert Finch, "Vital Statistics of Calcutta," *Journal of the Statistical Society of London* 13(2), 1850, pp. 168–82.

Imported shoes may have destroyed the custom of the handicraftsmen to some extent, but to a larger extent it helped them by creating a new demand for leather footwear among Indian consumers. Import substitution, therefore, was quite rapid and successful. In this process again, the Chinese of Calcutta proved remarkably entrepreneurial. They quickly bridged the gap between tanning and footwear manufacture, which remained wide for the Indian participants in the business, and vertically integrated the two sides. The difficult Sino-Indian relations after a war in 1962 placed great pressure on Calcutta's Chinese community and obscured their successes as a business group from public view. In its own unobtrusive way, the community reinvented itself as restaurateurs in the 1990s.

Science and technology

The examples in the previous section of the reinvention of the artisan tradition share a common emphasis on the cost of accessing useful knowledge. The empire was a facilitator of intellectual exchange. There were three important modes of exchange: European scholarship on Indian culture, European engineering and medicine traveling to India via public construction projects and colonial education, and technological choices made by private business.

The English East India Company embarked on a project of codification of Indian knowledge after the first governor-general, Warren Hastings, decided that the British Indian administration should be based on indigenous institutional traditions. For example, the future system would need to translate and transmit Indian knowledge in order to supply legal professionals to conduct court proceedings. It is often said that the hidden aim of the codification project was a political one. The argument is inspired by Edward Said, who believed that Western knowledge of the East supplied a justification for conquest.[19] The idea fits eighteenth-century European scholarship in its broad aims, but not necessarily in the scope of the output. A great deal of the research actually done on Indian language, literature, and science had no obvious connection with political purpose. Scholars gave the project a degree of autonomy from narrowly administrative uses. These scholars formed a diverse group.

[19] Edward Said, *Orientalism*, New York: Vintage, 1979.

7.4. European gentleman with his language teacher. In the late
eighteenth century, merchants and administrators in Bengal
collaborated with Indian intellectuals to create the foundation for a
legal system based on Indian codes. This collaboration led to loosely
coordinated scholarship on Indian science and culture. © British
Library Board

William Jones, who studied language, and James Mill, who studied
history, were driven by quite different intellectual goals.

The project could not get anywhere without the help of Indian trans-
lators and interpreters. Therefore, what the European scholars wrote about
India was often colored by the perceptions that the Indians held

about themselves and was influenced by that segment of the Indian intelligentsia that was rooted in indigenous systems of learning. In trying to understand European writings on India, historians have recently emphasized the context of collaboration and exchange between the Indians and the Europeans.[20] Another characteristic that distanced the knowledge project from politics was the role of late-Enlightenment sensibilities. For example, a strand in environmental history has seen the eighteenth century botanical research in India as an expression of an unfolding ecological sensibility.[21] An offshoot within this larger enterprise, and one led by the Scottish naturalists, also tried to identify fields in which commerce and science could form profitable collaboration. The East India Company wanted this collaboration to succeed because it saw itself not just as an administrator, but as an administrator that was market friendly.

The earliest example of mutually interactive growth in transactions was in botany, especially in the research by scientists and amateurs leading to a coding of knowledge about Indian plants and medicine.[22] The institutions at the forefront of the project were the Fort William College in Calcutta, established in 1800 to train company administrators; the botanic garden in Calcutta; the Asiatic Society of Bengal; and marginally, the Danish mission in Serampore. Among them, they shared the task of collecting and classifying information about Indian knowledge. The college was also a site of learning at which European scholars endeavored to develop a natural philosophy adapted to the Indian experience. These institutions and individuals within them established links with the Royal Society of Arts and the Kew Gardens. These links were important in the dissemination process. The company's court of directors played a role, if a random one, in the sponsorship of research and publication. *Philosophical*

---

[20] For two recent examples, see Thomas R. Trautmann, ed., *The Madras School of Orientalism: Producing Knowledge in Colonial South India*, Delhi: Oxford University Press, 2009; and Michael S. Dodson, *Orientalism, Empire, and National Culture. India, 1770–1880*, New Delhi: Foundation Books, 2010.

[21] Richard Grove, *Green Imperialism: Colonial Expansion, Tropical Island Edens and the Origins of Environmentalism, 1600–1860*, Cambridge: Cambridge University Press, 1995.

[22] Kapil Raj, "Colonial Encounters and the Forging of New Knowledge and National Identities: Great Britain and India, 1760–1850," *Osiris* 15(2), 2000, pp. 119–34. On the pioneers, especially in botany, medicine, and chemistry, see Mark Harrison, "Tropical Medicine in Nineteenth-Century India," *British Journal for the History of Science* 25(3), 1992, pp. 299–318; and Ray Desmond, *The European Discovery of the Indian Flora*, Oxford: Oxford University Press, 1992. A useful descriptive account that draws connections between early and late nineteenth-century chemical research is Aparajito Basu, "Chemical Research in India during the Nineteenth Century," *Indian Journal of History of Science* 24(4), 1989, pp. 318–28.

7.5. Botanical Garden, Calcutta, c. 1900. The botanical gardens were
started in 1787 by Robert Kyd, an officer in the East India Company's
army and the author of a series of reports on the vegetation along
the banks of the Hooghly. The gardens became a site for experiments
in adapting foreign plants for possible commercial use, including tea,
rubber, and cinchona. © Images of Asia

Transactions, the journal of the Royal Society, published some of the more
influential articles that came out of this project.

As fields of research, medicine, botany, chemistry, meteorology, cartography, and mineralogy were the most visible legacies of this exchange.
The pioneers were not confined to any one of these lines; rather, several
of them made their mark in more than one field. For example, Francis
Buchanan (1762–1829), who was a company surgeon, the director of an
abortive natural history project in India, and a director of the botanic
gardens in Calcutta, published annotated commentaries on works about
South Asian botany; but he became better known for his topographical
and economic surveys of Bengal and Mysore.[23] James Prinsep (1799–
1840), a son of the indigo planter John Prinsep, was an officer of the mint

---

[23] Marika Vicziany, "Imperialism, Botany and Statistics in Early Nineteenth-Century India:
The Surveys of Francis Buchanan (1762–1829)," *Modern Asian Studies* 20(4), 1986,
pp. 625–60.

and an architect of British Indian metrology. He was also a historian and an influential figure behind the Asiatic Society's research and dissemination activities. In his early life, Prinsep was a successful chemist. Both William Roxburgh (1751–1815) and the linguist William Jones (1746–1794) wrote on Indian ayurvedic medicine and its uses, especially for the treatment of ailments caused by local organisms and parasites. Roxburgh, a Scottish ship's surgeon, was associated with the Calcutta botanic gardens and in that capacity produced two treatises, *Flora Indica* and *Hortus Bengalensis*.

If these men were scientists by training, there were others who formed a bridge between science and commerce. What made Roxburgh special among the naturalists was his interest in making commercial plantations work in India. His studies in this direction included research on coffee, teak, tobacco, and hemp. Under Roxburgh's management, the Calcutta Botanical Garden became a laboratory for acclimatizing commercially viable plants imported into India from other parts of the tropical world. James Dinwiddie (1746–1815) was a mediator in international scientific exchanges at the turn of the nineteenth century. While teaching at Fort William College, Dinwiddie transported from China to India the tea plant, as well as a method of making tea. He also carried silkworms and Malayan rubber with him, but his role in popularizing these products commercially is rather more obscure than in the case of tea.

In contrast, several noteworthy individuals belonged mainly to the world of commerce rather than in academics or administration. They joined the scientific project because they had privileged access to observational data that they thought would be useful to business. Henry Piddington (1797–1858), an assayer in the Calcutta port and a man of no formal scientific training, systematized a vast number of observations on the cyclones in the Bay of Bengal that he gleaned from ships' logs and laid the foundation for scientific meteorology in India. Although he called his practical research the "science of cyclonology" and "the law of storms," his intended audience was not scientists, but the merchant marine.

Similar examples of knowledge transmission come from the European plantations in India. Amid the many failures and dead ends in the promotion of commercial plantations, indigo, cinchona, rubber, and tea were instances of a successful marriage between botanical research and high commerce, with the blessings of the company's state in Calcutta. In the case of indigo, knowledge seemed to have traveled from the French to the English colonies through channels that remain somewhat obscure. We do know that some of the early planters were Frenchmen. The research done, especially on cinchona, in the botanic gardens of Calcutta was also reportedly helpful. Cinchona was transplanted from South America to South India slightly later, and rubber, again, was a late nineteenth-century effort, as well as an immediate commercial success.[24]

The story behind tea is better known. Robert Bruce, an East India Company officer and amateur naturalist, started prospecting for tea in the most difficult terrains of Assam soon after the region became a British Indian province (1826). By using the services of a team of peripatetic informants, he collected reports of wild tea that grew in Assam, and he made notes on 120 such sites located within an area of several thousand square miles. He interviewed villagers who drank tea and found that some of them had brought the plant from China. Bruce planted what seemed to him the most promising varieties in eastern Assam, packed the dried leaves into ninety chests, and sent the consignment to London in 1839. Encouraged by these experiments, the first company-sponsored tea estate was started in 1839. John Masters, a poet and the head gardener in the botanic gardens of Calcutta, became the first superintendent of the estate. The estate was a commercial failure, but Masters left his mark on the classification of Assamese flora.

In the second half of the nineteenth century, the imperial connection facilitated mediated knowledge transfers in several areas, including the stationary steam engine, the telegraph, the railways, engineering education, medicine, and medical research and education.[25] Many more and lesser known technological transfers occurred in the marketplace, embodied in imported machinery and hired foreign technicians. The most consequential example of such a transfer was the cotton textile mill industry.

---

[24] Lucile H. Brockway, "Science and Colonial Expansion: The Role of the British Royal Botanic Gardens," *American Ethnologist* 6(3), 1979, pp. 449–65.

[25] Headrick, *Tools of Empire*, and Headrick, *The Tentacles of Progress: Technology Transfer in the Age of Imperialism, 1850–1940*, New York: Oxford University Press, 1990; Inkster, "Colonial and Neo-Colonial Transfers"; Baber, *Science of Empire*; Jennifer Tann and John Aitken, "The Diffusion of the Stationary Steam Engine from Britain to India, 1790–1830," *Indian Economic and Social History Review* 29(2), 1992, pp. 199–214; and S. Ambirajan, "Science and Technology Education in South India," pp. 153–76, Saroj Ghose, "Commercial Needs and Military Necessities: The Telegraph in India," pp. 112–33, and Arun Kumar, "Colonial Requirements and Engineering Education: The Public Works Department, 1847–1947," pp. 216–34, all in Roy Macleod and Deepak Kumar, eds., *Technology and the Raj: Western Technology and Technical Transfers to India, 1700–1947*, Delhi: Sage Publications. See also Satpal Sangwan, "Indian Response to European Science and Technology, 1757–1857," *British Journal for the History of Science* 21(2), 1988, pp. 211–32.

Historians rightly recognize that the empire channeled transactions in useful knowledge onto a fixed track. There was great dependence on British technology and standards. From the railways to manufacturing industry, hospitals, universities, even environmental management, British design and content were preferred. In part, the buy-British sentiment stemmed from a growing conservatism within the administration, whose services were increasingly "dominated by upright but slow thinking officers."[26] In part, the buy-British sentiment was a carryover from the mid-nineteenth-century mindset when British engineering defined best practice in the world. But it became outdated when technological leadership passed to Germany or the United States. And it may have acted as an obstacle to the kind of import substitution in machinery that the early Japanese mills practiced successfully. The dependence, therefore, imposed costs. For example, it led to an old-fashioned persistence with the mule in cotton spinning in the late nineteenth century, delaying the adoption of ring spindles.[27]

Yet this point about a dependent development can be taken too far. The close contact between Bombay and Manchester also enabled a quick and successful diversification into weaving in response to competition in spinning. As was true for nearly all the examples of "late" industrialization that began with the formation of a cotton mill industry, the interwar maturation of the industry saw import substitution in personnel, machines, and spare parts. The case of the cotton mill supervisory staff represents an impressive demonstration of capability building. Between the establishment of the first cotton mills in Bombay and 1925, the percentage of Europeans among mill supervisory staff decreased from 100 percent to less than 30 percent.[28] With the electric telegraph, a European idea needed to adapt to local materials. In the practice of medicine, even though the government tried to legitimize European systems of knowledge, the attempt succeeded only to a limited extent. Indian knowledge and European knowledge sometimes ran parallel to each other, and more often incorporated knowledge from one field into the other.[29] Insofar as British knowledge came in the shape of hired artisans and engineers,

---

[26] Ian Copland, cited by Michael Fisher, "Indirect Rule in the British Empire: The Foundations of the Residency System in India (1764–1858)," *Modern Asian Studies* 18(3), 1984, pp. 393–428 (quote on p. 397).

[27] See Dwijendra Tripathi, "Colonialism and Technology Choices in India: A Historical Overview," *Developing Economies* 34(1), 1996, pp. 80–97, for a discussion.

[28] Morris D. Morris, "The Recruitment of an Industrial Labor Force in India, with British and American Comparisons," *Comparative Studies in Society and History* 3(3), 1960, pp. 305–28.

[29] Poonam Bala, *Imperialism and Medicine in Bengal: A Socio-Historical Perspective*, New Delhi: Sage Publications, 1991.

informal and formal apprenticeship was possible, and the beneficiaries of such apprenticeships were Indians.

In India, learning from the first industrial nation was taking place inside railway workshops, arsenal factories, and cotton mills; during cadastral surveys, mineral prospecting, and geological surveys; in public works construction; and in the civil engineering colleges established in the mid-nineteenth century. Indianization of the technical and engineering workforce had been occurring steadily for more than fifty years when India became independent (1947). By then, the Indian contingent formed the majority in the engineering departments and the factory technical cadres. Indeed, the community of technicians was large enough to push for, and occasionally take leadership in, the development of formal scientific and technical education in postcolonial India, as we will see in Chapter 10.

Empire and law

Unlike in knowledge exchange, in law the state was more directly a participant in the production of public goods. It is not easy to define the European empires in Asia, America, and Africa as a common bundle of strategies and effects. But there can be no dispute that they all took law seriously. The common factor in the history of imperial governance was not violence, nor collaboration, nor cultural strategy for creating consent, but legislation. In making legislation a priority, the company's state was no different from European-ruled empires elsewhere in the world. Yet, the British Indian legislative project was a distinctive one.

The economic aims of colonial law can be quite diverse. In keeping with this diversity, modern empires pursued three types of institutional strategy, which can be called appropriation, incorporation, and standardization. By appropriation, I mean European settlers taking possession of non-European land and labor with the aid of property rights on land deemed *terra nullius* and property rights on labor through slavery or indenture. By incorporation, I mean securing loyalty with the offer of juridical autonomy to communities. In Africa, incorporation was a part of indirect rule; in India, incorporation stemmed from the adoption of indigenous religious codes as civil law; and in Russia, incorporation was allowing diverse ethnicities a share in local governance achieved at the same time as a hierarchical distinction between local and imperial elites.[30]

---

[30] Dominic Lieven, *Empire: The Russian Empire and Its Rivals*, New Haven, CT: Yale University Press, 2002.

The third strategy, standardization, is the opposite of incorporation. It refers to the practice of bringing diverse legal codes into conformity. If in property rights many practices could in principle coexist because most inheritance and succession were integrated into family and kin groups, in matters of contract between unrelated individuals, a reasonable uniformity needed to be established. Buyers and sellers in the same market could not possibly have access to different law. Thus, whereas empires often allowed some scope for personal or community autonomy in property rights, there was in commercial law a reverse bias for equivalence where no legal equivalence had been before. The clearest manifestation of standardization was in sales contracts, credit instruments, and company law.

The task of formulating a grand narrative of colonial law is complicated by the fact that no empire followed these three strategies with the same drive at the same time. Much depended on the character of the settler societies and the economic structure of the colonist power. Furthermore, the objectives themselves were mutually contradictory. Appropriation and incorporation were usually alternatives. Incorporation, or allowing one law for each ethnic group, did not fit easily with standardization, or allowing one law irrespective of the identity of the transactors.

How should we place India in this comparative history? If appropriation was crucial to the making of the Spanish and British Empires in the Americas, it was all but irrelevant in South Asian history. *Terra nullius* and slavery make more sense in the New World than in India. Creating settler landlords was not the aim of the British Empire in India. It did at times help European planters but only to the extent that such help was consistent with the overwhelmingly more important goal, market integration.[31] In India, property rights in land and labor continued to be private, free, and Indian owned.

If appropriation is irrelevant, incorporation fares better. The British legislative enterprise in eighteenth-century India carried a bias against interference in property and in favor of conserving indigenous rights. In India, the conservative bias in legislation was expressed initially in the form of a large-scale state-sponsored project that translated religious codes and reinterpreted these as positive laws, without much regard for actual practice. The policy was not seen as a great success in the mid-nineteenth century. Religion was a poor guide to substantive law, as there were many religions and many sects within them, and legal codes varied

---

[31] Marxist historiography of the expatriate-owned plantations tries to transpose a New World discourse of appropriation to the Indian context, but the project, which turns on a controversial reading of land laws and labor contracts, is a tenuous one at best.

not only by religion but also by community and region. For the law to be at all workable, the judges had to admit almost any claim to a distinctive custom, and making such claims had been made easier by a Westernization of procedural law. Colonial law followed a single judicial process and created one judiciary out of the decentralized and fragmented precolonial system. A strong referee ruled over many players, encouraging more players to make appeals to the referee. These anomalies slowed the judicial process and increased the costs of judicial redress. In short, incorporation failed in the presence of too many divisions within the society and a propensity for divisions to multiply in the presence of incorporative strategy. Thus early in the career of Crown rule, the bias shifted away from incorporation toward standardization.[32]

One radical example of this departure occurred in the context of land acquisition for tea estates in Assam. The principle of land legislation in 1830 was adapted to peasant cultivation, and not to estate ownership. Plantations were a capital-intensive business rather than a land-intensive one, and laws, it was felt, were needed to reduce the risks of a capital investment of an uncertain nature. Similarly, laws governing contractual relations between the estate laborer and the estate owner were also missing. Labor contract was deemed a crucial issue because in Assam the main difficulty in the way of large-scale plantation development was the availability of workers. Interventions in land law and indenture contract were therefore of great importance in making tea a viable idea.

In eighteenth-century trade, attempts to protect capitalist interests usually involved striking deals with the Indian headmen among artisan or merchant groups, leaving the enforcement of the contract to the social authority that the headman commanded over those who recognized him as a leader-cum-negotiator. The agency road was clearly inadequate. In the nineteenth century, transactions in cotton textiles, silk, opium, and indigo involved frequent disputes over the contract.[33] After the company

---

[32] A relevant parallel is the Chinese merchant in the Netherlands Indies. Alexander Claver discusses the tension between two principles of legislation, one that wanted communities to enjoy juridical autonomy in matters of property and contract, and another that aspired to create a universally applicable rule of legislation overriding ethnic law. Peter Boomgaard, Dick Kooiman, and Henk Schulte Nordholt, eds., *Linking Destinies: Trade, Towns and Kins in Asian History*, Leiden: KITLV Press, 2008.

[33] R. E. Kranton and A. V. Swamy, "Contracts, Hold-up, and Exports: Textiles and Opium in Colonial India," *American Economic Review* 98(5), 2008, pp. 967–89. See also M. Torri, "Mughal Nobles, Indian Merchants and the Beginning of British Conquest in Western India: The Case of Surat, 1756–1759," *Modern Asian Studies* 32(2), 1998, pp. 257–315, on the unstable relationship between East India Company officers and Indian brokers.

consolidated its political power, it tried to create a code of commercial law based on indigenous religious law books. But the Sanskrit, Arabic, and Persian codes that the British Indian courts used were largely silent on the subject of sale law and impersonal contracts. For a considerable time, therefore, contract was a subject that either was left alone or was addressed by means of ad hoc compilations, to be given up in actual practice.

In the mid-nineteenth century, special regulations added another instrument for contract performance, in addition to these informal means. In common with nineteenth-century English convention, breach of contract came to be addressed by means of criminal laws. The advantage of criminal law was that it delivered speedy justice through the magistrates' courts. The disadvantage was that it rarely delivered real justice. Inference of criminal intent was unjust when breach of contract happened because of accidents. Appearing in the magistrates' courts cost money. Disputants needed to employ lawyers, bribe officers, hire witnesses, and pay the stamp tax. These abuses reached scandalous proportions during particular disputes, especially during those concerning the indigo planters and peasants of Bengal in 1860, and the indentured workers going to Assam.

Contract in commodity and labor exchanges, therefore, was a leading field of legislative enterprise in the nineteenth century. In all cases, Indian custom or the principle of incorporation had to be abandoned. Act VIII of 1819, Act XIII of 1859, and Act IX of 1860, applicable to employment in the presidency towns, plantations, and public works, respectively, all treated breach of a contract of service as a criminal offense. In the indigo business, specifically, regulations passed in 1823, 1824, and 1830 increased the authority of the magistrate to prosecute defaulters. Some of these clauses were repealed later. But the general principle was reaffirmed in 1839, when the Law Commission reiterated the position that in settling disagreements over indigo contracts, criminal law should be in force.[34] Act XI of 1860 again made breach of contract in indigo a criminal offense. None of these regulations addressed contingency or accidents, and all of them failed to deliver stability during the Blue Mutiny. A partial response to the problem was the Contract Act (1872), which drew up a sales law after English and American practices, without making a reference to Indian custom or codes. Other spheres where this radical principle was extended included trusts, transfers of property, promissory notes, evidence, wills and

[34] Letter from J. P. Grant, Officiating Secretary to the Indian Law Commission, to W. H. Macnaghtan, Secretary to the Government of India, in the Legislative Department, 11 July 1837, in *Copies of the special reports* (pp. xxx, 1842), p. 266.

probates, and specific relief, all of which were codified in one major thrust between 1870 and 1890, and all of which drew on English rather than Indian precedents. After 1900, labor law was progressively incorporated into this corpus. The indenture was already long dead.

Conclusion

The Marxists are right in suggesting that the modern empires, and especially the British Empire in India, were keen to sustain market integration. But to jump from that premise to a state-dominated and state-directed process of transfer of social surplus that made the periphery poor would go against the grain of this project. This book is about markets before, during, after, with, and without European empires. Attributing special agency to markets under the European empire entails asking how these other times were different or similar. That question does not have an answer. Any argument about imperial markets that does not keep the nonimperial context in India in the picture is simply untestable.

I adopt a more neutral stance with regard to imperial agency. Of course, the empire mattered to markets, and it mattered differently from the past. This difference cannot be located in the force of arms or in the sponsored loot of social surplus. It should be located in the manner in which market integration was effected and the consequences thereof. The agents of integration of special interest are law, language, and knowledge. There was broad compatibility of law among parts of the British Empire. There was compatibility and exchange of skills. And because of the prioritization of law and of skills exchange, English had to become the lingua franca of the empire, eagerly embraced by upwardly mobile groups because the language was a road to new technology and new enterprise.

The consequences of the imperial umbrella of law, language, and skills exchange were various. At the broadest level, it created conditions for commodity and factor market transactions. If the imperial umbrella helped the Mauritian planters access Indian plantation workers, it was also crucial to the Bombay millowners' accessing Lancashire foremen. Technological spillover from the joining of British know-how with Indian capital, labor, and natural resources was considerable. India's precocious industrialization cannot be explained otherwise. On the other side, the empire achieved market integration only at the cost of an explosion of contractual disputes, driving legislation away from its indigenous roots toward what I have called in this chapter standardization.

The pursuit of market integration within an imperial framework was a potentially contradictory enterprise nevertheless. Market integration entailed a faith in liberalism and freedom, whereas the very act of subjection of other societies entailed a denial of freedom. All capitalistic empires struggled to find the right mix between unfreedom and liberalism, and with hindsight, failed in the end. The collapse of the world market during the Great Depression brought this conflict into the open in India, which is the subject of the next chapter.

8   Depression and Decolonization, 1920–1950

The period between the two world wars created a paradoxical scenario in India. Manufacturing and urban services flourished against the backdrop of a stagnant countryside staring at a food, credit, and wage crisis. The population growth rate, which had hovered between 0.5 and 0.8 percent per year in 1881–1921, exceeded 1 percent in the 1920s and accelerated. A few years before this demographic turning point, cultivated land area had stopped growing. In the late 1920s, the world demand forprimary goods collapsed. What the peasants sold to the world market was worth less than it was before in terms of manufactured goods. Manufacturing by and large escaped the worst effects of the turmoil. The Great Depression, however, drove a wedge between the mainly Indian-owned businesses that sold goods in India and the mainly foreign-owned businesses that sold goods in the world market, strengthening the one and weakening the other. In turn, the two groups developed conflicting interests in politics and saw themselves as potential competitors. The imperial umbrella was in tatters. The old mechanism of paying for service imports with export receipts broke down, adding fuel to a nationalistic upsurge.

In this chapter, the fall of the imperial system and the run-up to independence will be described. It is useful to begin with a snapshot of the domestic economy at the conclusion of World War I.

After the war

Against the backdrop of a few modern enterprises amid much that remained traditional, the First World War began in 1914. In common with other economies that did not directly take part in the conflict and yet had something useful to sell to those who did, India experienced the war as a massive demand boost. Demand for clothing or jute sacks made in India, for example, soared. In the initial year or two, imports of machinery, raw materials, spare parts, and chemicals by Indian industry from Britain and Germany stopped, and shipping was diverted. These supply constraints gradually eased, as domestic production adjusted. By the end of the war, industrial production had expanded, and conditions were ripe for the start of new industries and for diversification by old industries.

Until the end of World War I, trade between India and Britain was effectively free of tariffs. In the case of the Lancashire cloth that entered India, a 5 percent general tariff imposed in 1895 was neutralized by a countervailing excise duty of the same magnitude. Independently, however, both countries had been moving toward protectionism and dependence on customs for revenue. During the war, Britain imposed tariffs on a selected range of imports, fueling a similar demand in India. The call for protection from Lancashire had been made from time to time by individuals connected with the textile industry in western India, for whom the countervailing excise represented a great injustice.

Until this time, the government had followed a hands-off policy in respect of Indian industry, and a buy-British policy in respect of purchases for defense, railways, and administration. The war demonstrated the value of Indian manufacturing as an emergency reserve. After the war, therefore, the government looked to local sources and became more open to promoting such sources. The use of protective tariffs to help infant industry was sanctioned as part of the new measures. In the end, the industries that actually received protection consisted of some new ones, such as cement, but also some troubled mature ones, such as cotton textiles.

In the first half of the 1920s, the cotton textile mills in Bombay experienced an unprecedented fall in profitability, after having enjoyed a decade-long boom. What worried the millowners about the crisis was that it derived from Japanese and Chinese competition in certain grades of cloth in which Bombay found it impossible to match East Asian prices. Between 1913 and 1923, Japan's share of cotton yarn import had increased from 2 to 46 percent (in weight) and of cotton cloth import from 0.3 to 8.3 percent. Collectively, the three countries had an unassailable wage advantage over their Atlantic rivals. But among them, wage differentials were small. Price differences arose from efficiency and exchange-rate policies.

In principle, efficiency gains could be made in India. In 1940, 450,000 workers in cotton textile mills in India processed 3.5 million bales of cotton. In Japan, 190,000 workers processed the same quantity of cotton in that year. In practice, however, increasing productivity would mean persuading workers to work harder or to take a pay cut. Not an easy option in the best of times, it was complicated by the fact that the managers in India did not deal with the workers directly, but were used to dealing with them through headmen. The interests of these intermediaries were not identical with those of the employers. Attempts to cut wages or impose managerial authority, therefore, worsened an already tense industrial relationship.

In 1926, the Bombay Millowners Association made a representation before the Indian Tariff Board stating that the competition from Japan was an unfair one, deriving from manipulation of exchange and repressed labor in Japan. The millowners themselves did not all speak with one voice on the matter. A significant minority argued that the Japanese mills did better because they had better utilization of economies of scale in production and in marketing. Some of the provincial governments saw themselves as representing the interests of mill towns that hoped to compete with Bombay, or those of the consumer, or handloom weaver, who used a considerable quantity of imported yarn. Despite these divergent views, protection was granted to the Indian mills.

Tariffs led to rapid growth in India's sugar, steel, cement, matches, paper, and woolen textile industries. The integrated steel factory founded by the Tatas in 1907 received help in the form of tariffs and a railway contract that saved the firm from premature bankruptcy. On the eve of the Great Depression, then, India possessed an extensive and diversified manufacturing industry. The groups to have gained were businesses owned by Indians and serving domestic markets. A substantial banking industry had also emerged at the end of the war; again, new entry came mainly from local groups. Protection nevertheless slowed down the long-term trend. The level of Indian integration had increased in the preceding century, but it was still relatively small compared with other tropical export-oriented economies (exports were 7–9 percent of Net Domestic Product). With the railway boom essentially over, the share of foreign investment in national income in India stabilized at slightly less than 1 percent.[1] It was these two characteristics of the interwar economy – industrialization and retreat from the world market – that were to provide India with buffers against the Great Depression.

---

[1] On the construction of these numbers, see Tirthankar Roy, *The Economic History of India, 1757–2010*, Delhi: Oxford University Press, 2011.

Onset of the Depression

In common with many other open economies, India experienced the onset of the Depression in two main ways. First, demand for agricultural exports fell. And second, the existing currency system compelled a deflation. Real interest rates rose. Indebted households liquidated assets to repay loans when they could. Indebted businesses failed. And banks were left with unrecoverable assets. As elsewhere, wage depression, the end of the old currency regime, and the recovery of the banks returned the economy to health.

Although this general pattern occurred in India too, some aspects of India's Depression story were unique. Unlike the most severely affected regions, the Americas for example, real domestic product changed little in India during the peak of the Depression, 1929–1933 (see Figure 8.1). The slowdown in foreign trade had saved India from a sharper shock. Unlike in Latin America, where the Depression also worked upon American investment, in India a recession in foreign investment mattered little. And Indian banks were relatively insulated from bad debt because the major part of their portfolio was tied to the harvest, so that the books balanced every season.

These facts have generated a debate on the nature of the shock to India. One position argues, with India as one of its examples, that the effect was less damaging on the Third World than it was on the developed world.[2] This view is not widely shared among economic historians of India. The critics argue that the burden of adjustment fell more on the poor than on the wealthy in India.[3] Further, the uneven burden of Depression adjustment had political causes and far-reaching political consequences. The evidence in support of the second view comes mainly from prices, which show a comparatively large drop in India (Figure 8.2).

[2] Ian Brown, ed., *The Economies of Africa and Asia in the Inter-war Depression*, London: Routledge, 1989; N. Charlesworth, "The Peasant and the Depression: The Case of the Bombay Presidency, India," in Brown, *Economies of Africa and Asia*, pp. 59–73; C. J. Baker, "Debt and the Depression in Madras, 1929–1936," in C. Dewey and A. G. Hopkins, eds, *The Imperial Impact: Studies in the Economic History of Africa and India*, London: Athlone Press, 1978; C. Simmons, "The Great Depression and Indian Industry: Changing Interpretations and Changing Perceptions," *Modern Asian Studies* 21(3), 1987, pp. 585–623.

[3] See especially D. Rothermund, *India in the Great Depression, 1929–1939*, Delhi: Manohar, 1992, and Rothermund, *The Global Impact of the Great Depression, 1929–1939*, London: Routledge, 1996.

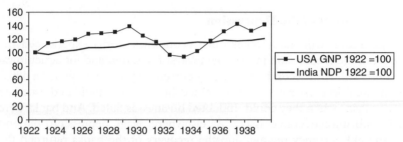

8.1. Real domestic product in India and the United States.

A tortuous policy response

Why did prices fall so much in India? Britain was India's principal trade and investment partner until World War I. Thereafter, the British Empire was no longer the main destination for commodities or labor of Indian origin. Increasingly, British capital markets looked to be an uncertain source both for government finance and for private business. Infrastructural investment in India more or less stopped. By 1929, for many influential opinion makers in India, London had become irrelevant to Indian interests. In this context, the conduct of Indian monetary policy during the Great Depression exposed the costs of imperial rule more than the gains.

The beginning of a fall in world commodity prices in the second half of the 1920s turned the balance of trade adverse for India. The relationship between balance of trade and money supply was close. A contraction in the balance of trade had an immediate effect on money supply because the Gold Exchange Standard fixed the value of the rupee with respect to the pound sterling. In that case, devaluation of the exchange was ruled out when the demand for the domestic currency fell, so that the burden of adjustment had to fall on the quantity of currency. Furthermore, the absence of a central bank made monetary policy too dependent on trade. Government budget deficits could not be financed by printing money. The trade contraction of 1929, therefore, reduced the money supply.

Official and nonofficial opinion in India favored depreciation of the rupee against sterling. But depreciation was not easy, nor was it acceptable to London. Indian balance of payments contained an annual factor income outflow on the government account (see Chapter 7). This component increased in the early 1930s because of interest payments. Most of

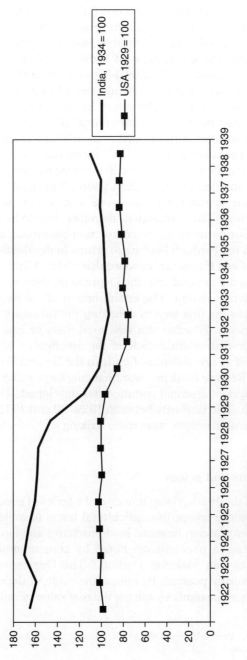

8.2. Implicit GDP deflators in India and the United States compared.

the other elements in external transactions (private remittance and investment) were individually small and did not matter much. Policy decisions,
then, rested on the need to meet official obligations. Depreciation, it was
feared, would lead the government of India to default on its external
obligations. The options usually available to the India Office for dealing
with a currency crisis – fresh borrowings from London – had become
difficult. The government's credit rating having fallen in the interwar
period, imports had become a major source of government revenues.
The loss of revenue from customs further strengthened official resistance
to devaluation. Eventually, on London's insistence, the government of
India carried out monetary contraction in the hope that this would reduce
prices and raise the demand for Indian goods. This goal was not easily
attainable, for the demand depression was not specific to India but a
global phenomenon. The contraction, therefore, had to be a deep and a
sustained one. Furthermore, as the contraction continued, and the less it
seemed to work, the harder it became to return to devaluation.

Although the Gold Exchange Standard that had tied Indian currency to
a sinking sterling did not end after the Depression, there was still a major
shift in the monetary system. The establishment of the Reserve Bank of
India in 1935 was the first step in delinking the monetary system from
balance of payments. Whether this was good news or bad news for the
Indians in the first turbulent decade of the functioning of this banking
institution is hard to say. Balance of trade in the Second World War was
in surplus. The Reserve Bank met war financing by printing money, even
as severe shortages of essential commodities developed. The result was
massive inflation. The similarity between 1929–32 and 1942–45 in monetary management, therefore, were quite striking.

Peasants and prices

In the middle of the 1920s, cheap money and a series of good harvests led
peasants in the more prosperous agricultural tracts to build up debt. In
Punjab, wealthier peasants financed land purchases and house construction by borrowing, a phenomenon noted by contemporary observers,
principally the civilian Malcolm Darling.[4] The Depression hurt these
rich and creditworthy peasants by raising the value of their outstanding
debt, and it hurt all peasants by raising the real value of rent. The fall in

---

[4] Malcolm Darling, "Prosperity and Debt in the Punjab," *Indian Journal of Economics* 3,
 1920–22, pp. 145–66.

prices was worsened by a good harvest. Gross acreage and the production of rice and coarse grains were stationary at the turn of the decade, whereas that of wheat expanded. The decline in prices made short-term borrowing costlier and thus reduced traders' stocks, further adding to the supply of goods in a falling market.

In the early 1930s, Indians, like many other agricultural exporters the world over, began to sell a large quantity of bullion under pressure from rising rents and debt values. Net sales were always unusual, and sales on this magnitude had been unknown for a century. The bullion export on the private account was consistent with the expected profitability of such a transaction. Britain's decision to leave the gold standard in 1931 depreciated the pound, and with it the rupee, against gold. These circumstances led to a rise in the price of gold in rupees. On the basis of an 18d rupee, the price of gold was lower in India than in the international market. Further, with greater institutionalization of the bullion market, gold became a more liquid asset in the interwar period.[5] In the next five years, these gold exports restored the balance of payments and provided the government of India with enough money to meet its sterling obligations. Nevertheless, the impoverishment of the peasant became a nationalist argument and left Britain-India relations seriously strained.

Price shock exposed one kind of contradiction in rural India. In urban India, a more political contradiction was unfolding at the same time.

Manufacturing

Between 1925 and 1935 capacity in some industries worldwide, including steel, paper, sugar, and cement, had expanded too fast. These industries had received tariff shelter in India. Some of the firms in these groups struggled to cope with the markets. Still, the Depression was not all bad news. Although real interest rates rose, the rise affected manufacturing industry only a little because it did not borrow much long-term capital. A wide range of capital goods was imported, and an overvalued currency had made imports lucrative. The Depression cheapened a variety of inputs for the manufacturing industries, including agricultural raw material. Between 1929 and 1931, cotton prices fell at a somewhat faster rate than did cotton yarn prices, and even more rapidly than average cloth prices did.

---

[5] I have shown that these developments had increased the price elasticity of net purchases substantially; see Tirthankar Roy, "Money Supply and Asset Choice in Interwar India," *Indian Economic and Social History Review*, 30(2), pp. 163–80.

The worst effects of the Depression were confined to those industries that were selling abroad. Troubled export businesses such as jute and tea had tried to shelter themselves from the fall in worldwide demand by forming cartels and voluntarily cutting production. The cartels formed along ethnic lines. Europeans dominated one chamber of commerce, the Indians another. The Indians, so far the smaller group and more marginal players, benefited from the voluntary restraints practiced by the dominant cartel, and grew to become competitors when the market improved.[6] In trying to meet this threat, some European firms sought state support. These moves polarized businesses into two lobbies along ethnic lines. The bitter aftertaste of this antagonism produced a series of hostile take-overs of British businesses in tea and jute by Indians soon after independence (1947), with the blessings of the political class.

Benefits for banks

Whereas the liquidation of gold assets dispossessed peasants of their capital, some of it flowed to the asset markets. A notable aspect of the restoration of stability was that the money supply expanded because deposit growth in private banks accelerated in the 1930s. How liquid these deposits were cannot be established with certainty. But there is ground to hypothesize that the money supply began to be more credit influenced and less influenced by foreign trade after the Depression. An increase in financial intermediation was a long-term tendency in early twentieth-century India, disturbed occasionally by bank failures, unstable interest rates, and two world wars. But the early-1930s represented a scale of development that cannot be explained by a modest long-term tendency.

One stimulus came from the sale of gold. If the sale was a sign of the impoverishment of the peasants, it improved the balance sheet of the informal bankers. In 1931–35, net gold sales were unusually high, and so was the growth of bank liabilities and the aggregate paid-up capital of joint-stock companies. Far from ushering in a banking crisis, the Depression created conditions for a banking boom. Of the total increase in paid-up capital in joint-stock companies, 47 percent was accounted for by financial companies. This was in contrast to the war period, when only 4 percent of incremental investment went to the financial sector, and to the

---

[6] Bishnupriya Gupta, "Why Did Collusion Fail? The Indian Jute Industry in the Inter-War Years," *Business History* 47(4), 2005, pp. 532–52.

1920s, when only 7 percent did. Until 1930, a boom or slump in banking showed up in large and sudden changes in the number of small and medium-sized banks. In 1930 and 1931, several large (in capital) banks failed. But the average and the total capital involved in bank failures was the lowest in 1932–35 compared to almost any year in the previous decade. Unlike the previous instances of a banking boom, the 1930s witnessed a relative growth of the larger and more reputable banks, which opened many new branches and operated more vigorously than before. This effect was combined, fortuitously, with drastic cuts in the lending rate of the government's banker, the Imperial Bank.

Where was the money going? How much of this growth in banking translated into new investments? The rate of savings in the Indian economy about doubled in the 1930s compared to the prewar average.[7] This corresponded to a sharp increase in the proportion of urban construction in total capital formation. Further, the agrarian crisis had turned the rural entrepreneurs' attention toward industries intensive in local resources. The early 1930s witnessed a remarkable growth of small-scale and local enterprise, and a great rise in the index of security prices.

A short-lived bonus for labor

The possibility of wage negotiation made the adjustment much easier for both rural and urban employers. In the early years of the Depression, 1929 and 1930, focus was on the net sellers in agriculture. In this indeterminate early phase of the shock, the main sufferers were exporters in the cities and the countryside. But wage workers experienced a bonus. Prices in these two years more than halved, but money wages were stable. Most real-wage indices for industrial and agrarian workers show increases until 1931. Sporadically from 1930, and generally from 1931, wages were falling across the board, a fall that continued halfway through the decade. The wage cuts spread from the countryside to the industries. Thus, textile mill real wages in Bombay and Ahmedabad rose sharply during 1929–31, but from 1932, money wage cuts were widespread, and large enough to almost completely neutralize the previous rise, such that real wages in 1934–37 were only 10 percent higher than their mid-1920s level.[8] These

[7] R. W. Goldsmith, *The Financial Development of India, 1860–1977*, New Haven, CT: Yale University Press, 1983.

[8] K. Mukerji, "Trends in Textile Mill Wages in Western India," *Artha Vijnana* 4(2), 1962, pp. 156–66.

adjustments did not happen peacefully. In the 1930s, when wage nego-tiations became a matter of survival for many cotton mills, major strikes and closures broke out. The newly elected provincial governments took the unrest seriously as it could derail the political mobilization efforts. The governments, therefore, were drawn deeper into the "conciliation" process.

Decolonization

To many Indian observers, the Depression demonstrated that an impe-rial union on nineteenth-century assumptions was no longer tenable. London, however, drew the opposite conclusion from the episode. At the turn of the twentieth century, the idea of imperial preference, wherein Indian goods would receive the same level of protection as British goods did in Britain, was under discussion. It proved as unpopular and con-troversial as the discriminatory excise on cotton textiles. Yet as the whole world moved toward aggressive tariff policy after the Great Depression, attempts revived to turn the British Empire into a customs union. The Imperial Economic Conference in Ottawa (1932) gave concrete shape to these sentiments by reducing duties on commodities traded within the empire. Initially welcomed by Indian business, the agreement quickly became controversial. It proved singularly ineffective in changing the two long-term trends in the direction of trade: increasing the dependence of the United Kingdom on imperial markets, and decreasing the depen-dence of the dominions and India on British markets. Although these trends were hardly checked by the Imperial Preference, as the new arrangement came to be known, the non-British partners in the arrange-ment feared that the preferential tariffs would see their goods discrimi-nated against in the new markets outside the empire that they had come to depend on. For India in the 1930s, both Japan and the United States, for example, were becoming more important than Britain as trade partners. Preferential trade, therefore, made the task of repairing India's external trade more difficult than before.

A different theater of economic nationalism was the countryside. The North Indian peasants were mobilized during the Civil Disobedience Movement (1930–31).[9] The peasant distress offered the Congress under M. K. Gandhi the chance to turn an elitist movement into a mass one.

[9] Gyanendra Pandey, *The Ascendancy of the Congress in Uttar Pradesh, 1926–1934: A Study in Imperfect Mobilization*, Delhi: Oxford University Press, 1978.

Agitation to reduce rents and waive debts joined local grievances in the first organized and broad-based movement against colonial policy in India. Interestingly, the scale of peasant participation varied with geographical zones. The intensity was greater in regions with fertile soil and more water, and consequently, the movement there attracted a relatively rich and politically ambitious class of peasants.[10] Such a situation obtained in the middle-Gangetic plains more than in the Deccan uplands. The Indian National Congress in the end delivered less than the tenant farmers had hoped for, especially because the movement was withdrawn somewhat abruptly soon after it began. And the Congress was still far from a mass-based party. But its wider reach, in evidence during this episode, made it the most promising platform from which to make demands for trade and exchange autonomy.

"By the 1930s the Congress had new committed allies – industrialists and big businessmen."[11] In a Marxist account, the Indian businesses appear as the oppressed minority in a business world dominated by European capital, pushing them into alliances with the Congress.[12] Such a construction presents a difficulty, however. It does not explain why Indian business would rally at a moment like this; the obvious answer is that European capital was now weaker than at any time before. To explain the timing of the political activism, we need to bring in the disruptions caused by the Depression, which made the empire less profitable for Indian business and raised the chances of influencing government policy.

In that endeavor, the Congress proved a highly imperfect vehicle. Although representing business and collecting donations from them, the Congress was constrained by its commitments to urban workers from

[10] The difference in the nature of political participation is illustrated for the "wet" and the "dry" regions of South India by David Washbrook, *The Emergence of Provincial Politics: The Madras Presidency, 1870–1920*, Cambridge: Cambridge University Press, 1976.

[11] T. Raychaudhuri, "Indian Nationalism as Animal Politics," *Historical Journal* 22(3), 1979, pp. 747–63 (quote on p. 756). Subsequent to this useful review article on the historiography of Indian nationalism, the literature diversified into new directions. The subaltern studies located nationalism in strategies of resistance by the peasants and the laborers, rather than in the enterprise of their elite representatives. On the subaltern studies, see David Ludden, ed., *Reading Subaltern Studies: Critical History, Contested Meaning and the Globalisation of South Asia*, Delhi: Permanent Black, 2001. Another trend analyzed nationalism through discursive formations that absorbed and contested colonial forms of knowledge. See Partha Chatterjee, *The Nation and Its Fragments: Colonial and Postcolonial Histories*, Princeton, NJ: Princeton University Press, 1993.

[12] Aditya Mukherjee, *Imperialism, Nationalism and the Making of the Indian Capitalist Class, 1920–1947*, New Delhi: Sage Publications, 2002.

playing a decisively pro-business role. Business lobbies were themselves far too divided in interests. Organized trade union resistance in Bombay unnerved prospective employers of labor. New factories, therefore, were set up "up-country," or deeper into the cotton cultivation zones, where wages were low and workers were unorganized. These up-country mills benefited from the labor troubles that plagued the Bombay mills. The Congress could succeed by incorporating varieties of class interests and, therefore, was not always ready to act with force.

Two major side effects of politics in the interwar period were the rise of communism and of communalism. A particular dimension of the many divisions within the business class – the division along Hindu-Muslim lines – assumed special significance in the 1940s. Claude Markovits has shown that differences between the elites within both business communities contributed to the idea of the Partition. The conflict developed between the Hindu business elite's preference for a strong central government, and the Muslim elite's preference for a strong federation and weak center.[13] The Communist Party of India was established in 1925. From then on, the idea of class struggle became linked with the nationalist movement. Such a connection was favored by Moscow and inspired by Lenin's thesis that imperialism was a mature stage of capitalism. And it appealed also to a section of the nationalists disillusioned with the Congress's leadership. The disillusionment grew after the withdrawal of the noncooperation movement (1920–22). The connection between class struggle and nationalism was for the communists a source of strength, because they could realistically hope to bring the working classes into the nationalist movement while retaining a distinct political identity from the Congress, which was seen by some as a platform for the bourgeoisie. But the joining of nationalism and trade unionism divided the communist movement. The Comintern of 1926 became an occasion for a stormy debate on India. The confusion between its two goals came back to hurt the party when the USSR joined in World War II as an ally of the British.

Against the backdrop of a beleaguered countryside and a restive urban economy, the Second World War began. Unlike in World War I, on this occasion India was a theater of war. Bengal, already weakened by deteriorating agriculture, became the eastern front of the war after the fall of Singapore, Burma, and the Andaman Islands to the Japanese forces in 1941. And also unlike in World War I, the commitment of ordinary Indians to the British political cause was now in question. The war was

[13] Claude Markovits, *Merchants, Traders, Entrepreneurs: Indian Business in the Colonial Era*, Basingstoke: Palgrave Macmillan, 2008.

fought by an imperial power that was politically hostile to Indian interests and had been driven into a corner by military debacles. Fearing a long-drawn battle, the government went into overdrive to procure rice for soldiers, unfortunately having to do so in a year of monsoon floods and crop failure. The newly established Reserve Bank of India funded the war by printing money. The resultant inflation worsened a famine in Bengal (1943) and caused distress everywhere.

Conclusion

If we only observe trends in production, then the Depression caused little damage. India's already limited and now falling engagement with the external sector sheltered much of its economy from collapse. And yet, politically, 1930 was a watershed. Underlying the tranquil picture, conflicts broke out between debtors and creditors, exporters and businesses selling in the home market, and, above all, Britain and India.

The situation destroyed trust between Indian business and the British Indian state, and forced European and Indian firms to take sides in the nationalist movement. The two world wars and the Depression empowered the one while weakening the other, deepened divisions along community lines, and strengthened the communists. The empire seemed to serve the interest of none. Politicians and businesses were writing manifestos outlining the shape of economic management to come after India gained its freedom. These documents displayed a barely concealed dislike for market integration, the emblem of British colonialism in India.

A few years after independence (1947), this vision was implemented with gusto, as we will see in the next chapter.

9   From Trade to Aid, 1950–1980

In the years after colonial rule ended (1947), the Indian state recast the international element in its economy. India steadily withdrew from foreign trade and investment. Labor migration flows slowed for about twenty years, before reviving from the 1970s. India also emerged as one of the world's largest recipients of foreign aid, and this aid had a well-defined role in the nation's strategy of development.

Before independence, a main current of intellectual thought within the Indian National Congress stressed the need for state control of productive resources to ensure a more equal distribution of income and wealth. This socialist strand was inspired by the Soviet developmental model. The accent was on state ownership, redistribution, and planning. Between the 1950s and the 1980s, these ideas became part of an informal consensus among Indian intellectuals. In this way, the communists and the mainstream came to a compromise. The country's first prime minister, Jawaharlal Nehru, represented this conjunction of two political traditions of interwar India.

The state established industries and nationalized some of them. Expansion in steel and heavy machinery was almost entirely in the state sector, whereas civil aviation was nationalized. The government retained for itself privileged access to imported capital goods. The government also became the main vehicle for bilateral technical collaboration agreements. Much foreign aid came in as capital goods and as an adjunct to these agreements. The private sector accepted the arrangement. In the division of labor between the state and the market, the market was allocated the task of supplying consumer goods. The restrictions imposed on foreign trade and foreign capital were an incentive. In return, employers had to swallow a legal regime that protected manufacturing jobs. Once again, a compromise was reached between the leftist and the centrist traditions in nationalism.

In short, the new regime did not turn against the world economy, but turned India's globalization into a state-managed aid-funded process. What was the rationale behind the choice? Why was it in the end given up? Chapter 9 answers these questions.

224

Aid-funded industrialization

Although the preference for aid over trade was shaped by decolonization and nationalism, discussions on the precise role for aid in industrialization were also conducted within technical discourses on development policy in the 1950s.[1] The technical discourse showed why money needed to be raised abroad in a capital-scarce nation. It did not offer a compelling reason why private foreign investment had to be curbed. It did suggest that an advantage of foreign aid was that it was low cost compared with sources of money accessible to the private sector, and that aid fitted a managed industrialization strategy better than did private investment. Foreign aid was integrated not with investment as such, but with the particular accent on capital-goods production in the public sector. Protective tariffs had antecedents in the decolonization experience. Further, the global development discourse of the 1950s, following on two decades of turmoil in world trade, was not too hopeful about free trade.

Foreign resources were needed not only because they were cheap but also because they were an adjunct to a policy of buying technology. Capital goods, if these were to be imported, had to be financed. If domestically produced, these needed foreign know-how and equipment, which had to be purchased from abroad. Given the obstacles to trade, India's export earnings were not going to be sufficient to finance such imports. Further, the accent on industrialization entailed some neglect of food production, and the avoidance of major food crises became an important priority, again needing foreign assistance.

In the first fifteen years after independence, two-thirds of India's net aid inflow went into industrial development, the rest into infrastructure. Oil and steel dominated the list of industries receiving foreign money. In steel, which accounted for a quarter of the aid into industrial development, the money went to new units set up by the government. Individual country commitments varied. Of total U.S. aid, approximately half consisted of food and commodity assistance under US P.L. 480 and 665 schemes.

[1] On the theory of aid, see H. B. Chenery and A. Strout, "Foreign Assistance and Economic Development," *American Economic Review* 1966; I. M. D. Little and J. M. Clifford, *International Aid: A Discussion of the Flow of Public Resources from Rich to Poor Countries with Particular Reference to British Policy*, London: George Allen & Unwin, 1965; V. Joshi, "Savings and Foreign Exchange Constraints," in P. Streeten, ed., *Unfashionable Economics: Essays in Honour of Thomas Balogh*, London: Weidenfield & Nicholson, 1970; and A. O. Krueger, C. Michalopoulos, and V. W. Ruttan, *Aid and Development*, Baltimore: Johns Hopkins University Press, 1989.

Table 9.1. *Net aid inflow in perspective, 1950–2003 (percentage).*

	Aid-GDP	Aid-investment	Aid as ratio of capital account balance	Investment–GDP ratio	Public sector's share in gross investment
1950	− 0.2	− 2.2	55	9.1	NA
1960	2.3	14.4	64	15.9	44.2
1970	1.1	6.1	116	17.4	37.8
1980	1.3	5.5	85	24.2	44.3
1990	0.8	2.9	31	26.5	38.4
2000	0.1	0.4	5	24.4	28.3
2003			− 14		

Note: Figures of gross outflow do not include rupee debt service.

These came in the form of wheat in the 1950s. Of the remaining amount, industrial development, including oil, gas, steel, and heavy machinery, all in the public sector, accounted for a little over half, and the rest went to railways, power, and irrigation development, again under the government. West German, Soviet, and British aid went to industrial development, and Canadian and International Bank for Reconstruction and Development (IBRD) aid to infrastructure. The first IBRD loan in Asia was a loan to India for railway development in 1949. In the late-1950s, a thirteen-member Aid India Consortium was established to facilitate and coordinate aid flow. The terms of concessional loans and conditionality did not seem to be a major point of concern.

The two principal industries receiving aid were oil and steel. Both were government priorities, and in both cases a storm was brewing between the Western donors and the Indian state over the uses of the aid. In the first half of the 1950s, the Indian government found it tough to negotiate import and exploration with the oil multinationals. Apart from some Italian assistance to building pipelines, Western aid did not enter the public-sector oil refinery and explorations project at all. By 1955, the Indian government had signed agreements with Burmah-Shell, Esso, and Caltex for refinery expansion. The Assam Oil Company was an already existing foreign firm in crude oil production and refining. It was soon felt that the private companies were not serving national interests well enough. In the next few years, therefore, the government painstakingly acquired a partnership in explorations projects in Assam through a new joint venture called Oil India Ltd. and began to establish itself as the main agency for exploration in Gujarat through a department called the

Oil and Natural Gas Commission (ONGC). Above all, India welcomed the emergence of the USSR as a major new oil producer in the world. In the late-1950s, Soviet aid began to enter into refinery projects, and India quickly increased its dependence on Soviet oil.

In the 1960s, the schism between the West and the East widened further. The issue in contention was the tying of aid with state leadership in the economy. There were growing divisions within American foreign policy over American aid becoming an instrument in India's socialism. American diplomatic circles in Delhi favored an Indo-U.S. partnership on Indian terms. But the second view failed to convince the U.S. Congress. The USSR faced no such dilemma. In India, the support for Soviet aid was growing. There was always resistance to Western capital, whether as a "handmaiden" to foreign aid or as an alternative to it. To the extent that foreign aid represented a dependence on privately controlled know-how, India's dependence on Western aid was never totally acceptable to the Indian politicians. Soviet aid seemed a lesser evil from this point of view. On some occasions, negotiation with Western firms and governments over oil and steel projects collapsed, and this made the Indian government even more wary. However, these conditions alone might not have pushed India toward ties with the USSR, had it not been for wars and famines.

In 1965 there occurred the worst episode of crop failure in postindependence India. A war with Pakistan, debt service, and food imports drained foreign reserves, forcing India to seek more consumption aid. The Aid India Consortium offered money on condition that India devalue its currency. A minority among India's economists saw the devaluation as economic realism. But almost everyone else was upset. Big business and the trade unions saw it as a move toward free trade, for which the country was not ready.[2] In Parliament, the government faced the charge that it had compromised freedom against food. The devaluation, then, at best was a temporary succor for the balance of payments, and at worst hardened autarkic sentiments. Again, Indo-Soviet trade was free of these worries.

By the late 1960s, the USSR had quietly entrenched itself as the main partner in India's quest for a socialistic industrial policy, whereas the increasing accent on public-sector industrialization strained relations with India's Western partners. More important than these ideological tensions was the fact that between 1965 and 1971, the years when India and Pakistan fought two wars, South Asia emerged as a theater of the Cold War. In the first half of the 1960s, Sino-Indian and Sino-Soviet conflicts

---

[2] Rahul Mukherji, "India's Aborted Liberalization – 1966," *Pacific Affairs* 73(3), 2000, pp. 375–92.

brought Indian and Soviet military interests in the region directly in line. India became dependent on Soviet arms.[3]

While the political situation pushed India toward Indo-Soviet friendship, the economy showed signs of strain. Export earnings were never enough to meet the cost of concessional debt. After the exchange crisis of the mid-1960s, the major part of new aid contracted went into debt service. Repayments of debt as a percentage of export earnings began to rise from 1964.

Interestingly, the response to this crisis was not a loosening of the system but a further hardening of it. India's trade and exchange policies grew more insular in the 1970s. Tariffs were raised, the exchange rate was controlled and overvalued, and import licensing was made tighter. The private sector could import only if it had licenses, which were hard to get. To maintain control over the sources of investment funds, banks and insurance companies were nationalized in 1969, and interest rates were regulated. The industrialization strategy needed more and more legs to stand on.

The two legs that helped the most in averting disaster in the 1970s were the so-called rupee trade and remittances from abroad. The rupee trade was an arrangement by which Soviet oil was paid for with Indian goods rather than with convertible currencies. It fostered a colonial pattern of commodity specialization, with the USSR selling machines and intermediates and India selling consumer goods and raw materials. Although the USSR was not India's largest trade partner (at the height of the rupee trade, the USSR was its fourth largest partner), some among India's economists saw the barter trade as a buffer against pressure from the West. Dependence quickly increased, and by the end of the 1960s, a quarter of India's exports went into servicing debts to the USSR. The second factor working for India was remittance. While the two oil shocks had recessionary effects on an economy heavily dependent on imported oil, the economic boom in the Persian Gulf saw massive recruitment there of Indian migrants.

All of these factors only delayed an impending crisis. Exports were depressing news. Growth rates in manufacturing faltered. There was joblessness all around in the industrial cities. Real wages had risen little, and that too in the public sector. The population growth rate accelerated,

---

[3] For a survey of the turn in Indo-Soviet relations, see Dietmar Rothermund, "India and the Soviet Union," *Annals of the American Academy of Political and Social Science* 386, 1969, pp. 78–88. See also Baldev Raj Nayar, "Treat India Seriously," *Foreign Policy* 18, 1975, pp. 133–54.

reaching a disastrous 2.3 percent per year in the 1970s. A successful green revolution in the 1970s eased the food crisis, but also increased regional inequality and stoked Maoist peasant movements.

An academic debate at the turn of the 1980s saw the first significant articulation of a neo-liberal voice. Inside academia, opinion had been divided on the origins of the stagnation. The Left blamed capitalist under-consumption and a coalition of foreign interests.[4] According to the neo-liberal alternative, excessive government investment in projects that yielded low private and social returns and led to capital wastage was responsible for industrial stagnation. By 1980, the USSR was in the throes of its own demise. The end of the rupee trade meant that any subsequent investment strategy that relied on imported technology would have to be financed with export income. Crisis was contagious, and injured one after another the many legs on which the autarkic policy then stood. Heavy investment in the state sector led to budget deficits, which were met by imports, giving rise to balance-of-payments problems that were "solved" by even more tighter exchange control.

A cautious easing of exchange rates began in the early 1980s. Selectively, private-sector import of technology was allowed in the mid-1980s. When both aid and remittance inflow declined in the late 1980s, the circumstances pushed a deep tariff reform (1992–95).

The whole story represents not so much the failure of India's insular strategy of industrialization, as the difficulties associated with leaving the state in charge of industrialization. The problem was not only that there was a small role for the market and a large role for the state, but that the little market that was allowed to function was exposed to political pressures. In the 1950s and the 1960s, liberal ideologues made a case that aid, like a cheap stimulant, could lead to aid addiction.[5] The argument became obsolete in its original form, but it returned in the shape of the moral hazard of gifts. A gift of money makes the recipient more relaxed about earning and saving money.[6]

---

[4] See essays in Deepak Nayyar, *Industrial Stagnation in India*, Bombay: Oxford University Press, 1990, on the extent of the industrial decline problem, and interpretations thereof.

[5] Milton Friedman, "Foreign Aid," *Yale Review* 47(4), 1958, pp. 500–516; Peter Bauer, "Foreign Aid Forever?," *Encounter* 42(3), 1971, pp. 15–30.

[6] The original statement of this problem is owed to K. Griffin, "Foreign Capital, Domestic Savings and Econometric Development," *Oxford Bulletin of Economics and Statistics* 32(1), 1970, pp. 99–112. Griffin argued, based on an empirical test that was critically received, that governments getting aid tended to reduce tax effort and/or to change the composition of their expenditure toward consumption.

So much for the direct effects of foreign aid; what about the positive externalities in the form of learning the know-how that came with aid?

Capability and knowledge

The extensive aid scholarship in India gave much attention to the benefits and costs of foreign know-how in particular projects. The experience varied. On the one hand, in those Western-aided steel factories that did not do well, the Indian officials blamed the foreign technicians, and the foreigners blamed Indian mismanagement. With Soviet aid, on the other hand, the problem was one of obsolescence and cost. Unit costs in Soviet-assisted steel and oil projects were higher than in their Western counterparts. Most projects financed by Soviet assistance were implemented on a large scale at one go. Though that practice saved on interest costs, it increased the dependence on a technology package that, by the 1970s, was falling behind global best practice. The more interesting effect of collaboration was the exchange of tacit knowledge, which remained less researched. The effectiveness of such exchanges depended on the quality of the interaction between foreign and domestic engineers and the opportunities for the Indianization of the technical cadre. Indians found it easy to interact with their Russian counterparts, whereas interaction with German and British engineers occurred on a more formal level and was restricted at the social level.

Private foreign investment was so low that it is almost futile to talk about capability building by the private sector. Nevertheless, sympathetic accounts showed that the little investment that came in allowed for some domestic learning.[7] Insularity is also said to have fostered innovation in the pharmaceutical industry. India's patent laws permitted production of drugs in competition with patented drugs if the competitor could claim to have made it with a different process. This implicit protection allowed a freer play of innovation in the domestic industry, in the end creating a cluster of firms with strong research infrastructures. These instances are outweighed, however, by a mountain of evidence showing how learning was obstructed in textiles, machine tools, consumer electronics, and a host of other industries.

---

[7] One example from the private sector was the truckmaker TELCO. A public-sector equipment maker, Bharat Heavy Electricals Ltd., was also cited as an example of domestic "learning by doing." R. Nagaraj, "Foreign Direct Investment in India in the 1990s: Trends and Issues," *Economic and Political Weekly* 38(17), 2003, pp. 1701–12.

Another kind of learning effect of the industrialization strategy was the social prioritization of engineering education. The decision to create technical universities, some of which were to be aid funded, was taken soon after independence, adding substantially to a small pool of colonial-period technical institutions that offered engineering degrees. Almost the whole output consisted of civil engineers. The number of engineering graduates increased from about one hundred per year in 1947 to more than forty thousand in 1987, and engineering graduates per million population increased from near zero in 1947 to thirty in 1980.[8] The major part of this growth occurred in government institutions and universities, and was concentrated in civil and mechanical engineering, which supplied engineers to the government public works departments and newly set up manufacturing industries. Although the scale of engineering education increased enormously, the predominance of civil engineering represented a shadow of the colonial pattern. The pattern was to remain in place until 1990, when a revolution in engineering education began (see Chapter 10).

Autarky and deindustrialization

The obscure side story of Indian industrialization was the deglobalization and consequent decline of India's best-known export-oriented manufactures. Tea, jute, and cotton textiles were the foremost examples. The withdrawal did not happen by choice, nor was it a simple outcome of trade policy. Rather, it resulted from the state's blocking the market-mediated import of knowledge in the shape of equipment trade, technical collaboration, and foreign investment. The nationalist sentiment that anything foreign was bad joined with the Gandhian sentiment that the small was beautiful, making the adaptation of India's manufacures to global standards difficult.

Despite outward concessions to foreign private capital, the general stance of the Indian Parliament on foreign investment was hostile throughout the 1960s and the 1970s, and hardened over time. At the same time, it was understood that the desired pattern of industrialization so heavily dependent on capital could not progress without concessions to foreign capital. The outcome was a deeply contradictory sentiment about foreign direct investment. Foreign private capital "in the [colonial] past," observed one participant in a policy seminar in the 1960s, represented "the shadow of

---

[8] Rangan Banerjee and Vinayak P. Muley, "Engineering Education in India" (mimeo), Indian Institute of Technology Bombay, Mumbai, 2008.

serfdom." But, whereas "the doses of vitamins might have been bad for a sick and diseased India in the past, ... the same vitamins now possess vitality."[9] Not many multinational firms were reassured by this logic.

As the Soviet safety valve came into operation, foreign firms were placed under the purview of two restrictive laws in the 1970s, the Monopolies and Restrictive Trade Practices Act (most multinational firms fell within the definition of a "monopoly," which followed the benchmark of average size), and the Foreign Exchange Regulation Act, which made repatriation of profits difficult. The high tariff barrier had provided an opportunity to the world's leading producers of consumer goods to open branches in India. In that scenario, consumer good and drug manufacturing firms such as Hindustan Levers, Philips, Johnson and Johnson, Nestle, and Glaxo continued to do business in India under diluted holding. A few others, including Coca Cola and Du Pont, had a presence before 1973 and left India thereafter. The real cost of the policy cannot be estimated by those who left India, but by those who stayed away. It is likely that a large number of those that stayed away were specialized firms in possession of niche technologies, tools, and processes.

In tea and jute industries, and in a host of other fields where Indians could potentially create a competitive edge, the capital had already been largely foreign owned. India's share in global tea exports fell continuously, with exports reaching a historic low in 2003. Much of the colonial-period market was captured by Sri Lanka, Kenya, and China. The retreat was acute in the western markets. Tea, by contrast, was a favored item in the rupee trade system. Indian tea export, therefore, developed a dependence on East European markets. Because the larger foreign firms did not want to invest in a business where repatriation of profits had been made difficult, growth concentrated in small estates. The small estates produced a large quantity of common, or plainer, tea in green-leaf condition and sent this to bought-leaf factories for processing. These teas were unbranded and subject to little quality control. Their plucking standards were rudimentary, as was their handling of the plucked leaf and its transportation. In short, production of finished tea in India developed a bias toward low quality, low price, and the unbranded – together a recipe for failure in the international consumer market.

Deglobalization in cotton mills followed a slightly different pathway. In 1948, the Cotton Textiles (Control) Order, introduced with a view to protecting Indian handloom weavers, froze mill capacity in weaving,

---

[9] Indian Council of Current Affairs, *Foreign Aid: A Symposium, a Survey and an Appraisal*, Calcutta: Oxford Book and Stationery, 1968, p. 351.

taxed mill cloth production more heavily than before, and reserved goods for exclusive production on the handlooms. In the next decades, this policy furthered the decline of the mills. The Indian cotton textile industry as a global brand was destroyed, and India receded from exports just when East and Southeast Asia built their industrialization on textile export. The restriction on capacity was a disincentive to technological modernization. The quality and range of Indian cotton cloth remained primitive. Not surprisingly, consumption declined. Owners and managers stripped the assets of the firms that they believed would sink anyway. The majority of the colonial-era mills were left with obsolete machines and too little money to buy new machines. Mills continued to produce and export a certain quantity of yarn. In cloth production, the retreat was complete.

Between 1950 and 1970, the jute industry had to battle a whole range of adversities. Shortly after independence, jute speculators and fly-by-night stockbrokers colluded to carry out hostile takeovers of the leading foreign firms of Calcutta, frequently with an eye toward the liquid assets that the firms contained. The operation received the tacit approval of the regime in Delhi and Calcutta. Jute also faced competition from a synthetic substitute in bulk packaging. The competition failed to elicit any worthwhile response owing to the already weak state of the industry. The official reaction to the crisis was a government order forcing packagers in India to buy jute bags, spreading the malady wider. There was justified criticism of this order, and some industries disregarded it openly.

One of the far-reaching changes in agriculture was a thorough recasting of the relationship between the peasants and the world economy. Export of agricultural goods was prohibited, or was licensed to government vendors. The overriding objective was the avoidance of famines. To that end, the government also intervened in the sphere of food distribution. Whereas the peasants lost access to the world market, an elaborate infrastructure was established to facilitate the import of green revolution seeds under the direction of the state. In short, agriculture was not deprived of globalization, but the agency changed from market to state, and from trade to knowledge.

New ties

The Cold War split up the world into trading blocs. The Indian experience in the formation of trade blocs can be divided into two phases, a shadow of communism in the first phase, and an abortive beginning of regionalism in the second.

In 1949, the task of securing collaborative and commercial ties within the now-disappearing British Empire was handed over to the Commonwealth of Nations, an association of Britain and her former and existing colonies. The term "commonwealth" came from its use by a nineteenth-century British statesman as a positive description of the empire. Initially, London's hopes in creating the association were to mitigate the effects of the 1947 partition of India and to keep South Asia from veering toward communism. In the long run, the Commonwealth did not succeed in the task of mediation within South Asia, but it did play an important role in matters of knowledge exchange where the formerly colonized countries could collaborate.[10]

The influence of the USSR, the United States, and China on South Asian affairs nevertheless increased during the Cold War. After 1970, India's defense policy turned closer to the USSR, partly in response to Pakistan's closeness to the United States and China, and partly as an extension of India's stronger socialist leanings in economic ideology. Britain's membership in the North Atlantic Treaty Organization (NATO) distanced Britain from India in the Cold War alignments. As more Commonwealth members gained independence, Britain's informal headship of the body, and consequently British foreign policy interests in the affairs of the Commonwealth, tended to weaken. The United Nations, the Nonaligned Movement, and, finally, the South Asian Association for Regional Cooperation (SAARC) emerged as competing bodies.

In securing economic ties between Britain and India, the Commonwealth could not possibly be very relevant given that the two nations' interests diverged. Trade and investment connections between India and Britain grew weaker in the forty years after independence. The presence of British capital in India shrank. There was a change in the direction of India's external transactions away from Britain to the United States, Germany, the USSR, and Japan. In 1947, Britain was by far the most important supplier of machinery to India, but other industrial countries gradually overtook Britain in this role. The British external sector became more closely integrated with Europe and tended to disengage itself from the former colonies.

The Nonaligned Movement was an organization that avowed cooperation among developing nations. This loose and contentious federation, which was a poor training ground for constructive collaboration, became

---

[10] Its potential role as a body for dispute settlement was compromised because mediation was resisted in the most critical disputes that beleaguered South Asia: Kashmir and the citizenship of Sri Lankan Tamils.

obsolete with the end of the Cold War. In the South Asia region, the immediate aftermath was the formation of SAARC in 1985 by the governments of Bangladesh, Bhutan, India, Maldives, Nepal, Pakistan, and Sri Lanka. The aim was to achieve cooperation in areas of common economic interest. The examples of the European Union and the Association of Southeast Asian Nations were a source of inspiration. However, unlike in those two groups, the members of SAARC did not share a common security concern. Because they did not, progress toward cooperation proved to be a challenge. The overwhelming dominance of India in population, resources, and production made other members apprehensive about economic exchange. And political differences among members, especially the conflict between India and Pakistan over Kashmir, also posed barriers. For nearly two decades after it was established, SAARC had little more than symbolic value. Negotiations were often protracted and fruitless. The idea of a preferential trade zone, mooted in 1994, saw concrete action only in 2006.

Interestingly, the idea of regional collaboration was never given up; the tenacity of the belief in positive economic exchange stemmed from the fact that individually the major nations of the region reembraced globalization, even as they remained bogged down in seemingly intractable political disputes.

Migration and diaspora

Amid so many examples of retreat from integration and aborted integration, labor export accelerated. South Asia continued to be one of the largest exporters of workers in the postwar world. The numbers were much larger than in colonial times. The number of persons of Indian origin living outside India is now estimated at close to five million, of which less than a quarter live in the tropical colonies that received Indian workers in the nineteenth century. Along with their numbers, the migrants' destinations changed. The older pattern of circulation within the tropics ended. The major postwar flows went to the United States (possibly two million Indian-origin residents) and Britain (one to two million). The motivations changed too. Indian migration indirectly contributed to the postwar reconstruction of Europe and helped sustain the steady growth of the Western economies.

Demand for workers being highly diversified along a whole spectrum of skilled services, migrants tended to have diverse profiles. Labor-intensive service industries, such as retailing, hotels, and restaurants, received more migrant workers than wage employment in agriculture or industry had before. Britain received Indian doctors, and the United States received Indian engineers. Many of the skilled migrants were retrained in the United States. Within one generation, the worker-migrants produced a substantial number of entrepreneurs, again rooted in the same industries where migrant workers predominated.

Despite the differences, there were also some similarities between the postcolonial and the colonial migrations. Perhaps the most important one was the systematic use of ethnicity in constructing labor relations. In many businesses, older migrants owned the firm and newer migrants worked as employees. Special labor relations developed in situations where the employers and the employees belonged in the same social set. The shared ties offered security to the new migrants, especially after migration restrictions made their legal status more contingent, and offered peaceful and predictable industrial relations to the employers. And yet, dependence could be perceived as exploitation, and where dependence joined with illegality, the scope of exploitation increased. Ethnicity in the workplace, therefore, was an unreliable form of glue. On that point too, colonial and postcolonial migrations might share similarities.

Diaspora ties between India and Britain took over as the main driver of a relationship earlier mediated by goods, capital, and labor. By 1980, the Indian diaspora in Britain was a highly differentiated population, and yet the different segments or communities within it displayed common patterns in the way they adapted their Indianness to their presence in Britain. These processes of transformation-transplantation became the subject of a large and growing literature in the 1990s, of which travel, mixed identities, displacement, and nostalgia were the major themes. Immigration controls were half-hearted and only partially effective until the early 1970s, but they became increasingly stringent from 1973 on. Twenty years later, when migration from Europe had been made considerably easier compared to migration from the former colonies, Britain's economic realignment away from its former colonies was complete. Integration with Europe and immigration controls weakened the relative importance for Britain of the poorer nations in the Commonwealth as partners in trade, investment, and labor exchange.

Migrations from South Asia have not stopped. But permanent moves have been replaced by an almost explosive growth in temporary migrations, as we will see in the next chapter.

Conclusion

In India, the thirty-odd years from 1950 were a time when a radical experiment in external relations was tried and then was abandoned. The point of that experiment was to end market integration and encourage aid-tied knowledge inflow as a necessary part of a policy giving leadership in capital-intensive manufacturing industry to the state. The restriction on market integration served a dual role, to protect domestic private businesses and to conserve foreign exchange for use by the state. These were political choices. But the choices were consistent with the drift of the 1950s development discourse.

On the one hand, many costs were associated with these choices. Economic growth developed a dysfunctional dependence on political decisions. Formerly export-oriented industries decayed. The private sector lost access to market-mediated transfer of knowledge. On the other hand, perhaps the most significant achievement of the statist regime was the spread of useful agricultural knowledge from foreign laboratories to the Indian farmers.

The only area of unrestrained market integration was labor. Migration responded to the demand for labor in the West. Consistent with the West's own technological trajectory, there was growth in the demand for scientists and engineers as well as for relatively unskilled and semiskilled service professionals. By the 1990s, a section of the Indian diaspora abroad had graduated from workers to entrepreneurs. These two independent trends – the growth of the knowledge industry in India and the growth of diaspora capital – joined together to construct one of the most dramatic returns to the world market, which we discuss in Chapter 10.

10   Return to Market, 1980–2010

When did India begin to reintegrate with the world economy? When did the Indian state begin to embrace the market again? Much confusion prevails in the academic discourse on these questions.[1] The confusion derives from a belief that the questions are necessarily related. They are not. The reintegration did not stem from any formally announced reforms. In fact, the reintegration began informally, in the late 1970s, when two trends came together, an accumulation of capital and competitiveness in small-scale labor-intensive industry, and an unannounced easing of the value of the Indian currency. The exporting opportunities that the latter step created were utilized by the former group. An official reform that extended to all aspects of trade and investment policy did not happen before 1992. Its effects encompassed foreign investment, import of technology, and export of knowledge-based industry in the 2000s. The door that was opened slightly in the late 1970s was now fully ajar.

The precise contents of the economic liberalization process announced for 1992–95 were similar to "structural adjustments" elsewhere in a developing world burdened with bankrupt governments and unsustainable balances of payments. Exchange rates were formally devalued. Tariffs were reduced. A basketful of industrial regulations was removed. The government stepped away from business commitments, a move resisted by the organized trade unions. The broad result, nevertheless, was market integration at all levels, and a fall in the size of the government in the national economy, in short, a return to the nineteenth-century liberal ideal.

The return to market integration shifted between the small opening and the wide opening of the door. One important distinction is that between

---

[1] The debates around these issues are summarized and extended in an innovative direction in R. G. Maluste, "Endogenous Origins of Economic Reforms in India and China: Role of Attitudinal Changes: India (1980–1984) and China (1978–1982)," Ph.D. diss., London School of Economics and Political Science, 2011. See also Tirthankar Roy, *The Economic History of India, 1857–1947*, New Delhi: Oxford University Press, 2011.

238

labor-intensive industry, which played a vanguard but unsung role in the earlier reintegration phase, and the knowledge economy, which dominated the more recent upsurge. These two transitions are described in this chapter.

Trading again

From 1950 to 1970, foreign trade declined in importance in India. Over the next twenty years, there was a mild revival, and the 1990s and 2000s saw an upsurge (Table 10.1). During the upsurge, commodity markets were joined by foreign investment and remittances (Table 10.2). In colonial India, foreign capital inflow was in the range of 1–2 percent of national income. Independent India drove the proportion down to zero. The revival, when it came, pushed foreign investment to a level above that achieved in British India.[2] Inflow of labor income from abroad, if the Gulf

Table 10.1 *Export–income ratio, 1900–2009 (percentage).*

	Undivided India (Export/GDP)	Indian Union (Export/GNP)
1900	7.8	
1910	10.8	
1920	6.8	
1930	8.0	
1939	7.2	
1950		6.3
1960		3.9
1970		3.6
1980		5.1
1990		6.4
2000		10.7
2009		13.8

Sources: For Tables 10.1–3, official statistics supplied in India, *Economic Survey*, New Delhi: Ministry of Finance, various issues; and India, *Statistical Abstracts of India*, New Delhi: Central Statistical Office, various issues.

[2] V.N. Balasubramanyam and Vidya Mahambare, "India," in Yingqi Wei and V.N. Balasubramanyam, eds., *Foreign Direct Investment: Six Country Case Studies*, Cheltenham: Edward Elgar, 2004, pp. 47–68.

Table 10.2. *Investment, remittances, and aid in GNP, 1950–2009 (percentage).*

	Net foreign investment inflow	Net invisibles inflow	Net foreign aid inflow
1950	0.0	0.4	−0.1
1960	0.2	0.5	1.3
1970	0.1	−0.1	1.2
1980	NA	3.0	0.8
1990	0.0	−0.1	0.8
2000	1.6	2.4	0.1
2009	5.0	6.2	0.2

Table 10.3. *Main exports, 1955–2009 (percentage of export value).*

	Traditional manufacturing: Tea and jute	Textiles and clothing	Labor-intensive industry (except clothing): Gems, leather, handicrafts	Knowledge industry: Software	Total of these goods
1955	41.7	11.9	4.8	0.0	58.4
1960	40.3	11.4	6.2	0.0	57.9
1970	22.0	9.4	12.9	0.0	44.4
1980	11.3	13.9	29.2	0.0	54.4
1990	4.2	18.8	43.0	0.7	66.7
2000	1.4	20.4	23.5	11.9	57.2
2009	0.5	8.1	18.8	28.4	55.8

boom of 1980 and the Gulf War of 1990 are both excluded, surged in the 1990s and the 2000s. In this round, labor services paid for by foreign buyers became a complementary input to the export of knowledge goods. Both rose together. One constant factor between these phases was the continued decline in the colonial pioneers of tea, jute, and cotton.

The composition of exports (Table 10.3) shows how deeply the colonial pattern was restructured by three distinct drivers – outright closure (1955–1970), a mild revival led by labor-intensive manufactures including textiles (1970–2000), and a revival led by the knowledge industry (2000–2010). In the first phase, the composition of exports was similar to that in colonial times. The heroes of the second phase were small firms based in small towns, who straddled the old and the new regimes of trade. The strength of these industries derived from the maturing of what one historian calls "small-town capitalism."[3] In the late 1970s, limited trade reform enabled these firms to access the export market. Obstacles to foreign investment continued for another decade, so that the road to new technology and new capital was still blocked. The main beneficiary of the currency reform, then, was the small labor-intensive firms that did not rely on complex technology and capital.

Beginning in 1990, the end of the Cold War and a retreat from socialism removed some of the old irritants between India and Western markets. India's trade with the former USSR and with Eastern Europe collapsed. In a throwback to the colonial pattern, Britain reemerged as the fourth largest market for Indian goods in the 1990s, and if oil imports are excluded, among the four largest sources of imports. Again in a throwback to the past, India's Asian trade revived. Between 1800 and 1860, India's second most important trading partner had been China. After a century-long wilderness, India-China trade began to grow again in the 1990s. On this occasion, the revival was driven by prospects of intraindustry trade. For example, in the 1990s, India supplied cotton cloth and yarn to clothing manufacturers in East Asia. But the rising integration with East Asia hurt Indian producers in 1997 when East Asia experienced an economic crisis. For the first time since the Great Depression, an external recession was transmitted to India.

Table 10.3 leaves a large percentage of exports unaccounted for, because these other goods are too diverse to be discussed item by item. Within this group, one commodity is fast emerging as a leading export. In the last thirty-odd years, global agricultural trade faced barriers to entry into the developed-country markets owing to subsidies paid to farmers. In the Uruguay Round Agreement on Agriculture (1995), tariffs in the developed markets were reduced by 35–45 percent on fruits and vegetables, flowers, and other agricultural products. Following on this change, farmers and orchard owners in some regions in India began diversifying into high-value-added products such as fruits and flowers. Floriculture emerged as a moneymaker in southern India and is set to become much more so. Another success story has been basmati rice. Overall, agricultural exports form 10–15 percent of India's agricultural production today,

[3] Douglas Haynes, *The Making of Small-Town Capitalism: Artisans, Merchants and the Politics of Cloth Manufacture in Western India, 1870–1960*, Cambridge: Cambridge University Press, 2011.

which is close to the best figures of export intensity in the nineteenth century.

Table 10.2 reveals the increased importance of remittances to the new economy. Labor migration to West Asia began in the 1970s. An interesting feature of the migration to the Gulf was the corresponding rise in the export of manufactured consumer goods from India. Some of this export went to meet the needs of the immigrants themselves. As in the past, when Tamil laborers in Ceylon and Malaya insisted on buying rice grown in South India and handloom cloth manufactured in South India, a portion of the export to West Asia reflected the proximity of tastes between the average resident worker in the Gulf region and the middle class in India. Consumption and tastes seemed to drive the trade, with migration playing a facilitating role.[4]

Growth and decline in traditional manufacturing

The three tables in this chapter conceal the painful adjustments that manufacturing had to make to rejoin world markets. Industries such as machinery that had been sheltered from international competition before, faced bankruptcy when trade policy changed. There were closures in machinery and metallurgy. Huge unemployment developed in the cotton and jute textile mills. At the end of 2000, 1.9 million workers were on the rolls of factories that had registered themselves with agencies in charge of bankruptcy and liquidation. A little less than half of these workers were employed in textiles and engineering. Not all of these closures were an effect of the economic reform. Throughout the 1980s, the rate of employment growth was small in the formal sector, a phenomenon known to economists as "jobless growth." By contrast, in the first half of the 1990s, closures occurred selectively, and gross jobs lost were of small order (2 percent of 1991 employment).

The reforms led to some positive changes in traditional businesses. Tea and jute gained, though far from enough to be reestablished as major export goods. The volume of production of jute had been declining prior to 1980, but it steadied thereafter. The main product of the industry was still commercial packaging. But there was now a growing consumer market for jute bags and furnishings, which were often wanted for their eco-friendly qualities. As with cotton textiles, the direct effect of

---

[4] S. B. Karayil, "Does Migration Matter in Trade? A Study of India's Exports to the GCC Countries," *South Asia Economic Journal* 8(1), 2007, pp. 1–20.

the reforms on jute was the encouragement of export and modernization. A small number of mills were renovated in response to these opportunities. These mills manufactured good quality yarn/twine, decorative fabrics, hessian cloth, bags, and blended fabrics.

From the mid-1990s, tea production on the large colonial-era estates experienced an organizational reshuffle. Through mergers and acquisitions, many old plantations consolidated into a more concentrated structure. The domination by a few firms enabled global branding in the packaged tea business. The major players in the branded tea industry are Hindustan Lever Ltd. and Tata Tea; a distant third is Duncans Tea. The market still consists of a large number of small and regional firms. But in 2000, Tata Tea acquired Tetley, the brand name owned by the United Kingdom's Tetley Group, and the company embarked on a global expansion plan by acquiring brands in North America.

The leadership in the reintegration phase, however, came from an unexpected source: small labor-intensive firms engaged in the clothing, jewelry, leather, and handicraft industries. Within the textile industry, the manufacture of cotton yarn in small factories, small-scale garment factories, and knitwear makers gained. Between 1985 and 1996, cloth production increased about 80 percent in volume and 400 percent in value. Exports in volume increased 500 percent. Share of export in production increased from 11 to 30 percent. India's share of the world market in cotton yarn rose from zero to 13 percent. Almost all of this growth occurred in small firms. A surprising feature of the turnaround was a revival of the domestic market, showing how deeply export capacity and domestic consumption had been connected all along. After 1990, domestic consumption of clothing started growing again (see also Chapter 9). Meanwhile, easier import of machinery, marketing tie-ups, and foreign investment made it possible for the domestic small firm to improve the quality and the range of goods available, which stimulated domestic demand for clothing. The products that began to define casual wear in urban India in the 1990s, jeans, printed shirts, T-shirts, shorts, gabardines, chinos, polos, a host of knitted goods, and all sorts of undefined clothing that imitated these, were new varieties.[5]

A second industry to join the world market quickly was diamond polishing. Rough diamonds were mined in Angola, Botswana, Namibia, and

---

[5] Not all of this expansion occurred in small units. Between 1990 and 2000, denims, which were among the fastest-growing products in casual wear, were made by an old Ahmedabad cotton mill company. However, the downstream users of denim were often small garment factories.

Russia, and sent to Antwerp, where the hub of the international diamond trade was located. From here, stones were sent to other locations for cutting and polishing. Where would one find such work at its cheapest and most reliable? The answer once was New York, Amsterdam, Johannesburg, and Tel Aviv. Bombay began to cut into this market in the 1970s, but as wages increased in Bombay, the industry moved to Surat. At first, the bigger stones continued to be cut and polished in Antwerp, New York, or Tel Aviv, and Surat was engaged in working with the cheaper stones. But in the mid-2000s, the capability in Surat had increased sufficiently for it to move into the larger and costlier stones segment. The wages of a diamond cutter in the mid-2000s were the highest among manual laborers in India, but among the lowest for diamond polishing in the world. The industry was controlled by Palanpuri Jains. Their community relationship of trust enabled the Jains, like their counterparts in Antwerp, the Hasidic Jews, to carry out transactions worth millions of rupees with little fuss and paperwork. Their increasing clout in the industry led a number of firms to set up bases in the global centers of the diamond trade. "You cannot," it was said, "throw a stone in Antwerp without hitting a Shah." In the late 2000s, the maturing of India's own consumer market provided added stability to the trade, which it had lacked during the era of export dependence.

The leather industry in India was another export success of the 1990s. The industry succeeded owing to a historic advantage, that is, an abundance of its main raw materials, the hides of cattle and buffalo, and the skins from sheep and goats. From the 1980s, the industry grew rapidly by exporting. The exports, in turn, created the technological capability to allow diversification into footwear manufacture, which generated strong interest in the home consumer market. There was a shift from customizing footwear to supplying wholesalers and large retailers.

Another cluster of small firms to lead the market integration in the 1990s was that of traditional handicrafts. The closure of the world market had deprived the crafts of access to exports, even though friendly government policy made available some concessions. Soon after international trade opened up, the crafts jumped out of the world of patronage into the commercial center stage. They became an export success. The world market for ethnic goods rediscovered Indian designs and products, and entrepreneurial merchants forged a closer link between craft production, craft markets, and international tourism. In the course of the revival, craft concentrations moved from South India toward western India, which was a hub of tourism and of trade in ethnic goods.

Much of the early dynamism came to an end in 1997, during the Asian crisis. The suddenly receding interest in Indian goods exposed the weak foundation on which the boom had stood. From the point of business organization and infrastructure, India was not yet ready to take on the world. The labor-intensive export came from the small towns. Some of these towns had grown far too rapidly, leading to environmental disasters. Textile-processing towns ran short of water for the main business and then polluted the water for drinking. The journey from the port to a small industry cluster could become interminable because of narrow potholed roads and heavy traffic. It took a few hours to load a shipping container in a Southeast Asian port; it took days in an Indian one. Furthermore, customs regulations were still in place, so that for a small business importing equipment could become a challenging job. Years of neglect of the urban infrastructure, even as public money was diverted into agriculture, threatened to take its toll on a fledgling globalization too heavily reliant on the small firms.

Elsewhere in Asia, a more open foreign investment policy had mitigated the continuing scarcity of organizational and technological know-how to an extent. India's policy toward foreign capital was still rigid in the 1990s. In the face of such difficulties, importers of Indian goods preferred to do business, in the fashion of colonial trading regimes, via middlemen and contractors. The distance between the final market and the producer created ample scope for information problems to develop and, therefore, for the fraudulent or careless execution of a contract. Complaints were frequently heard about lack of standardization and lack of due care in the quality of the goods delivered. A single innovative and successful textile design would attract hundreds of interlopers who then supplied poor quality cloth.

In short, transaction costs in doing business with the small firms of India were large, which kept many of these firms outside the mainstream commercial infrastructure even as their goods become globalized. When markets revived from the early 2000s, an easier foreign investment regime eased these costs. At the same time, comparative advantage shifted from manufacturing to services.

The knowledge economy

One of the visible changes between the first and the second phases was the much larger entry of foreign investment in the second. Whereas the older multinationals were consumer industries, the newer entrants were mainly technology-intensive ones. Multinational company (MNC) investment in machinery, intermediates, automobiles, and consumer electronics increased enormously. Areas where MNC investment was completely restricted, such as power generation and telecom, were also opened up. Among the more recent sectors to open up was construction.

These new steps were important, no doubt, but they produced results only in conjunction with another factor that had been silently taking shape in the previous twenty years. During India's retreat from world trade, 1947–80, engineering graduates per million persons increased from near zero to thirty. Over the next ten years, the number more than doubled, to seventy-five, and at the end of the next decade it exceeded three hundred. Whereas the government engineering education institutions remained tied to a conventional course offering dominated by mechanical and civil engineering, the thousands of new institutions offered specialized professional courses dominated by electrical engineering, electronics, and increasingly, information technology. Little in this growth was owed to the state-sponsored engineering education of the earlier era. Rather, it reflected the extraordinary flexibility of private educational markets to adapt to an anticipated and incipient globalization. However, the money invested in private technical schools and colleges came partially from money accumulated during the green revolution in agriculture and the first phase of the reforms. A new breed of entrepreneurs took steps to produce a new breed of technology workers.

In this way, India's key advantage in the global technology expertise built on an extremely flexible market for technical training supplied at an unassailably low cost. The state had little role in making this happen. There is no evidence in official pronouncements to suggest that the state understood, planned, or even adapted to this transformation in any serious sense. It simply let it happen.

After 1999–2001, the combination of globalization and the boom in engineering education took an unexpected course, the export of software services and products. Firms developing software for export, captive software-user organizations, and business process outsourcing mushroomed. A whole package of professional jobs began to be created. The firms employed software analysts, domain specialists, information security experts, integration specialists, database administrators, network specialists, communication engineers, software programmers, design and architecture experts, and data warehousing and semiconductor design specialists. The job market recruited a young workforce, in their twenties mostly, and employed more women workers than almost any of the manufacturing industries. In 2000, the number employed did not exceed a few hundred thousand; in 2006, the number was placed at one million;

in 2010, estimated employment exceeded three million. Although the industry concentrated in a few cities, most professionals tended to be trained in small towns. The concentration (in Bangalore, Hyderabad, Pune, and Gurgaon) resulted from the fact that well-functioning systems of telecom, power, and roads were distributed unequally. But there was also a role for networking advantages in the exchange of tacit knowledge.

Even though the vast majority of the software workers came from private technical schools, many of the leading entrepreneurs and firms were set up by graduates of the Indian institutes of technology sponsored by the state. In the previous decades, the institutes of technology served two aims, that of producing technical workers needed by domestic industrial firms, and that of serving as a finishing school for doctoral candidates in American universities. The second goal was an implicit one. The government railed in public about the "brain drain" at the cost of the Indian taxpayer, but had no clue about what should be done about it. Meanwhile, engineers formed a large component of the Indian diaspora in the United States, well over a million strong in 2004 (see also Chapter 9). Some of them invested money in starting firms in the Silicon Valley. Some of the others worked in the existing firms. The Indian workforce pool was familiar to these individuals, and recruits could in principle receive training and mentoring from them.[6] A relationship that began in this way matured in the late 2000s as many firms, irrespective of the ethnicity of ownership or management, purchased services and products made by India-based firms.

Behind the boom, there worked two global trends. One of these is known as the death of distance: a great fall in the costs of transportation and communication dispersed businesses widely from the late twentieth century, undermining many of the world's core manufacturing hubs and creating new ones in the developing world. Satellite communication could theoretically drive communication costs over long distances close to zero, making it likely that a knowledge-intensive business could be carried out from anywhere in the world. This was indeed one of the reasons for the wide and quick dispersal of the technology worldwide. The second process was the clustering of networked businesses. "Network" lends itself to different meanings, from an international satellite communication system, to a cluster of firms located close together, to a city cafe where knowledge holders might meet for a chat. Common to some of the modern

---

[6] Abhishek Pandey, Alok Aggarwal, Richard Devane, and Yevgeny Kuznetsov, "India's Transformation to Knowledge-Based Economy – Evolving Role of the Indian Diaspora," online report available from Evalueserve, 2004.

meanings of network is an element of physical proximity and personal exchanges, which is one peculiar advantage that cities possess even when the cost of transmitting information over long distances via cable falls to near zero. Both these effects were at work behind the dispersal of software services worldwide and yet their clustering in a few hubs. India displays this dual tendency.

That said, the visible foundation for a boom in the supply of trained information technology professionals was a simultaneous growth in the supply of engineering education in private schools. This dramatic example of capability building invites sociologists to rethink their theories about how capability is created during the development process. One strand in sociological theories of the role of knowledge in modern societies focuses on the quality of knowledge as a public good, which can be acquired and developed through a mechanism called network. A second strand focuses on the capacities of individuals to make knowledge produce value. The former literature is concerned mainly with the process of exchange and the costs of exchange; the latter, with capability and entitlements.[7]

India after 1990 suggests that the approaches are complementary rather than rivals. India is a good example of how network building and capability building could reinforce each other. Mass education in information technology exploded after the trade liberalization. As international networking costs fell, and Indian knowledge labor acquired a potential value, millions of students paid the cost of a private education to equip themselves with the required skills. The lesson is that, by enhancing the expected market value of knowledge labor, networks induced acquisition of the required capability from the market. Educational entrepreneurs joined in, in anticipation of a global demand.

We should perhaps end with a note of caution. Like the first export boom, the second one too carried a great deal of slack. Industry professionals complain of the poor quality of the education offered in the vast majority of private technical schools, and of the specific investments that any recruiting firm needs to make in training people on the job. Private enterprise of the kind that the small towns in India nurture are good for raising supply quickly, but not necessarily good for raising quality. Good trained teachers are in short supply, a lack that money cannot meet. Growing foreign competition, and worse, an industry recession, could expose the underbelly of private enterprise in technology education.

---

[7] Alberto Corsin Jimenez, "Relations and Disproportions: The Labor of Scholarship in the Knowledge Economy," *American Ethnologist* 35(2), 2008, pp. 229–42.

Conclusion

How much of this story from the turn of the twenty-first century should remind us of India's colonial past? There are similarities between the pattern of globalization in the 2000s and that in the late 1900s. Export-income proportion was high in 1900, low in 1970, and high again in 2000. Market integration today is similar to the colonial pattern of integration in its reliance on multiple axes of trade, capital, and labor, with significant externalities flowing in the shape of knowledge exchange. After lying low for nearly a century, India-Asia trade has risen again.

We should not overdo the continuity. The postcolonial globalization is reliant on a different set of profit opportunities than the colonial was. Much of the dynamism in the current phase, for example, derives from reduction in costs of communication rather than in cost of transportation, contributing to trade in services. Foreign direct investment is again prominent in India today, but unlike the jute and tea companies of the nineteenth century, foreign capital today are carriers of niche technologies. Commodity export and service export are now joined in a tighter interdependence than was true for the colonial period.

Having discussed the unfinished transition, it is time to look backward again.

11   Conclusion: A New India?

A decade into the economic reforms, India had earned the right to be
called an "emerging economy." "Emergence" is a comparative term with
explicit reference to trade and competitiveness in the world market. But it
raises more questions than it answers. From the perspective of world
history, when did India's emergence really begin? And what depths of
stagnation and obscurity did Indian business emerge from? Did emergence begin with the rise of the modern knowledge economy in the 2000s?
Did an offbeat industrialization in the nineteenth century mark the
moment of emergence? Did it happen in the seventeenth and eighteenth
centuries when Indian textile artisans sold cloth all over the world? Or
should we push back the beginning of emergence even earlier, in Indo-
Roman trade of the first century CE perhaps?

Equally vexing is "underdevelopment," as well as the theories that once
sought to discover the historical origins of poverty in the long-term pattern
of trade and investment. When and where should the roots of poverty and
underdevelopment be found – the feudalism of late antiquity? the deindustrialization of the nineteenth century? the British Empire? or, the
insular and statist development paradigm of the 1960s and the 1970s?
Arguments can be found to show that each one of these moments of
transition was the real break, and arguments can be found to show that
it was a break for the better or for the worse.

Rather than pursuing such a course at all, we should perhaps acknow-
ledge that queries such as these reveal the risk global history runs of falling
into a rhetorical trap if it tries too hard to explain world economic inequality with reference to global contact. The methodological lesson I draw
from the present narrative is that we should keep the globalization story
distinct from the growth story. The quest for the origins of comparative
economic growth within an account of cross-cultural exchange is not a
promising project. At any rate, it is an unproductive tool in making sense
of the economic history of India in the very long run.

The present work is about doing business beyond the borders; it is a
business history. For a region that has been doing business beyond the

borders for two thousand years, it is unnecessary to justify the enterprise by making reference to comparative growth in the last two hundred years. Merchants, peasants, artisans, and professionals, some of them foreigners but the majority of them Indians or naturalized Indians, are the main actors and agents making this story. I do not deny that the opportunities and constraints that they faced were sometimes exogenous, and that the makeup of the world economy itself changed in ways that are relevant to the present story and that lend themselves to comparative historical analysis. But the region's own makeup placed big limits too, and offered significant opportunities as well.

One general conclusion suggested here is that for much of Indian history, doing business beyond the borders was a question of either making use of favorable geographical conditions or overcoming the obstacles of unfavorable geographical conditions. Where proximity to the coastline, riverine access to the interior, and the monsoon winds seemed to offer prospects of safe and profitable trade, the opportunities never went unutilized. But these resources, or comparable conditions for land-locked regions, were unequally distributed within the subcontinent. Most parts of central and southern India remained poorly integrated into the highways that led to the coasts. Moreover, geography – the overwhelming need to make safe use of the monsoons, for example – left Indian shipping with a limited horizon confined to the relatively short-haul routes and small-sized ships.

A second hypothesis follows from the first. Empires in general were an agent in integrating regions and therefore in reducing trade costs. All empires initiated road building to facilitate the passage of armies, and these roads then facilitated trade. The Turko-Afghan, the Vijayanagar, and the Mughal Empires connected north-south and east-west land routes to the major ports of their time. The history of the late-medieval ports Saptagram, Hooghly, and Surat illustrates the connections wrought by the Indo-Islamic empires of the Gangetic plains. Similarly, the early East India Company state unleashed a process of integration of newly created ports with overseas buyers and sellers of goods. In the end, the costs of trade were still great, and the scale of the early modern commercial expansion would still pale into insignificance if we measured what was traded beyond the borders against what was traded locally.

The third hypothesis is that, despite these attempts by regional states to integrate the land and the sea, the relationship between the two worlds changed decisively only in the nineteenth century. The railways achieved the land and sea connection with an effectiveness that prior systems of carriage had lacked. Far more than just bridging distances, rail was the first truly effective way to overcome the obstacles to travel that the uplands, the forests, and the rivers had earlier posed to the transportation of goods.

The fourth hypothesis concerns the British Empire. In earlier times, the direct aim of empires was to maintain taxes and tribute; market integration was a byproduct of this fiscal enterprise. The British Empire had market integration as its aim. The empire not only created a global market for commodities and factors of production but also cemented it with a compatible, if not a common, institutional framework. These effects made the nineteenth-century globalization different from the past patterns of exchange; it extended beyond commodity trade and involved also large-scale labor transfer, foreign investment, and transactions in knowledge. These multiple channels of contact led in India to industrialization and laid the foundations for a world-competitive service economy.

The fifth hypothesis considers the pattern of integration under way in India in the postcolonial times. Excepting a brief thirty years of a largely failed experiment in state-mediated foreign contact, a part of what is happening in India today builds on a foundation created in earlier times. The 2000s witnessed a return to the market-integration process that had been the long-standing and never-ending part of life in the subcontinent. More than that, the connections between the present and the colonial past were more than obvious in the first phase of reintegration, when craft industries, almost all of them with a history, led the export resurgence. This was a success story written by small-town merchants, skilled craft labor, and informal capital markets.

What followed in the second phase of the reintegration was a more complex episode. So often do today's analysts of the knowledge economy harp on the Indians' command of the English language as a source of their advantage in the knowledge industry that one would be tempted to give all credit to the British colonialists for the software industry in India. But this advantage is exaggerated. It is not English proficiency that matters. What matters more are engineering and university education, in the reinvestment of profits from trade into education, in the readiness with which the literate elites used university education as a means of moving up, and in the location of some of the hubs of the knowledge economy in the metropolitan cities. But then, technical education already had a precocious beginning in colonial India, the literate upper-caste elites had been using education in this way for centuries, and some of the hubs today are cities established by the East India Company. The present-day profile of the vast and burgeoning world of private technical education bears little resemblance to anything the colonial or the precolonial past could offer.

Education has a value in the new world economy that it had lacked in the older ones. The Indian education market responded to that rising value with remarkable speed. A historian, however, should not be surprised that India supplied a fertile bed for such efflorescence.

The narrative remains incomplete. Hopefully, it still offers a way to studying cross-cultural exchanges that is more sensitive to the region's own situation, more realistic in describing the big structural breaks, and less mythological in dealing with the meaning of these break points.

References

Abu-Lughod, Janet (1991). *Before European Hegemony: The World System, A.D. 1250–1350*. New York: Oxford University Press.

Alam, Muzaffar (1994). "Trade, State Policy and Regional Change: Aspects of Mughal-Uzbek Commercial Relations, c.1550–1750." *Journal of the Economic and Social History of the Orient* 37(3), pp. 202–27.

Alam, Muzaffar, and Sanjay Subrahmanyam (2004). "The Deccan Frontier and Mughal Expansion, ca. 1600: Contemporary Perspectives." *Journal of the Economic and Social History of the Orient* 47(3), pp. 357–89.

Ambirajan, S. (1995). "Science and Technology Education in South India." In Macleod and Kumar, *Technology and the Raj*, pp. 153–76.

Andrabi, Tahir, and Michael Kuehlwein (2010). "Railways and Price Convergence in British India." *Journal of Economic History* 70(4), pp. 351–77.

Anon. (1840). *East India Bank* (pamphlet).

Anon. (1845). "Journal of a Residence in Great Britain, by Jehungeer Nowrajee and Hirjeebhoy Merwanjee, of Bombay, Naval Architects. London. 1841." *Calcutta Review* 4, Miscellaneous Notices, pp. i–xii.

Anon. (1848). *Indian Railways and Their Probable Results*. London: E. Newby.

Anon. (1870). *The Opium Trade between India and China in Some of Its Present Aspects*. London: The Aborigines' Protection Society.

Arasaratnam, Sinnapah (1980). "Weavers, Merchants and Company: The Handloom Industry in Southeastern India, 1750–1790." *Indian Economic and Social History Review* 17(3), pp. 257–81.

Arasaratnam, Sinnapah, and Aniruddha Ray (1994). *Masulipatnam and Cambay: A History of Two Port Towns, 1500–1800*. New Delhi: Munshiram Manoharlal.

Arnold, David (2000). *Science, Technology and Medicine in Colonial India*. Cambridge: Cambridge University Press.

Asiaticus (1912). "The Rise and Fall of the Indigo Industry in India." *Economic Journal* 22(86), pp. 237–47.

Baber, Zaheer (1996). *The Science of Empire: Scientific Knowledge, Civilization, and Colonial Rule in India*. Albany: State University of New York Press.

Bagchi, Amiya Kumar (1982). *The Political Economy of Underdevelopment*. Cambridge: Cambridge University Press.

Baker, C. J. (1978). "Debt and the Depression in Madras, 1929–1936." In C. Dewey and A. G. Hopkins, eds., *The Imperial Impact: Studies in the Economic History of Africa and India*. London: Athlone Press, pp. 233–42.

Bala, Poonam (1991). *Imperialism and Medicine in Bengal: A Socio-Historical Perspective*. New Delhi: Sage Publications.

Balasubramanyam, V. N., and Vidya Mahambare (2004). "India." In Yingqi Wei and V. N. Balasubramanyam, eds., *Foreign Direct Investment: Six Country Case Studies*. Cheltenham: Edward Elgar, pp. 47–68.

Bandopadhyay, Rakhal Das (1908). "Saptagram" (in Bengali), *Bangiya Sahityaparishatpatrika*, pp. 15–41.

Banerjee, Rangan, and Vinayak P. Muley (2008). "Engineering Education in India" (mimeo). Indian Institute of Technology Bombay, Mumbai.

Barbosa, Duarte (1866). *A Description of the Coasts of East Africa and Malabar*. London: Hakluyt Society.

Basak, R. K. (1981). "Robert Wight and His Botanical Studies in India." *Taxon* 30(4), pp. 784–93.

Basu, Aparajito (1989). "Chemical Research in India during the Nineteenth Century." *Indian Journal of History of Science* 24(4), pp. 318–28.

Bauer, P. T. (1974). "Foreign Aid Forever?" *Encounter* 42(3), pp. 15–30.

Begley, Vimala (1983). "Arikamedu Reconsidered." *American Journal of Archaeology* 87(4), pp. 461–81.

   (1988). "Rouletted Ware at Arikamedu: A New Approach." *American Journal of Archaeology* 92(4), pp. 427–40.

Begley, Vimala, and Richard Daniel de Puma, eds. (1991). *Rome and India: The Ancient Sea Trade*. Madison: University of Wisconsin Press.

Bhaduri, Amit (1991). *On the Border of Economic Theory and History*. Delhi: Oxford University Press.

Bhattacharya, S. (1966). "Cultural and Social Constraints on Technological Innovation and Economic Development: Some Case Studies." *Indian Economic and Social History Review* 3(3), pp. 240–67.

Biswas, A. K. (1994). "Iron and Steel in Pre-modern India – A Critical Review." *Indian Journal of the History of Science* 19(4), pp. 579–610.

Blake, Stephen (1991). *Shahjahanabad: The Sovereign City in Mughal India, 1639–1739*. Cambridge: Cambridge University Press.

Boomgaard, Peter, Dick Kooiman, and Henk Schulte Nordholt, eds. (2008). *Linking Destinies: Trade, Towns and Kins in Asian History*. Leiden: KITLV Press.

Bopearachch, Osmund (2004). "New Archaeological Evidence on Cultural and Commercial Relationships between Ancient Sri Lanka and Tamil Nadu." *Journal of Interdisciplinary Studies in History and Archaeology* 1(1), pp. 60–72.

Bowen, H. V. (2006). *The Business of Empire: The East India Company and Imperial Britain, 1756–1833*. Cambridge: Cambridge University Press.

References   257

(2010). "Bullion for Trade, War, and Debt-Relief: British Movements of
   Silver to, around, and from Asia, 1760–1833." *Modern Asian Studies* 44(3),
   pp. 445–75.
Bowrey, Thomas (1895). *A Geographical Account of Countries round the Bay of
   Bengal, 1669 to 1679*. Cambridge: Cambridge University Press.
Boxer, C. R. (1969). "A Note on Portuguese Reactions to the Revival of the Red
   Sea Spice Trade and the Rise of Atjeh, 1540–1600." *Journal of Southeast Asian
   History* 10(3), pp. 415–28.
Boyajian, James (2007). *Portuguese Trade in Asia under the Habsburgs, 1580–1640*.
   Baltimore: Johns Hopkins University Press, 2007.
Brennig, Joseph (1986). "Textile Producers and Production in Late Seventeenth
   Century Coromandel." *Indian Economic and Social History Review* 23(4),
   pp. 333–55.
Briggs, John (1819). "Account of the Origin, History, and Manners of the Race of
   Men Called Bunjaras." *Transactions of the Literary Society of Bombay*, vol. 1.
   London: John Murray, pp. 170–97.
British Parliamentary Papers, 1773. *Seventh Report from The Committee Of Secrecy
   Appointed To Enquire Into The State Of The East India Company. Together with
   an Appendix referred to in the said Report.*
   1812–13 (152). *An Account of Bullion and Merchandize Exported by the East India
   Company to India and China Respectively, from 1708 to the Latest Period;
   Distinguishing Each Year, and the Several Presidencies: with a Statement of the
   Mode in which the Value of the Merchandize is Calculated.*
   1812–13 (306). *Papers relating to Revenues of India, and on Growth of Hemp and
   Cotton.*
   1831–32 (734) (735-I) (735-II) (735-III) (735-IV) (735-V) (735-VI). *Report
   from the Select Committee on the Affairs of the East India Company; with minutes of
   evidence in six parts, and an appendix and index to each.* London.
   1852–53 (634). *Despatches, Minutes and Reports from Madras Government on
   Origin and Transactions of Porto Novo Iron Company.*
   (1859), Session 1 (198). *Select Committee to Inquire into Progress and Prospects for
   Promotion of European Colonization and Settlement in India Report, Proceedings,
   Minutes of Evidence, Appendix, Index.*
   1874 (314). *Mr. Geogheghan's Report on Coolie Emigration from India*. London.
   1895 (C.7723) (C.7723–1). *Royal Commission on Opium*. Vol. 6, *Final Report
   of the Royal Commission on Opium. Part 1, The Report, with annexures.*
   London.
Brockway, Lucile H. (1979). "Science and Colonial Expansion: The Role of the
   British Royal Botanic Gardens." *American Ethnologist* 6(3), pp. 449–65.
Brogan, C. (1951). *James Finlay & Company Limited*. Glasgow: Jackson.
Brown, Ian, ed. (1989). *The Economies of Africa and Asia in the Inter-war Depression*.
   London: Routledge.
Bulley, Anne (1986). *The Bombay Country Ships, 1790–1833*. Richmond, UK:
   Curzon Press, 2000.

Cain, P. J., and A. G. Hopkins (1986). "Gentlemanly Capitalism and British Expansion Overseas I: The Old Colonial System, 1688–1850." *Economic History Review* 39(4), pp. 501–25.

"Calcutta in the Olden Times. Its Localities" (1852). *Calcutta Review* 18, pp. 275–321.

Chakravarti, Ranabir (1991). "Horse Trade and Piracy at Tana (Thana, Maharashtra, India): Gleanings from Marco Polo." *Journal of the Economic and Social History of the Orient* 34(3), pp. 159–82.

(1999). "Early Medieval Bengal and the Trade in Horses: A Note." *Journal of the Economic and Social History of the Orient* 42(2), pp. 194–211.

(2000). "Nakhudas and Nauvittakas: Ship-Owning Merchants in the West Coast of India (c. AD 1000–1500)." *Journal of the Economic and Social History of the Orient* 43(1), pp. 34–64.

Champakalakshmi, R. (1987). "Urbanisation in South India: The Role of Ideology and Polity." *Social Scientist* 15(8/9), pp. 67–117.

(1996). *Trade Ideology and Urbanization: South India, 300 BC to AD 1300*. New York: Oxford University Press.

Chapman, S. D. (1985). "British-Based Investment Groups before 1914." *Economic History Review* 38(2), pp. 230–51.

(1998). "British Free Standing Companies and Investment Groups in India and the Far East." In Mira Wilkins and Harm Schroter, eds., *The Free Standing Company in the World Economy, 1830–1996*. Oxford: Oxford University Press, pp. 202–17.

Charlesworth, N. (1989). "The Peasant and the Depression: The Case of the Bombay Presidency, India." In Brown, *Economies of Africa and Asia*, pp. 59–73.

Chase-Dunn, Christopher K., Thomas D. Hall, and E. Susan Manning (2000). "Rise and Fall: East-West Synchronicity and Indic Exceptionalism Reexamined." *Social Science History* 24(4), pp. 727–54.

Chatterjee, Partha (1993). *The Nation and Its Fragments: Colonial and Postcolonial Histories*. Princeton, NJ: Princeton University Press.

Chaudhuri, K. N. (1978). *The Trading World of Asia and the English East India Company, 1660–1760*. Cambridge: Cambridge University Press.

(1985). *Trade and Civilisation in the Indian Ocean: An Economic History from the Rise of Islam to 1750*. Cambridge: Cambridge University Press.

Chaudhury, Sushil (1995). *From Prosperity to Decline: Eighteenth-Century Bengal*. Delhi: Manohar.

(1995). "International Trade in Bengal Silk and the Comparative Role of Asians and Europeans, circa.1700–1757." *Modern Asian Studies* 29(2), pp. 373–86.

Chenery, H. B., and A. Strout (1966). "Foreign Assistance and Economic Development." *American Economic Review* 56(4), pp. 679–733.

Cheong, W. E. (1980). *Mandarins and Merchants: Jardine Matheson and Co., A China Agency of the Early Nineteenth Century*. Atlantic Highlands, NJ: Humanities Press.

Cheong, Weng Eang (1997). *Hong Merchants of Canton: Chinese Merchants in Sino-Western Trade, 1684–1798*. Richmond, UK: Curzon Press.

Christie, Jan Wisseman (1998). "Javanese Markets and the Asian Sea Trade Boom of the Tenth to Thirteenth Centuries." *Journal of the Economic and Social History of the Orient* 41(3), pp. 344–81.

Chung, Tan (1974). "The Britain-China-India Trade Triangle (1771–1840)." *Indian Economic and Social History Review* 11(4), pp. 411–31.

Clark, Colin (1940). *The Conditions of Economic Progress*. London: Macmillan.

Claver, Alexander (2008). "Struggling for Justice: Chinese Commerce and Dutch Law in the Netherlands Indies, 1800–1942." In Boomgaard, Kooiman, and Nordholt, eds., *Linking Destinies: Trade, Towns, and Kins in Asian History*, pp. 99–118.

Colebrooke, H. T. (1804). *Remarks on the Husbandry and Internal Commerce of Bengal*. Calcutta.

Connell, C. M. (2003). "Jardine Matheson & Company: The Role of External Organization in a Nineteenth-Century Trading Firm." *Enterprise and Society* 4(1), pp. 99–138.

Crawford, D. G. (1908). "Satgaon or Triveni," *Bengal Past and Present* 3(1), pp. 18–26.

Dale, Stephen F. (2009). "Silk Road, Cotton Road or . . . Indo-Chinese Trade in Pre-European Times." *Modern Asian Studies* 43(1), pp. 79–88.

Dasgupta, Ashin (2001). *The World of the Indian Ocean Merchant, 1500–1800*. New Delhi: Oxford University Press.

Dasgupta, Atis (2004). "Islam in Bengal: Formative Period." *Social Scientist* 32 (3/4), pp. 30–41.

Dash, K. C. (1997). "Economic Life of Orissa under the Imperial Gangas." In N. R. Patnaik, ed., *Economic History of Orissa*. New Delhi: Indus, pp. 49–61.

De Vries, Jan (1973). "On the Modernity of the Dutch Republic." *Journal of Economic History* 33(1), pp. 191–202.

Derbyshire, I. D. (1987). "Economic Change and the Railways in North India, 1860–1914." *Modern Asian Studies* 21(3), pp. 521–45.

Desmond, Ray (1992). *The European Discovery of the Indian Flora*. Oxford: Oxford University Press.

Deyell, John (1990). *Living without Silver: The Monetary History of Early Medieval North India*. New Delhi: Oxford University Press.

(1994). "The China Connection: Problems of Silver Supply in Medieval Bengal." In Sanjay Subrahmanyam, ed., *Money and the Market in India, 1100–1700*. Delhi: Oxford University Press.

Dodson, Michael S. (2010). *Orientalism, Empire, and National Culture: India, 1770–1880*. New Delhi: Foundation Books.

Dodwell, H., ed. (1922). *The Private Diary of Ananda Ranga Pillai*, vols. 1–8, Madras.

During Caspers, Elisabeth C. L. (1979). "Sumer, Coastal Arabia and the Indus Valley in Protoliterate and Early Dynastic Eras: Supporting Evidence for a

Cultural Linkage." *Journal of the Economic and Social History of the Orient* 22(2), pp. 121–35.

Dutt, A. K. (1992). "The Origins of Uneven Development: The Indian Subcontinent." *American Economic Review* 82(2), pp. 146–50.

Eaton, Richard (1985). "Approaches to the Study of Conversion to Islam in India." In R. C. Martin, ed., *Approaches to Islam in Religious Studies*. Tucson: University of Arizona Press, pp. 107–23.

(1993). *The Rise of Islam and the Bengal Frontier, 1204–1760*. Berkeley: University of California Press.

Edye, John (1834). "Description of the Various Classes of Vessels Constructed and Employed by the Natives of the Coasts of Coromandel, Malabar, and Ceylon." *Journal of the Royal Asiatic Society of Great Britain and Ireland*. London: W. Parker, pp. 1–14.

Eggermont, P. H. L. (1966). "The Murundas and the Ancient Trade-Route from Taxila to Ujjain." *Journal of the Economic and Social History of the Orient* 9(3), pp. 257–96.

Eswaran, M., and A. Kotwal (1994). *Why Poverty Persists in India: A Framework for Understanding the Indian Economy*. New Delhi: Oxford University Press.

Fichter, James (2010). *So Great a Proffit: How the East Indies Trade Transformed Anglo-American Capitalism*. Cambridge, MA, and London: Harvard University Press.

Fieldhouse, D. K. (1961). "'Imperialism': An Historiographical Revision." *Economic History Review* 14(2), pp. 187–209.

Finch, Cuthbert (1850). "Vital Statistics of Calcutta." *Journal of the Statistical Society of London* 13(2), pp. 168–82.

Findlay, Ronald, and Kevin H. O'Rourke (2007). *Power and Plenty: Trade, War, and the World Economy in the Second Millennium*. Princeton, NJ, and Oxford: Princeton University Press.

Fisher, Michael (1984). "Indirect Rule in the British Empire: The Foundations of the Residency System in India (1764–1858)." *Modern Asian Studies* 18(3), pp. 393–428.

Flynn, Dennis O., and Arturo Giráldez (2002). "Cycles of Silver: Global Economic Unity through the Mid-Eighteenth Century." *Journal of World History* 13(2), pp. 391–427.

Foltz, Richard C. (1998). *Mughal India and Central Asia*. Oxford and Karachi: Oxford University Press.

Forbes Royle, J. (1851). *On the Culture and Commerce of Cotton in India*. London: Smith, Elder.

Fort William–India House Correspondence. New Delhi: National Archives, vols. 1–7.

Frank, André Gunder (1998). *ReOrient: Global Economy in the Asian Age*. Berkeley and Los Angeles: University of California Press.

Frasca, Richard (1975). "Weavers in Pre-Modern South India." *Economic and Political Weekly*, 10(30), pp. 1119–23.

Friedman, Milton (1958). "Foreign Aid." *Yale Review* 47(4), pp. 500–516.

Furber, Holden (1951). *John Company at Work: A Study of European Expansion in India in the Late Eighteenth Century*. Cambridge MA: Harvard University Press.

Ghose, Saroj (1995). "Commercial Needs and Military Necessities: The Telegraph in India." In Macleod and Kumar, *Technology and the Raj*, pp. 112–33.

Goitein, S. D. (1954). "From the Mediterranean to India: Documents on the Trade to India, South Arabia, and East Africa from the Eleventh and Twelfth Centuries." *Speculum* 29(2), pp. 181–97.

(1961). "The Main Industries of the Mediterranean Area as Reflected in the Records of the Cairo Geniza." *Journal of the Economic and Social History of the Orient* 4(2), pp. 168–97.

(1987). "Portrait of a Medieval India Trader: Three Letters from the Cairo Geniza." *Bulletin of the School of Oriental and African Studies* 50(3), pp. 449–64.

Goldsmith, R. W. (1983). *The Financial Development of India, 1860–1977*. New Haven, CT: Yale University Press.

Gommans, Jos (1994). "The Horse Trade in Eighteenth-Century South Asia." *Journal of the Economic and Social History of the Orient* 37(3), pp. 228–50.

(1998). "The Silent Frontier of South Asia, c. A.D. 1100–1800." *Journal of World History* 9(1), pp. 1–23.

(2002). *Mughal Warfare: Indian Frontiers and High Roads to Empire, 1500–1700*. London: Routledge.

Gopal, Lallanji (1961). "Textiles in Ancient India." *Journal of the Economic and Social History of the Orient* 4(1), pp. 53–69.

Great Britain (1888–89). *Reports and Papers on Impurities in Indian Wheats*. London: HMSO.

(1910). *Report of the Committee on Emigration from India to the Crown Colonies and Protectorates*. London: HMSO.

Green, Gillian (2000). "Indic Impetus? Innovations in Textile Usage in Angkorian Period Cambodia." *Journal of the Economic and Social History of the Orient* 43(3), pp. 277–313.

Greenberg, Michael (1969). *British Trade and the Opening of China, 1800–1842*. Cambridge: Cambridge University Press, 1969.

Greif, Avner (2006). *Institutions and the Path to the Modern Economy: Lessons from Medieval Trade*. Cambridge: Cambridge University Press.

Grieco, Elizabeth M. (1998), "The Effects of Migration on the Establishment of Networks: Caste Disintegration and Reformation among the Indians of Fiji." *International Migration Review* 32(3), pp. 704–36.

Griffin, K. (1970). "Foreign Capital, Domestic Savings and Economic Development." *Oxford Bulletin of Economics and Statistics* 32(1), 1970, pp. 99–112.

Grose, John Henry (1757). *A Voyage to the East Indies*. London: S. Hooper. 2 vols.

Grove, Richard (1995). *Green Imperialism: Colonial Expansion, Tropical Island Edens and the Origins of Environmentalism, 1600–1860.* Cambridge: Cambridge University Press.

Guha, Amalendu (1972). "Raw Cotton of Western India: 1750–1850." *Indian Economic and Social History Review* 9(1), pp. 1–41.

Gupta, Bishnupriya (2005). "Why did Collusion Fail? The Indian Jute Industry in the Inter-War Years." *Business History* 47(4), pp. 532–52.

Habib, Irfan (1964). "Usury in Medieval India." *Comparative Studies in Society and History* 6(4), pp. 393–419.

(1969). "Potentialities of Capitalistic Development in the Economy of Mughal India." *Journal of Economic History* 29(1), pp. 32–78.

(1975). "Colonialization of the Indian Economy, 1757–1900." *Social Scientist* 32(3), pp. 20–53.

(1980). "Technology and Economy of Mughal India." *Indian Economic and Social History Review* 17(1), pp. 1–34.

(1983). "The Peasant in Indian History." *Social Scientist* 11(3), pp. 21–64.

(1992). "Akbar and Technology." *Social Scientist* 20(9/10), pp. 3–15.

(1992). "Pursuing the History of Indian Technology: Pre-modern Modes of Transmission of Power." *Social Scientist* 20(3/4), pp. 1–22.

Hall, Kenneth (1978). "International Trade and Foreign Diplomacy in Early Medieval South India." *Journal of the Economic and Social History of the Orient* 21(1), pp. 75–98.

(1999). "Coinage, Trade and Economy in Early South India and Its Southeast Asian Neighbours." *Indian Economic Social History Review* 36(4), 431–59.

(2004). "Local and International Trade and Traders in the Straits of Melaka Region: 600–1500." *Journal of the Economic and Social History of the Orient* 47(2), pp. 213–60.

Hamilton, Alexander (1995). *A New Account of the East Indies being the Observations and Remarks of Capt. Alexander Hamilton from the year 1688–1723,* vol. 1. Delhi.

Harnetty, Peter (1970). "The Cotton Improvement Program in India, 1865–1875." *Agricultural History* 44(4), pp. 379–92.

Harrison, Mark (1992). "Tropical Medicine in Nineteenth-Century India." *The British Journal for the History of Science* 25(3), pp. 299–318.

Hatekar, Neeraj (1996). "Information and Incentives: Pringle's Ricardian Experiment in the Nineteenth-Century Deccan Countryside." *Indian Economic and Social History Review* 33(4), pp. 437–57.

Haynes, Douglas (2001). "Artisan Cloth-Producers and the Emergence of Powerloom Manufacture in Western India, 1920–1950." *Past and Present* 172, pp. 170–98.

(2008). "The Labor Process in the Bombay Handloom Industry, 1880–1940." *Modern Asian Studies* 42(1), pp. 1–45.

(2011). *The Making of Small-Town Capitalism: Artisans, Merchants and the Politics of Cloth Manufacture in Western India, 1870–1960*. Cambridge: Cambridge University Press.

Haynes, Douglas, and T. Roy (1999). "Conceiving Mobility: Migration of Handloom Weavers in Precolonial and Colonial India." *Indian Economic and Social History Review* 36(1), pp. 35–68.

Headrick, Daniel (1981). *The Tools of Empire: Technology and European Imperialism in the Nineteenth Century*. New York: Oxford University Press.

(1990). *The Tentacles of Progress: Technology Transfer in the Age of Imperialism, 1850–1940*. New York: Oxford University Press.

Heitzman, James (1987). "Temple Urbanism in Medieval South India." *Journal of Asian Studies* 46(4), pp. 791–826.

Holman, J. (1840). *Travels in Madras, Ceylon, Mauritius, etc.* London: G. Routledge.

Hossain, H. (1979). "The Alienation of Weavers: Impact of the Conflict between the Revenue and Commercial Interests of the East India Company." *Indian Economic and Social History Review* 16(3), pp. 323–45.

Hurd, John, II (1975). "Railways and the Expansion of Markets in India, 1861–1921." *Explorations in Economic History* 12(4), pp. 263–88.

Ibn Battuta (1929). *Travels in Asia and Africa, 1325–1354*. London: Routledge.

Indian Council of Current Affairs (1968). *Foreign Aid: A Symposium, a Survey and an Appraisal*. Calcutta: Oxford Book and Stationery.

Inikori, Joseph (2007). "Africa and the Globalization Process: Western Africa, 1450–1850." *Journal of Global History* 2(1), pp. 63–86.

Inkster, Ian (1995). "Colonial and Neo-Colonial Transfers of Technology: Perspectives on India before 1914." In Macleod and Kumar, *Technology and the Raj*, pp. 25–50.

(2007), "Science, Technology and Imperialism in India." In S. Irfan Habib and Dhruv Raina, eds., *Social History of Science in Colonial India*. Delhi: Oxford University Press, pp. 196–228.

Israel, Jonathan I. (1989). *Dutch Primacy in World Trade, 1585–1740*. Oxford: Clarendon Press.

Jacobs, Els M. (2006). *Merchant in Asia: The Trade of the Dutch East India Company during the Eighteenth Century*. Leiden: Brill.

Jeffery, Roger (1982). "Merchant Capital and the End of Empire: James Finlay, Merchant Adventurers." *Economic and Political Weekly* 17(7), pp. 241–48.

Jimenez, Alberto Corsin (2008). "Relations and Disproportions: The Labor of Scholarship in the Knowledge Economy." *American Ethnologist* 35(2), pp. 229–42.

Jones, Geoffrey (1993). *British Multinational Banking, 1830–1990*. Oxford: Clarendon Press.

Jones, Geoffrey, and Judith Wale (1998). "Merchants as Business Groups: British Trading Companies in Asia before 1945." *Business History Review* 72(3), pp. 367–408.

Joshi, Maheshwar P., and C. W. Brown (1987). "Some Dynamics of Indo-Tibetan Trade through Uttarākhanda (Kumaon-Garhwal), India." *Journal of the Economic and Social History of the Orient* 30(3), pp. 303–17.

Joshi, V. (1970). "Savings and Foreign Exchange Constraints." In P. Streeten, ed., *Unfashionable Economics: Essays in Honour of Thomas Balogh*. London: Weidenfield & Nicholson.

Kanaka Durga, P. S. (2001). "Identity and Symbols of Sustenance: Explorations in Social Mobility of Medieval South India." *Journal of the Economic and Social History of the Orient* 44(2), pp. 141–74.

Kane, P. V. (1946). *History of Dharmasastra (Ancient and Medieval Religious and Civil Law in India)*. Poona: Bhandarkar Oriental Research Institute, vols. 1–6.

Karayil, S. B. (2007). "Does Migration Matter in Trade? A Study of India's Exports to the GCC Countries," *South Asia Economic Journal* 8(1), pp. 1–20.

Kaur, Amarjit (2006). "Indian Labor, Labor Standards, and Workers' Health in Burma and Malaya, 1900–1940." *Modern Asian Studies* 40(2), pp. 425–75.

Kay, Geoffrey (1975). *Development and Underdevelopment: A Marxist Analysis*. New York: St. Martin's Press.

Kenoyer, M. (1997). "Trade and Technology of the Indus Valley: New Insights from Harappa, Pakistan." *World Archaeology* 29(2), pp. 262–80.

Keswick, M., ed. (1982). *The Thistle and the Jade: A Collaboration of 150 Years of Jardine, Matheson and Co*. London: Octopus Books.

Khan, I. A. (1981). "Early Use of Cannon and Musket in India: A.D. 1442–1526." *Journal of the Economic and Social History of the Orient* 24(2), pp. 146–64.

Kirk, William (1975). "The Role of India in the Diffusion of Early Cultures." *Geographical Journal* 141(1), pp. 19–34.

Kling, B. B. (1966). *The Blue Mutiny: The Indigo Disturbances in Bengal, 1859–1862*. Philadelphia: University of Pennsylvania Press.

Kosambi, D. D. (1955). "The Basis of Ancient Indian History." In two parts. *Journal of the American Oriental Society* 75(1), pp. 35–45, and 75(4), pp. 226–37.

  (1956). *An Introduction to the Study of Indian History*. Bombay: Popular Book Depot.

Kranton, R. E., and A. V. Swamy (2008). "Contracts, Hold-up, and Exports: Textiles and Opium in Colonial India." *American Economic Review* 98(5), pp. 967–89.

Krueger, A. O., C. Michalopoulos, and V. W. Ruttan (1989). *Aid and Development*. Baltimore: Johns Hopkins University Press.

Krugman, Paul, and Anthony J. Venables (1995). "Globalization and the Inequality of Nations." *Quarterly Journal of Economics* 4, pp. 857–80.

Kulke, Hermann (1993). "'A Passage to India': Temples, Merchants and the Ocean." *Journal of the Economic and Social History of the Orient* 36(2), pp. 154–80.

Kumar, Arun (1995). "Colonial Requirements and Engineering Education: The Public Works Department, 1847–1947." In Macleod and Kumar, *Technology and the Raj*, pp. 216–34.

Kumar, Deepak (2000). "Science and Society in Colonial India: Exploring an Agenda." *Social Scientist* 28(5/6), pp. 24–46.

Lamb, G. (1859). *The Experiences of a Landholder and Indigo Planter in Eastern Bengal.* London: Edward Stanford.

Lambourn, Elizabeth (2003). "Of Jewels and Horses: The Career and Patronage of an Iranian Merchant under Shah Jahan." *Iranian Studies* 36(2), pp. 213–41, 243–58.

Lane, Frederic C. (1968). "Pepper Prices before Da Gama." *Journal of Economic History* 28(4), pp. 590–97.

  (1979). *Profits from Power: Readings in Protection Rent and Violence-Controlling Enterprises.* Albany: State University of New York Press.

Larrain, Jorge (1990). *Theories of Development: Capitalism, Colonialism, and Dependency.* Oxford: Basil Blackwell.

Levi, Scott (1999). "The Indian Merchant Diaspora in Early Modern Central Asia and Iran." *Iranian Studies* 32(4), pp. 483–512.

Lewis, Archibald (1973). "Maritime Skills in the Indian Ocean, 1368–1500." *Journal of the Economic and Social History of the Orient* 16(2/3), pp. 238–64.

Lieven, Dominic (2002). *Empire: The Russian Empire and Its Rivals*, New Haven, CT: Yale University Press.

Little, I. M. D., and J. M. Clifford (1965). *International Aid: A Discussion of the Flow of Public Resources from Rich to Poor Countries with Particular Reference to British Policy.* London: George Allen & Unwin.

Little, J. H. (1920–21). "The House of Jagatseth." *Bengal Past and Present* 20, 1920, pp. 1–200, and 22, 1921, pp. 1–119.

Liu, Xinru (1988). *Ancient India and Ancient China: Trade and Religious Exchanges, A.D. 1–600.* New York: Oxford University Press.

Logan, F. A. (1965). "India's Loss of the British Cotton Market after 1865." *Journal of Southern History* 31(1), pp. 40–50.

Ludden, David, ed. (2001). *Reading Subaltern Studies: Critical History, Contested Meaning and the Globalisation of South Asia.* Delhi: Permanent Black.

Machado, Pedro (2009). "A Regional Market in a Globalised Economy: East Central and South Eastern Africans, Gujarati Merchants and the Indian Textile Industry in the Eighteenth and Nineteenth Centuries." In Riello and Roy, *How India Clothed the World*, pp. 53–84.

MacLeod, Roy (2000). "Nature and Empire: Science and the Colonial Enterprise." *Osiris* 15(1), pp. 1–13.

Macleod, Roy, and Deepak Kumar, eds. (1995). *Technology and the Raj: Western Technology and Technical Transfers to India, 1700–1947.* Delhi: Sage Publications.

Macpherson, Kenneth (2004). *The Indian Ocean: A History of People and the Sea.* New Delhi: Oxford University Press, 2004.

Maluste, R. G. (2011). "Endogenous Origins of Economic Reforms in India and China: Role of Attitudinal Changes: India (1980–1984) and China (1978–1982)." Ph.D. diss., London School of Economics and Political Science.

Manian, Padma (1998). "Harappans and Aryans: Old and New Perspectives of Ancient Indian History." *History Teacher* 32(1), pp. 17–32.

Margabandhu, C. (1965). "Trade Contacts between Western India and the Graeco-Roman World in the Early Centuries of the Christian Era." *Journal of the Economic and Social History of the Orient* 8(3), pp. 316–22.

Margariti, Roxani Eleni (2007). *Aden and the Indian Ocean Trade: 150 Years in the Life of a Medieval Arabian Port*. Chapel Hill: University of North Carolina Press.

(2008). "Mercantile Networks, Port Cities, and 'Pirate' States: Conflict and Competition in the Indian Ocean World of Trade before the Sixteenth Century," *Journal of the Economic and Social History of the Orient* 51(4), pp. 543–77.

Markovits, Claude (2008). *Merchants, Traders, Entrepreneurs: Indian Business in the Colonial Era*. Basingstoke: Palgrave Macmillan.

Marshall, P. J. (2005). *The Making and Unmaking of Empires: Britain, India, and America, c. 1750–1783*. Oxford: Oxford University Press.

McAlpin, M. B. (1974). "Railroads, Prices, and Peasant Rationality." *Journal of Economic History* 34(3), pp. 662–84.

McCusker, John J., and Kenneth Morgan, eds. (2000). *The Early Modern Atlantic Economy*. Cambridge: Cambridge University Press.

Meloy, John L. (2003), "Imperial Strategy and Political Exigency: The Red Sea Spice Trade and the Mamluk Sultanate in the Fifteenth Century." *Journal of the American Oriental Society* 123(1), pp. 1–19.

Mirkovich, Nicholas (1943). "Ragusa and the Portuguese Spice Trade." *Slavonic and East European Review* 2(1), pp. 174–87.

Moosvi, Shireen (2002). "The Mughal Encounter with Vedanta: Recovering the Biography of 'Jadrup.'" *Social Scientist* 30(7/8), pp. 13–23.

Moreland, William H. (1920). *India at the Death of Akbar: An Economic Study*. London: Macmillan.

(1929). *The Agrarian System of Moslem India: A Historical Essay with Appendices*. Cambridge: W. Heffer & Sons.

Morony, Michael G. (2004). "Economic Boundaries? Late Antiquity and Early Islam." *Journal of the Economic and Social History of the Orient* 47(2), pp. 166–94.

Morris, Morris D. (1960). "The Recruitment of an Industrial Labor Force in India, with British and American Comparisons." *Comparative Studies in Society and History* 3(3), pp. 305–28.

(1963). "Towards a Reinterpretation of Nineteenth-Century Indian Economic History." *Journal of Economic History* 23(4), pp. 606–18.

(1979). "South Asian Entrepreneurship and the Rashomon Effect, 1800–1947." *Explorations in Economic History* 16(4), pp. 341–61.

(1983). "Growth of Large-scale Industry to 1947." In Dharma Kumar, ed., *The Cambridge Economic History of India*, vol. 2. Cambridge: Cambridge University Press, pp. 553–676.

Morrison, Kathleen D. (1997). "Commerce and Culture in South Asia: Perspectives from Archaeology and History." *Annual Review of Anthropology* 26, pp. 87–108.

Mortel, Richard (1995). "Aspects of Mamluk Relations with Jedda during the Fifteenth Century." *Journal of Islamic Studies* 6(1), pp. 1–13.

Mukerji, K. (1962). "Trends in Textile Mill Wages in Western India." *Artha Vijnana* 4(2), pp. 156–66.

Mukherjee, Aditya (2002). *Imperialism, Nationalism and the Making of the Indian Capitalist Class, 1920–1947*. New Delhi: Sage Publications.

(2008). "The Return of the Colonial in Indian Economic History: The Last Phase of Colonialism in India." *Social Scientist* 36(3/4), pp. 3–44.

Mukherjee, Mukul (1980). "Railways and Their Impact on Bengal's Economy, 1870–1920." *Indian Economic and Social History Review* 17(2), pp. 191–208.

Mukherji, Rahul (2000). "India's Aborted Liberalization – 1966." *Pacific Affairs* 73(3), pp. 375–92.

Munro, J. Forbes (1998). "From Regional Trade to Global Shipping: Mackinnon Mackenzie & Co. within the Mackinnon Enterprise Network." In Geoffrey Jones, ed., *The Multinational Traders*. London: Routledge, pp. 48–65.

(2003). *Maritime Enterprise and Empire: Sir William Mackinnon and His Business Network, 1823–1893*. Woodbridge, UK: Boydell Press.

Nagaraj, R. (2003). "Foreign Direct Investment in India in the 1990s: Trends and Issues." *Economic and Political Weekly* 38(17), pp. 1701–12.

Nandy, Ashis (1990). *Science, Hegemony and Violence*. Delhi: Oxford University Press.

Naqvi, Hameeda Khatoon (1967). "Progress of Urbanization in United Provinces, 1550–1800." *Journal of the Economic and Social History of the Orient* 10(1), pp. 81–101.

Nayar, Baldev Raj (1975). "Treat India Seriously." *Foreign Policy* 18, pp. 133–54.

Nayyar, Deepak (1990). *Industrial Stagnation in India*. Bombay: Oxford University Press.

Newman, R.K. (1995). "Opium Smoking in Late Imperial China: A Reconsideration." *Modern Asian Studies* 29(4), pp. 765–94.

Nightingale, Pamela (1970). *Trade and Empire in Western India, 1784–1806*. Cambridge: Cambridge University Press.

North, Douglass (1991). *Institutions, Institutional Change and Economic Performance*. Cambridge: Cambridge University Press.

O'Brien, Patrick K. (2006). "Historiographical Traditions and Modern Imperatives for the Restoration of Global History." *Journal of Global History* 1(1), pp. 3–39.

Osterhammel, J., and N. Peterson (2005). *Globalization: A Short History.* Princeton, NJ: Princeton University Press.

Pandey, Abhishek, Alok Aggarwal, Richard Devane, and Yevgeny Kuznetsov (2004). "India's Transformation to Knowledge-Based Economy – Evolving Role of the Indian Diaspora." Online report available from Evalueserve.

Pandey, Gyanendra (1978). *The Ascendancy of the Congress in Uttar Pradesh, 1926–1934: A Study in Imperfect Mobilization.* Delhi: Oxford University Press.

Parker, Grant (2002). "*Ex Oriente Luxuria*: Indian Commodities and Roman Experience." *Journal of the Economic and Social History of the Orient* 45(1), pp. 40–95.

Parthasarathi, Prasannan (2001). *The Transition to a Colonial Economy: Weavers, Merchants and Kings in South India, 1720–1800.* Cambridge: Cambridge University Press.

(2008). "Iron-smelting in the Indian Subcontinent, c. 1800," Paper presented at the S. R. Epstein memorial conference. London: London School of Economics and Political Science.

(2011). *Why Europe Grew Rich and Asia Did Not: Global Economic Divergence, 1600–1850.* Cambridge: Cambridge University Press.

Pearson, M. N. (1976). *Merchants and Rulers in Gujarat: The Response to the Portuguese in the Sixteenth Century.* Berkeley and Los Angeles: University of California Press.

(1987). *The Portuguese in India.* Cambridge: Cambridge University Press.

The Periplus of the Erythraen Sea. Trans. Wilfred Schoff. London: Longmans Green, 1912.

Pirenne, Henri (1969). *Medieval Cities: Their Origins and the Revival of Trade.* Princeton, NJ: Princeton University Press.

Plüss, C. (2011). "Baghdadi Jews in Hong Kong: Converting Cultural, Social and Economic Capital among Three Transregional Networks." *Global Networks* 11(1), pp. 82–96.

Pomeranz, Kenneth (2000). *The Great Divergence: China, Europe, and the Making of the Modern World Economy.* Princeton, NJ: Princeton University Press.

Prakash, Gyan (1999). *Another Reason: Science and the Imagination of Modern India.* Princeton, NJ: Princeton University Press.

Prakash, Om (1985). *The Dutch East India Company and the Economy of Bengal, 1630–1720.* Princeton, NJ: Princeton University Press.

(1998). *European Commercial Enterprise in Pre-colonial India.* Cambridge: Cambridge University Press.

(2007). "From Negotiation to Coercion: Textile Manufacturing in India in the Eighteenth Century." *Modern Asian Studies* 41(5), pp. 1331–68.

Qaisar, Ahsan Jan (1982). *The Indian Response to European Technology and Culture (A.D. 1498–1707).* Delhi: Oxford University Press, pp. 10–13.

Raj, Kapil (2000). "Colonial Encounters and the Forging of New Knowledge and National Identities: Great Britain and India, 1760–1850." *Osiris* 15(2), pp. 119–34.

Rajamani, V. (1989). "Trade Guilds." *Journal of Tamil Studies*, pp. 1–11.

Rawlinson, H. C. (1868–69). "On Trade Routes between Turkestan and India." *Proceedings of the Royal Geographical Society of London* 13(1), pp. 10–25.

Rawlinson, H. G. (1916). *Intercourse between India and the Western World*. Cambridge: Cambridge University Press.

Ray, Aniruddha (2008). "The Rise and Fall of Satgaon: An Overseas Port of Medieval Bengal." In S. Jeyaseela Stephen, ed., *Indian Trade at the Asian Frontier*. Delhi: Gyan Publishing, pp. 69–102.

Ray, Himanshu Prabha (1985). "Trade in the Western Deccan under the Satavahanas." *Studies in History* 1(1), pp. 15–35.

(1996). "Seafaring and Maritime Contacts: An Agenda for Historical Analysis." *Journal of the Economic and Social History of the Orient* 39(4), pp. 422–31.

Ray, Rajat Kanta (1995). "Asian Capital in the Age of European Domination: The Rise of the Bazaar, 1800–1914." *Modern Asian Studies* 29(3), pp. 449–554.

Raychaudhuri, Tapan (1962). *Jan Company in Coromandel, 1605–1690: A Study in the Interrelations of European Commerce and Traditional Economiecs*. The Hague: Martinus Nijhoff.

(1979). "Indian Nationalism as Animal Politics." *Historical Journal* 22(3), pp. 747–63.

Reid, Anthony (1988). *Southeast Asia in the Age of Commerce*. Vol. 1, *The Lands below the Winds*. New Haven, CT: Yale University Press.

Reins, Thomas D. (1991). "Reform, Nationalism and Internationalism: The Opium Suppression Movement in China and the Anglo-American Influence, 1900–1908." *Modern Asian Studies* 25(1), pp. 101–42.

Rhodes, R. I. (1971). *Imperialism and Underdevelopment: A Reader*. New York: Monthly Review Press.

Riello, Giorgio (2010). "Asian Knowledge and the Development of Calico Printing in Europe in the Seventeenth and Eighteenth Centuries." *Journal of Global History* 5(1), pp. 1–28.

Riello, Giorgio, and Prasannan Parthasarathi, eds. (2010), *The Spinning World: A Global History of Cotton Textiles, 1200–1850*, Oxford: Oxford University Press.

Riello, Giorgio, and Tirthankar Roy, eds. (2010). *How India Clothed the World: The World of South Asian Textiles, 1500–1850*. Leiden: Brill.

Rizvi, Janet (1994). "The Trans-Karakoram Trade in the Nineteenth and Twentieth Centuries." *Indian Economic and Social History Review* 31(1), pp. 27–64.

Rothermund, Dietmar (1969). "India and the Soviet Union." *Annals of the American Academy of Political and Social Science* 386, pp. 78–88.

(1992). *India in the Great Depression, 1929–1939*. Delhi: Manohar.

(1996). *The Global Impact of the Great Depression, 1929–1939*. London: Routledge.

Roy, Tirthankar (1993). "Money Supply and Asset Choice in Interwar India." *Indian Economic and Social History Review* 30(2), pp. 163–80.

(1999). *Traditional Industry in the Economy of Colonial India.* Cambridge: Cambridge University Press.

(2002). "Acceptance of Innovations in Early Twentieth-Century Indian Weaving." *Economic History Review* 55(3), pp. 507–32.

(2007). "Out of Tradition: Master Artisans and Economic Change in Colonial India." *Journal of Asian Studies* 66(4), pp. 963–91.

(2008). "Knowledge and Divergence from the Perspective of Early Modern India." *Journal of Global History* 3(3), pp. 361–87.

(2009). "Did Globalization Aid Industrial Development in Colonial India? A Study of Knowledge Transfer in the Iron Industry." *Indian Economic and Social History Review* 46(4), pp. 579–613.

(2011). "Indigo and Law in Colonial India." *Economic History Review* 64(S1), pp. 60–75.

(2011). *The Economic History of India, 1857–1947.* 3rd ed. New Delhi: Oxford University Press.

(2012). *The East India Company: The World's Most Powerful Corporation.* New Delhi: Allen Lane.

Rudner, David West (1987). "Religious Gifting and Inland Commerce in Seventeenth-Century South India." *Journal of Asian Studies* 46(2), pp. 361–79.

Rungta, R. S. (1970). *The Rise of Business Corporations in India, 1851–1900.* Cambridge: Cambridge University Press.

Said, Edward (1979). *Orientalism.* New York: Vintage.

Sangwan, Satpal (1988). "Indian Response to European Science and Technology, 1757–1857." *British Journal for the History of Science* 21(2), pp. 211–32.

Sanyal, Hiteshranjan (1968). "The Indigenous Iron Industry of Birbhum." *Indian Economic and Social History Review* 5(1), pp. 101–8.

Sastri, Pandit Haraprasad (1893). "Reminiscences of Sea-voyage in Ancient Bengali Literature." *Journal of the Asiatic Society of Bengal*, pp. 20–24.

Satyanarayana, Adapa (2002). "'Birds of Passage': Migration of South Indian Laborers to Southeast Asia." *Critical Asian Studies* 34(1), pp. 89–115.

Schechter, S. (1901). "Geniza Specimens." *Jewish Quarterly Review* 13(1), pp. 218–21.

Scott, Jonathan (1794). *Ferishta's History of the Dekkan.* 2 vols. London: Shrewsbury.

Sewell, Robert (1900). *A Forgotten Empire (Vijayanagar): A Contribution to the History of India.* London: Swan Sonnenschein.

Sharma, R. S. (1958). "The Origins of Feudalism in India (c. A.D. 400–650)." *Journal of the Economic and Social History of the Orient* 1(3), pp. 297–328.

Sharma, R. S., and D. N. Jha (1974). "The Economic History of India Up to AD 1200: Trends and Prospects." *Journal of the Economic and Social History of the Orient* 17(1), pp. 48–80.

Shrimali, K. M. (2002). "Money, Market and Indian Feudalism: AD 600–1200." In Amiya Kumar Bagchi, ed., *Money and Credit in Indian History: From Early Medieval Times*. New Delhi: Tulika Books.

Simmons, C. (1987). "The Great Depression and Indian Industry: Changing Interpretations and Changing Perceptions." *Modern Asian Studies* 21(3), pp. 585–623.

Singh, Anjana (2010). *Fort Cochin in Kerala, 1750–1830: The Social Condition of a Dutch Community in an Indian Milieu*. Leiden and Boston: Brill.

Sivasubramonian, S. (2000). *National Income of India in the Twentieth Century*. Delhi: Oxford University Press, 2000.

Smith, Monica L. (1999). "'Indianization' from the Indian Point of View: Trade and Cultural Contacts with Southeast Asia in the Early First Millennium." *Journal of the Economic and Social History of the Orient* 42(1), pp. 1–26.

Stargardt, Janice (1971). "Burma's Economic and Diplomatic Relations with India and China from Early Medieval Sources." *Journal of the Economic and Social History of the Orient*, 14(1), pp. 38–62.

Steensgaard, Niels (1974). *The Asian Trade Revolution of the Seventeenth Century: The East India Companies and the Decline of the Caravan Trade*. Chicago: University of Chicago Press.

(1981). "Violence and the Rise of Capitalism: Frederic C. Lane's Theory of Protection and Tribute." *Review (Fernand Braudel Center)* 5(2), pp. 247–73.

Stein, Burton (1977). "Circulation and the Historical Geography of Tamil Country." *Journal of Asian Studies* 37(1), pp. 7–26.

(1980). *Peasant State and Society in Medieval South India*. New York: Oxford University Press.

Stillman, Norman A. (1973). "The Eleventh-Century Merchant House of Ibn 'Awkal (A Geniza Study)." *Journal of the Economic and Social History of the Orient* 16(1), pp. 15–88.

Stone, Lawrence (1949). "Elizabethan Overseas Trade." *Economic History Review* 2(1), pp. 30–58.

Subrahmanyam, Sanjay (1988). "A Note on Narsapur Peta: A 'Syncretic' Shipbuilding Center in South India, 1570–1700." *Journal of the Economic and Social History of the Orient* 31(3), pp. 305–11.

(1988). "Persians, Pilgrims and Portuguese: The Travails of Masulipatnam Shipping in the Western Indian Ocean, 1590–1665." *Modern Asian Studies* 22(3), pp. 503–30.

(1993). *The Portuguese Empire in Asia, 1500–1700: A Political and Economic History*. London and New York: Longman.

(1995). "Of *Imarat* and *Tijarat*: Asian Merchants and State Power in the Western Indian Ocean, 1400 to 1750." *Comparative Study of Society and History* 37(4), pp. 750–80.

(1997). *The Career and Legend of Vasco da Gama*. Cambridge: Cambridge University Press.

(2000). "A Note on the Rise of Surat in the Sixteenth Century." *Journal of the Economic and Social History of the Orient* 43(1), pp. 23–33.

Subrahmanyam, Sanjay, and C. A. Bayly (1988). "Portfolio Capitalists and the Political Economy of Early Modern India." *Indian Economic and Social History Review* 25(4), pp. 401–24.

Subramanian, Lakshmi (1996). *Indigenous Capital and Imperial Expansion: Bombay, Surat and the West Coast*. Delhi: Manohar.

Sugihara, Kaoru (2009). "The Resurgence of Intra-Asian Trade, 1800–1850." In Riello and Roy, *How India Clothed the World*, pp. 139–70.

Swarnalatha, P. (2001). "Revolt, Testimony, Petition: Artisanal Protests in Colonial Andhra." *International Review of Social History* 46, pp. 107–29.

Tagliacozzo, Eric (2004). "Ambiguous Commodities, Unstable Frontiers: The Case of Burma, Siam, and Imperial Britain, 1800–1900." *Comparative Studies in Society and History* 46(2), pp. 354–77.

Talbot, Cynthia (1991). "Temples, Donors, and Gifts: Patterns of Patronage in Thirteenth-Century South India." *Journal of Asian Studies* 50(2), pp. 308–40.

Tann, Jennifer, and John Aitken (1992). "The Diffusion of the Stationary Steam Engine from Britain to India, 1790–1830." *Indian Economic and Social History Review* 29(2), pp. 199–214.

Temple, Richard, ed. (1911). *The Diaries of Streynsham Master, 1675–1680*. London: John Murray.

Thakur, V. K. (1987). "Trade and Towns in Early Medieval Bengal (c. A.D. 600–1200)." *Journal of the Economic and Social History of the Orient*, 30(2), pp. 196–220.

Thapar, Romilla (1992). "Patronage and Community." In Barbara S. Miller, ed., *The Powers of Art: Patronage in Indian Culture*. Delhi: Oxford University Press, pp. 19–34.

Thomas, P. J., and B. Natarajan (1936). "Economic Depression in the Madras Presidency (1825–54)." *Economic History Review* 7(1), pp. 67–75.

Thorner, Daniel (1950). *Investment in Empire: British Railway and Steam Shipping Enterprise in India*. Philadelphia: University of Pennsylvania Press.

Tomber, Roberta, Lucy Blue, and Shinu Abraham (2009). *Migration, Trade and Peoples*. London: British Association of South Asian Studies.

Torri, M. (1998). "Mughal Nobles, Indian Merchants and the Beginning of British Conquest in Western India: The Case of Surat, 1756–1759." *Modern Asian Studies* 32(2), pp. 257–315.

Trautmann, Thomas R., ed. (2009). *The Madras School of Orientalism: Producing Knowledge in Colonial South India*. Delhi: Oxford University Press.

Tripathi, Dwijendra (1996). "Colonialism and Technology Choices in India: A Historical Overview." *Developing Economies* 34(1), pp. 80–97.

Trivedi, K. K. (1994). "The Emergence of Agra as a Capital and a City: A Note on Its Spatial and Historical Background during the Sixteenth and Seventeenth Centuries." *Journal of the Economic and Social History of the Orient* 37(2), pp. 147–70.

Unstead, J. F. (1913). "Statistical Study of Wheat Cultivation and Trade, 1881–1910." *Geographical Journal* 42(3), pp. 254–73.

Vickers, Michael (1994). "Nabataea, India, Gaul, and Carthage: Reflections on Hellenistic and Roman Gold Vessels and Red-Gloss Pottery." *American Journal of Archaeology* 98(2), pp. 231–48.

Vicziany, Marika (1986). "Imperialism, Botany and Statistics in Early Nineteenth-Century India: The Surveys of Francis Buchanan (1762–1829)." *Modern Asian Studies* 20(4), pp. 625–60.

Wales, J. A. G. (1902). *A Monograph on Wood Carving in the Bombay Presidency.* Bombay: Government Press.

Wallerstein, Immanuel (1980). *Mercantilism and the Consolidation of the European World-Economy, 1600–1750.* New York: Academic Press.

(1986). "Incorporation of the Indian Subcontinent into Capitalist World-Economy." *Economic and Political Weekly* 21(4), pp. PE28–PE39.

(2004). *World-Systems Analysis: An Introduction.* Durham, NC: Duke University Press.

Washbrook, David (1976). *The Emergence of Provincial Politics: The Madras Presidency, 1870–1920.* Cambridge: Cambridge University Press.

Watson, E. R. (1907). *A Monograph on Iron and Steel Works in the Province of Bengal.* Calcutta: Government Press.

Webster, Anthony (2005). "An Early Global Business in a Colonial Context: The Strategies, Management, and Failure of John Palmer and Company, 1780–1830." *Enterprise and Society* 6(1), pp. 98–133.

(2006). "The Strategies and Limits of Gentlemanly Capitalism: The London East India Agency Houses, Provincial Commercial Interests, and the Evolution of British Economic Policy in South and South East Asia, 1800–1850." *Economic History Review* 59(4), pp. 743–64.

Wilkins, Mira (1988). "The Free-Standing Company, 1870–1914: An Important Type of British Foreign Direct Investment." *Economic History Review* 41(2), pp. 259–82.

Wilson, H. H. (1830). *A Review of the External Commerce of Bengal, 1813–14 to 1827–28.* Calcutta: Baptist Mission Press.

Wink, André (1991). *Al-Hind: The Making of the Indo-Islamic World.* Vol. 1, *Early Medieval India and the Expansion of Islam, 7th–11th Centuries.* Leiden: E.J. Brill.

Yule, H., ed. (1887). *The Diary of William Hedges.* 2 vols. London: Hakluyt Society.

References

Index